OXFORD ENGLISH MONOGRAPHS

General Editors

OXFORD ENGLISH MONOGRAPHS

Bodleian MS. Digby 41 f. 13ᵛ. The body of the page contains *FDR* 731–60; the lower margin contains *UR* 350–63. The writing in the upper margin is the work of an interpolator: see *UR* 349 n.

JACK UPLAND
FRIAR DAW'S REPLY
AND
UPLAND'S REJOINDER

EDITED BY

P. L. HEYWORTH

OXFORD UNIVERSITY PRESS

1968

Oxford University Press, Ely House, London W. 1

GLASGOW NEW YORK TORONTO MELBOURNE WELLINGTON
CAPE TOWN SALISBURY IBADAN NAIROBI LUSAKA ADDIS ABABA
BOMBAY CALCUTTA MADRAS KARACHI LAHORE DACCA
KUALA LUMPUR SINGAPORE HONG KONG TOKYO

PRINTED IN GREAT BRITAIN
AT THE UNIVERSITY PRESS, OXFORD
BY VIVIAN RIDLER
PRINTER TO THE UNIVERSITY

TO
THE MEMORY OF
BERTRAM RYCE
1931–1953

PREFACE

I T is necessary to apologize both for the length of a work which has the unhappy distinction of being the bulkiest monograph in the series in which it appears, and for the economies practised in an attempt to reduce it to more modest proportions. The length results from the bringing together of these texts in a single volume, and I hope that the arguments in favour of this are self-evident. Of the economies I regret especially the omission of a glossary, and the limited treatment accorded the language in the Introduction. I rest my defence on the claim that the language is neither difficult enough to inconvenience those who are likely to want to read these texts, nor interesting enough to engage the attention of specialist philologists. My plan to include a verbatim reprint of the black-letter edition of *Upland* I abandoned with less reluctance since prints of it are available. These are the chief sacrifices, and I would like to think that what remains justifies them. *Alii aliter judicent.*

I am grateful to the Trustees of the British Museum and the Curators of the Bodleian Library for permission to publish the manuscripts in their custody. I owe thanks to Professor J. A. W. Bennett for encouragement when I first thought to edit these texts, and later for the loan of a pair of shoes on an important occasion in connexion with them. For help on particular points I am grateful to Miss Pamela Gradon, Mr. Philip Grierson, Dr. R. W. Hunt, the late Professor W. A. Jackson, Mr. N. R. Ker, the late K. B. McFarlane, Father J. R. O'Donnell, C.S.B., Mr. William O'Sullivan, Professor Robert Raymo, Mr. John Reidy, and Professor C. L. Wrenn. More substantial help I owe to the Revd. H. K. Moulton and Miss Joan Watson. Bill and

Sheila Walter and Mr. Alan Harrison subsidized my work at an early stage, as did the Humanities Research Fund of the University of Toronto more recently. My profoundest debts are to Professor Norman Davis who has overseen my work from the beginning; and to my wife for simply putting up with it.

CONTENTS

ABBREVIATIONS

FROM *Select English Works of John Wyclif*, ed. T. Arnold, 3 vols. (Oxford, 1869–71) I quote the following: 'Fifty Heresies and Errors of Friars', 'Of Mynystris in þe Chirche', 'De Blasphemia, Contra Fratres', 'Vae Octuplex'; from *The English Works of Wyclif Hitherto Unprinted*, ed. F. D. Matthew, EETS, OS 74 (revd. edn. 1902), I quote 'Tractatus de Pseudo-Freris'. These are abbreviated as:

> *Fifty Heresies*
> *Of Mynystris*
> *De Blasphemia*
> *Vae*
> *Tractatus*

References are given in the form: *Fifty Heresies*, Arnold, iii. 379, *Tractatus*, Matthew, p. 320, etc.

Other abbreviations are:

CT	*The Canterbury Tales: Text*, ed. W. W. Skeat, *The Complete Works of Geoffrey Chaucer*, iv (Oxford, 1894)
EETS	Early English Text Society
EPS	*English Philological Studies*
Friedberg, *Corpus*	A. Friedberg, *Corpus Iuris Canonici*, 2 vols. (Leipzig, 1879–81)
HLQ	*Huntington Library Quarterly*
JEGP	*Journal of English and Germanic Philology*
MÆ	*Medium Ævum*
MED	*Middle English Dictionary*
Migne, *PL*	J.-P. Migne, *Patrologia Latina*
Mustanoja	T. F. Mustanoja, *A Middle English Syntax*. Part i (Helsinki, 1960)
ODCC	*The Oxford Dictionary of the Christian Church*, ed. F. L. Cross (London, 1957)
ODEP	*The Oxford Dictionary of English Proverbs*, ed. W. G. Smith, 2nd edn. revd. P. Harvey (Oxford, 1948)
OED	*Oxford English Dictionary*
PBA	*Proceedings of the British Academy*

PP	*Piers the Plowman,* ed. W. W. Skeat, 2 vols. (Oxford, 1886)
PPC	*Pierce the Ploughmans Crede,* ed. W. W. Skeat, EETS, os 30 (1867)
PT	*The Plowmans Tale,* ed. W. W. Skeat, *Chaucerian and Other Pieces* (Oxford, 1897), pp. 147–90
RES	*Review of English Studies*
WV 1, 2	*The Holy Bible . . . in the Earliest English Versions . . . by John Wycliffe and His Followers,* ed. J. Forshall and F. Madden, 4 vols. (Oxford, 1850): the earlier (1) and later (2) versions

INTRODUCTION

THE MANUSCRIPTS

Jack Upland survives in two manuscripts:

B.M. MS. Harley 6641. Vellum, 25 leaves,[1] measuring 11·4 × 8·3 cm. Collation: 1–3⁸, 4¹. Text area 7·8 to 8·5 cm. × 5·3 to 5·5 cm.; 16–17 lines to the page. Catchwords, no signatures. Folios numbered in sixteenth-century hand. Text within single vertical rules: single pricking in outside margins. Book hand, probably fifteenth century; writing above the line. Paragraph marks in red inserted after writing. Inscription erased head and foot f. 1ʳ. Name 'J. Wartor' (?) in elaborate sixteenth-century hand f. 25ᵛ; vertical doodle in right-hand margin f. 9ʳ. Binding eighteenth century.

C.U.L. MS. Ff. vi. 2. Paper, a composite volume; ii (flies, blank)+84+ii (flies, blank), measuring 20 × 14·5 cm. Collation: 1–17⁴, 18² (ff. 1–70; sigs. A–R⁴, S²); 19–20⁴, 21² (ff. 71–80; sigs. A–B⁴, C²); 22⁴ (ff. 81–84; no sigs.). Text area 15·5 to 16·5 cm. × 11·5 to 13 cm.; 26–29 lines to the page. No catchwords. Folios numbered 1–70 in ink, sixteenth-century hand; 71–84 in pencil, modern hand. English current hand, early sixteenth century. The three pieces that make up the volume (divided ff. 1–70, 71–80 (*Upland*), 81–84) are written by the same hand but, on the evidence of the signatures, at different times. In first piece and *Upland* some cross ruling and occasional underlining in faint red ink; the red ruling appears also beneath title (f. 81ʳ) and at end (f. 84ʳ) of third piece. At end of first piece (f. 70ʳ) is written *finis laus detur deo*; end of *Upland* (f. 80ʳ) *schortly wᵗ all spedynes*; end of third piece (f. 84ᵛ) an illegible word; all in red ink, probably hand of text. Head of

[1] I ignore a number of paper leaves at beginning and end, probably inserted during binding in the eighteenth century.

f. 1^r 'Vol 103' in seventeenth-century hand; head f. 71^r (beginning of *Upland*) 'Chaucer' in sixteenth-century hand. Binding probably seventeenth century, end-papers from printed book with running title 'Against Bellarmine Touching Antichrist'. Inside margin f. 1^r in seventeenth-century hand 'A Theological treatis in English'; on spine 'Theol: Treatis M.S.'

Friar Daw's Reply and *Upland's Rejoinder* survive in a unique copy:

Bodleian MS. Digby 41. Vellum, a composite volume, 104 leaves, pieces dated from twelfth to fifteenth centuries.[1]

The *Reply* is on ff. 2–17, 16 leaves measuring 18·8 × 12·4 to 13 cm. Collation: 1–2^8 (last leaf blank). Between 1^8 and 2^1 leaf cut out, conjoint with f. 1 preceding *FDR*.[2] An untidy book hand, fifteenth century, in alliterative long lines: ff. 2–7 as verse, ff. 7^v–16^v continuously as prose. Text area of prose 13 cm. × 8·5 to 9·5 cm.; 29 to 33 lines to the page. Catch-phrase (f. 9^v), some signatures, no rubrics.[3] Folios numbered in modern hand. Head f. 2^r '67' in seventeenth-century hand; head f. 10^r 'A. 234' in sixteenth-century hand.[4] Binding seventeenth century.

The *Rejoinder* is written in the margins (variously upper, lower, and side) of the *Reply*, beginning f. 2^r ending f. 15^r. Alliterative long lines written continuously as prose, current

---

[1] For an account of the other pieces in the MS., see W. D. Macray, *Catalogi Codicum Manuscriptorum Bibliothecae Bodleianae . . . Codices a . . . Kenelm Digby* (Oxford, 1883), cols. 38–39. I do not attempt a full description or collation of the MS. here.

[2] The bifolium was presumably bound in to provide a front cover; the back cover is provided by the blank leaf (f. 17) at the end of the second quire of *FDR*. This front cover (f. 1) contains a list of medicinal recipes.

[3] The first three lines of text are indented to leave space for a rubricated capital *W*, and the flecks of red ink between 489 and 491 (f. 9^v) suggest that at some time it was in a rubricator's hands.

[4] The numbers, presumably press-marks, in the composite volume are of some interest. They are: 67 (f. 2^r); A. 234—after original 235 cancelled —(f. 10^r); 43, A. 175 (f. 57^r); A. 235 (f. 91^r). The Digby Catalogue in a headnote describes the MS. as 'olim in tres codices divisus; "67"; "43. A. 175"; et "A. 235"'. Thus A. 234 is omitted while 43 and A. 175 are run together, although in the MS. they are quite distinct.

hand, mid fifteenth century. A second hand beginning f. 13ʳ (upper margin), continued f. 13ᵛ (upper), f. 14ᵛ (lower), ff. 15ᵛ and 16ʳ (both lower), f. 16ʳ (upper), is that of an inter-polator.[1]

The Harley MS. was known in the eighteenth century to William Thomas, secretary to Robert Harley, first Earl of Oxford, the elder of the two brothers who, after the death of John Urry, saw Urry's edition of Chaucer through the press.[2] Attention is drawn to it in the Preface to Urry, written by William Thomas's brother, Timothy:

I had also an opportunity by the favour of an ingenious Friend, of collating a MS. of *Jack Upland*, on Vellom in a very small Volume, which was of use to explain some, and correct other Passages in it; but the Text is generally so different there from that which is exhibited in this, as well as former Editions of *Chaucer*, that it may deserve to be printed entire as it is in that MS. which is now in the possession of that indefatigable Collector, *Thomas Rawlinson* Esq.[3]

The collation was done by William Thomas in March 1719/20, and is extant in B.M. Addit. MS. 38180 on ff. 279 f.[4]

William Thomas transcribed the readings gathered from his collation into his own copy of Urry, now in the British Museum.[5] A note in that book says that Rawlinson was given the *Upland* MS. by William Jones (1675–1749), mathematician and anti-quary. There is no evidence of its earlier history except the name 'J. Wartor' (or Warton) written in a sixteenth-century hand on the verso of the last folio (f. 25). This may be the John Warter who in 1608 owned a copy of the Gospels of Matthew, Mark, and Luke in the later version of the Wycliffe

[1] See pp. 40–44 for a discussion of this hand; f. 13ᵛ is reproduced in the frontispiece. In what follows, the abbreviation UR stands both for the first hand of the MS. and (since I take the MS. to be holograph) the author of the *Rejoinder*, the abbreviation FDR for the scribe of the *Reply*.

[2] Chaucer, *Works*, ed. John Urry (Oxford, 1721). For a full account of the genesis and sad history of this edition, see 'Christ Church and Chaucer', *Oxford Magazine*, 21 June 1962, pp. 386–7.

[3] Urry, sig. l.1ᵛ.

[4] The MS. collections for Urry's edition are in B.M. Addit. MSS. 38178–81 and Harley MS. 6895.

[5] Press-mark 643. m. 4.

translation.[1] I have been unable to discover anything about him, but *Upland* and the Wyclifite gospels would be at home in the library of the same man.

At the dispersal of Rawlinson's library the *Upland* MS. appeared in the last sale, which began on 4 March 1733/4. It brought £4, the second highest price of the ninth day, and one exceeded only by the £4. 5s. 0d. paid for an illuminated copy of the Wyclifite New Testament. The purchaser was one Barker, who was presumably acting as agent for Edward Harley, second Earl of Oxford, into whose collection the manuscript passed.[2]

Nothing is known of the history of the Cambridge MS. until it came into the University Library. It was no. 103 in the collection of Richard Holdsworth, D.D., Master of Emmanuel College, who died in 1649, and whose library was assigned to the University in 1664.

The Digby MS. was part of a bequest to Sir Kenelm Digby from his tutor, Thomas Allen of Gloucester Hall, in 1632. Two years later Digby presented the collection, on Laud's persuasion, to the Bodleian.[3]

In this century the manuscripts have languished in a privacy afforded few medieval texts. Much of the thanks for this must go to Skeat for his blunt statement about *Upland* in 1897, that 'of this piece, no MS. copy is known'.[4] In 1908 Miss Hammond

---

[1] Now Oriel MS. 80 (Forshall and Madden, no. 100). On f. v^r is the signature 'J. Warter' in an ornate form as in Harley 6641; on f. vi^r it occurs twice as a simple signature 'J. Warter' and 'John Warter' with date 1608. The signature is doubtfully that of 'M^r J [or G] Warter' in Bodleian MS. Auct. F. inf. 1.1, f. iii (SC 2439), a fifteenth-century copy of the commentary of Dionysius de Burgo on the last six books of the *De factis et dictis memorabilibus* of Valerius Maximus, acquired by the library not later than 1602.

[2] See *Codicum Manuscriptorum Bibliothecae Rawlinsonianae Catalogus* [London, 1733]. The *Upland* MS. was lot 695. The Bodley copy of the catalogue has the prices and buyers' names inserted. In the whole sale of over a thousand lots only six manuscripts brought a higher price than *Upland*.

[3] The collection was received by the library on 30 December 1634; it consisted of 233 volumes, 5 rolls, and a bound MS. catalogue of the collection. In this catalogue the MS. is numbered 67 (MS. Digby 234^a, p. 74; see also p. 2, n. 4 above). The collection was renumbered in 1641.

[4] *Chaucerian and Other Pieces*, supplement to Chaucer's *Complete Works* (Oxford, 1897), p. xxxv.

drew attention to the existence of both manuscripts.[1] They are not recorded by Wells, the *Cambridge Bibliography*, or its Supplement, but are noted by Robbins and Cutler, *Supplement to the Index of ME Verse* (1965), no. 3782.5.

THE PRINTED EDITIONS

The earliest printed text of *Upland* is a small octavo black-letter volume probably to be dated 1536;[2] two copies survive, one in the Huntington Library, the other in the library of Gonville and Caius College, Cambridge:

Iack vp Lande | Compyled by the | famous Geoffrey | Chaucer. | Ezechielis. xiii. | Wo be vnto you that | dishonour me to me peo | ple for an handful of bar | lye & for a pece of bread | Cum priuilegio | Regali.

The colophon reads:

Prynted for Ihon Gough. | Cum Priuilegio Regali.[3]

Bale in his manuscript *Index* lists a copy *Ex officina Ioannis Daye*, but no copy has survived.[4] John Foxe printed *Upland* in the second edition (1570) of his *Actes and Monumentes.*[5]

[1] *Chaucer: A Bibliographical Manual*, ed. E. P. Hammond (New York, 1908), p. 430. Miss Hammond is misled by the entry in Bernard's *Catalogus* (1697), p. 79, and lists the Digby MS. as a copy of *Upland*. Bernard was presumably misled by the inscription 'Jak Upland' on the first flyleaf of Digby 41. C. F. E. Spurgeon, *Five Hundred Years of Chaucer Criticism and Allusion, 1357–1900* (Cambridge, 1925), i. 83, lists the Harley but not the Cambridge MS. A third MS., B.M. MS. Sloane 3205 ff. 70ᵛ–71ʳ, contains a seventeenth-century transcript of the opening of the black-letter print of *Upland* published by John Gough, probably in 1536.

[2] See 'The Earliest Black-letter Editions of *Jack Upland*', *HLQ*, xxx (1967), 307–14.

[3] *STC* 5098, where only the Huntington copy is recorded. A copy entitled *Jack by Lande*, mentioned by Spurgeon, *Chaucer Criticism*, i. 83, is a ghost caused by misreading lower-case *vp* as *by*; the error probably derives from W. C. Hazlitt, *Hand-Book to the Popular, Poetical, and Dramatic Literature of Great Britain* (London, 1867), p. 98.

[4] *Index Britanniae Scriptorum*, ed. R. L. Poole and M. Bateson (Oxford, 1902), p. 274. For Gough's and Day's editions, see *HLQ*, xxx (1967), 307–12.

[5] i. 341–5. Foxe's *Actes* was printed by Day, but Bale could not have been referring to it, since *Upland* appears only in the second and subsequent editions, and Bale died in 1563.

Gough and Foxe attribute *Upland* to Chaucer,[1] and in his second edition of 1602 Speght formally admitted the text to the Chaucer canon[2] and it was retained in the reprint of 1687. Urry printed Speght's text in his edition of 1721, but thereafter it was banished from the canon. Skeat included it in his volume of Chaucer apocrypha.[3]

Daw's *Reply* and Upland's *Rejoinder* have been printed in full only once—by T. Wright in *Political Poems and Songs*, ii (Rolls Series, 1861)—and only on this occasion have all three texts appeared together.[4]

THE AUTHORS

There is no clue to the identity of the author either of *Upland* or of the *Rejoinder*. There is no reason to assume that one man was responsible for both: 'Jack Upland' is as much an assumed *persona* as that of the ploughman in such a work as *Pierce the Ploughmans Crede*. My dating of the two pieces, if accepted (see pp. 17–19), makes single authorship highly improbable if not impossible. In any case, the *Rejoinder*'s vigorous alliterative verse, its cogent argument, and its latinity set it apart from the

[1] This is the usual ascription in the sixteenth century. 'Chaucer' is written at the head of the first folio (f. 71ʳ) of the text of *Upland* in the Cambridge MS., in a hand probably of the sixteenth century. Bale, however, condemns the attribution to Chaucer and gives the author as Wyclif (*Index*, p. 274). In his zeal Foxe includes Chaucer and Gower with Wyclif, Purvey, and Swinderby as 'faithful witnesses' of the Church (*Actes* (1570), i. sig. iiij). See further *HLQ*, xxx (1967), 312–14.

[2] Ff. 348–50ᵛ. Speght in his headnote (f. 348) identifies *Upland* with *Pierce the Ploughmans Crede*, and quotes *Plowman's Tale*—in Skeat, *Chaucerian and Other Pieces*, ll. 1065–8.

[3] *Chaucerian and Other Pieces*, pp. 191–203.

[4] *Upland* on pp. 16–39, the *Reply* and the *Rejoinder* in (more or less) parallel texts on pp. 39–114. Wright followed Speght for his text of *Upland*, the unique Digby MS. for the *Reply* and the *Rejoinder*. I do not take account of Wright's or Skeat's readings except for special reasons. Wright's printing of the *Reply* and the *Rejoinder* is very inaccurate and to be trusted neither for spelling nor for substantive readings. In the first ten lines of the *Rejoinder* as printed by Wright, leaving aside substitution of *and* for &, *th* for þ, *v* for *u* (and vice versa), and erroneous introduction of *Jak* at the beginning of l. 10 (see p. 50, n. 2), there are six errors of transcription. A. S. Cook, *A Literary Middle English Reader* (Boston, 1915), pp. 366–7, reprints *FDR* 451–74 from Wright.

colourless and rather flaccid prose and the generally unlearned quality of *Upland*.¹ It is difficult to believe that they are by the same person.

The *explicit* to Daw's *Reply* declares that the author was one John Walsingham, and this suggests that his family may have come from Walsingham in Norfolk. Daw himself claims (at 725) to have been 'a manciple at Mertoun Halle' where he 'lernede Latyn bi roote of clerkes'. Bale lists Robert and John Walsingham, two Carmelites living at the beginning of the fourteenth century, but Emden condemns John as a ghost.² The only other Walsingham from Oxford recorded by Emden is Thomas, chronicler of St. Alban's. What is known of his dates, opinions, and provenance would qualify him as author of the *Reply*: he was still living *c.* 1422, he was rabidly anti-Lollard, and he may have been an Oxford man. But he was a monk not a friar, and a pattern of orthodoxy; it is extremely unlikely that he was the author of the *Reply*. It may be that the piece, originally anonymous for discretionary reasons, was attributed to Walsingham because of his known antagonism to Lollardy, his Christian name being either imperfectly remembered or corrupted in the course of transmission.³

If the author was a native of Walsingham and a Norfolk man

---

¹ The author of *Upland* has more in common with the interpolator of the *Rejoinder* (see pp. 40–44, *UR* 349 n., 374 n., 393 n.) than with its author; they share, for example, either an innocence of, or a reluctance to use, Latin, which contrasts with UR's facility in the language and his effective use of it.

² Bale, *Scriptorum Illustrium maioris Brytanniae*, i. 364–5, 378–9. A. B. Emden, *A Biographical Register of the University of Oxford to A.D. 1500*, iii (Oxford, 1959), 1970–1.

³ G. Kane, *Piers Plowman: The A Version* (London, 1960), p. 137, n. 1, quotes the observation of G. Pasquali, *Storia della Tradizione e Critica del Testo* (Florence, 1934 and 1952), pp. 18–19, that proper names are certain to be corrupted. Cp. Sir Maurice Powicke's suggestion that the reference in a late fourteenth-century dialogue of the Italian humanist Leonardo Bruni, to an English scholar named Ferabrick, may be to William Heytesbury, the distinguished Oxford logician, whose name was often reduced to Tisberus; Suisset in the same context refers to another Oxford scholar, Roger Swineshead. He points out that scholars' names must have been largely familiar only through colophons in manuscripts, where their names were hopelessly corrupted ('Bologna, Paris, Oxford: Three *Studia Generalia*', *Ways of Medieval Life and Thought* (London, [1949]), pp. 162–3).

he may have been a graduate of Cambridge; but Emden's list[1] does not contain a John Walsingham, and of the other candidates with the surname none seems very probable. Of course, he may not have been a graduate at all and his reference to Merton may be merely a device to give authority to his claim of proficiency in Latin; yet the author's learning and his rhetorical skill both argue for a training in the schools.[2]

In his catechism Upland seems primarily to have in mind the Franciscans; this is suggested by his references to the *knottid girdel* (141), to the Minors' claims for the efficacy of burial in their habit (204–8), and to the controversy over the *usus pauper* (298–306);[3] but the Dominicans find a place in his net, as at 288–90, where he presses on his friar the uncharitableness of accepting men as brothers only if they 'haue on moornynge cloþis & be of ȝoure sett'—presumably a reference to the Dominican habit;[4] and, if I am right in my interpretation of 157–8, so do the Carmelites. The author of the *Rejoinder* seems to have thought that he was controverting a Dominican in ascribing to his habit 'þe coloure þat signifieþ sadnes' (178) and imputing to him *Dominikis reules* (299).

It seems likely that Daw was a Dominican. At 380–1 he refers Upland to the Franciscans for an explanation of the significance of the knotted girdle, since he can provide none; at 529–32 he disclaims on behalf of the Austins and Dominicans the fable that those buried in a friar's habit are saved from hell, and says that perhaps Carmelites or Franciscans might maintain such an error. This suggests that he is neither a Carmelite nor a

---

[1] *A Biographical Register of the University of Cambridge to 1500* (Cambridge, 1963), pp. 613–14.

[2] John Walsingham's absence from the records of Oxford and Cambridge graduates is not, in any case, decisive. Professor Norman Davis points out to me that Walter Paston certainly took his degree in 1479 but there is no *university* record of it. For Cambridge graduates, see also the remarks of H. Peek and C. Hall, *The Archives of the University of Cambridge* (Cambridge, 1962), pp. 30–31.

[3] See the notes to these lines for an explanation of their significance. The interpolator of *Upland* (see *JU* 411 n.) seems to have been a Franciscan, indignant at what he takes to be an attack on his order.

[4] Cp. *JU* 289 n.

Franciscan. At 623 f., in pointing out that every deed is known by its end, he adds that God knows that the preaching of friars has been directed towards making this clear. In thus calling attention to that for which of all the mendicant orders the Dominicans especially were famous, it is possible that Daw intended to identify himself with them.

Indeed, in the light of the local knowledge that Daw displays in his reference to the Hospitals of St. Thomas of Acres, St. Anthony, and St. Mary Rouncivall and their privileges (481–2 and *n*.),[1] and the vehemence of his attack on them, it seems likely that he was a member of the great house of the London Blackfriars.[2]

THE DATES

The evidence is treacherous. The credentials of no single allusion are unexceptionable, and such allusions as there are— of unequal weight and none decisive in itself—when taken together make it possible to fix for only one of the three texts a date for which can be claimed any degree of probability.

Wright, followed by Skeat, argues that the latest probable date of composition for the three pieces can be fixed by an allusion in Upland's *Rejoinder* (at 271–2): 'And þe kyng by his juges trwe execute his lawe / As he did now late whan he hangid ʒou traytoures.' Skeat (correcting Wright, see *Chaucerian and Other Pieces*, p. xxxvii) suggests that this refers to the hanging of eight Franciscan friars at Tyburn in June 1402 for being implicated in a plot against the life of Henry IV. Skeat also agrees with Wright that 'it was necessary that Friar Daw...should produce his reply at once; and we may be sure that Jack's rejoinder was not long delayed'. On the basis of these assumptions he declares (p. xxxvii) that we 'may, accordingly, safely refer all three pieces to the year 1402'.

Skeat's and Wright's neglect of the supplementary evidence makes this statement far from safe. The most important is

---

[1] For the distinction between roman and italic in references see p. 52.

[2] See pp. 10–17 for an argument which, if accepted, goes far towards supporting Daw's claims to membership of this house.

Daw's remark, in a passage (499–505) discussing the taxation of
the clergy, that while 'prelatis & persouns aftir her state / Ben
stended to paien what þat nede askip' it was not true of 'freres ne
annuellers saue now late'. That *UR* 271–2 refers to the hanging
of 1402 cannot be regarded as proved unless this event can be
related to one of the years in which it is known that those religious
normally exempt were, in fact, taxed.

On a number of occasions at the end of the fourteenth
century and in the early fifteenth, levies were imposed on the
'exempt': in 1371, 1404, 1419, and 1429.[1] Skeat's and Wright's
dating of the *Rejoinder* necessarily excludes those of 1419 and
1429, since if Daw refers to either one of them, the *Rejoinder*
must be later than 1419 or 1429 and the allusion in it to the
hangings (as 'now late') cannot refer to the executions of 1402.
The levy of 1371 is ruled out by (among other things) the
attacks on Wyclif in the *Reply*:[2] his career as a reformer (much
less as heresiarch) had barely begun at that date. Only the levy
of 1404 remains. But it is difficult to see how, if this levy of
November 1404 can be described by Daw as 'now late', the
author of the *Rejoinder* writing after him can refer to the execution of the Franciscans in June 1402, at least two and a half
years earlier, in exactly the same words—as having occurred
'now late'. It is very difficult to reconcile the usual meaning of
the phrase in ME.—'recently'—with a lapse of time that cannot
be much less than three years.

If the *Reply* is freed from having to support Skeat's and
Wright's conjecture, reasons against dating the *Reply* and the
Rejoinder as early as 1404 (or shortly thereafter) are not slow to
appear, and although largely negative, they cannot easily be

---

[1] For the levy of 1371, see D. Wilkins, *Concilia Magnae Britanniae et
Hiberniae* (London, 1737), iii. 91; for 1404, W. Stubbs, *Constitutional History
of England* (5th edn.), iii. 46, n. 4, 48, n. 5; 1419 and 1429, E. F. Jacob,
Register of Henry Chichele, iii (Oxford, 1945), 523, 525; I take 1429 as the
latest probable date for the *Reply*. The date is arbitrary, but it seems to me
that a very corrupt text (as the *Reply* is) in a MS. to be dated a little before
1450 can hardly be allowed a period of transmission of less than twenty
years if its extensive corruptions are to be accounted for.

[2] At 150–8, also 71–74, 660–1.

discounted. Thus, the attacks on Wyclif in the *Reply* have a vehemence that is hardly to be expected as early as this: the first embargo on the teaching of Wyclif was that passed by the Southern Convocation in 1407, and his official condemnation by his own university was not carried through (and then reluctantly) until 1410. Daw's attacks would best suit a date after Wyclif's condemnation at the Council of Constance in May 1415; and if Daw's description of Wyclif (at 155) is to be taken literally it must refer to his excommunication there. So too (but less convincingly) Daw's remarks about Lollard craftsmen (865–8) may be held to argue for a date after the failure of Oldcastle's rebellion in 1414, when for the first and only time the enthusiasm of the artisan class for Lollardy spilled over into political action.[1] Nor does the reference to Wyclif in the *Rejoinder* as one who was '*in hys tyme* knowen wel a vertuouse man' (86) suggest that the author was what a man who had gone through the schools (as the learning of the author of the *Rejoinder* implies that he had), writing in the middle of the first decade of the fifteenth century, must have been—a near contemporary; and it may be argued that it would take the posthumous martyrdom inflicted on Wyclif at Constance, and perhaps also the exhumation and burning of his bones thirteen years later, to account for the reverence of the description of him in *UR* as a 'seint þat lyued & tauȝt so truly' (91).[2]

If the decisiveness demanded of it by Skeat and Wright is denied the allusion to the hangings, both its authority and its usefulness are much diminished,[3] and in attempting to date the

[1] See *FDR 865–7 n.*

[2] William White in his trial at Norwich in September 1428 was accused of quoting words of 'beatus Wyccliff' in support of unlicensed preaching. William Emayn of Bristol in March 1429 abjured before the bishop of Bath and Wells heresies which included the opinion that 'Maister John Wyclif was holier and now is more in blisse and hier in heven glorified than Seint Thomas of Canterbury the glorious Martir' (M. Aston, 'John Wycliffe's Reformation Reputation', *Past and Present*, xxx (1965), 43 and n. 65).

[3] I must in fairness state here that the late K. B. McFarlane (to whose kindness I owe some of my facts about ecclesiastical taxation, but who is responsible for none of my arguments) declared in a private communication that in the case of the reference in the *Rejoinder* he knew of no episode so apt as the execution of the Franciscans in 1402.

texts on historical grounds[1] it is wiser to look to the limited alternatives offered by Daw's remark about the recent taxation of the exempt.

The levy of 1371 is ruled out and that of 1404 is, if my argument is accepted, improbable. Between the levies of 1419 and 1429 it is difficult to decide, but on balance that of 1419 seems the more likely. If both are distant enough from the last occasion on which the exempt were taxed for Daw to insist that such a levy was unprecedented, a stronger case can be made for the fifteen years that had elapsed in 1419 than the ten years of 1429. If both stand in the shadow of denunciations of Wyclif that might be expected to colour Daw's references to him, it is his condemnation at Constance with the full weight behind it of the Church assembled in solemn Council that one would expect to impress the memory, rather than the exhumation and burning of his bones at Lutterworth in 1428, finally executed on no greater authority than that of the diocesan. The levy of 1429 is within range of no incident which would explain Daw's references to craftsmen as satisfactorily as Oldcastle's revolt of 1414 does.[2] Finally, my emendation *sorcerie* for the meaningless *snowcrie* at *FDR* 900 restores sense to the passage and provides an allusion which, if accepted, makes a date late in 1419 or early 1420 very probable.

Since the argument is important both for date and text it must be set out in full. In my restored text *FDR* 898–901 reads:

> But good Iak, ʒour grace, where be ʒe foundid?
> Not in Goddis gospel but in Sathanas pistile,
> Wher of sorowe & of sorcerie noon is to seken,
> But al maner of dolosite to ʒou is enditid.

---

[1] See pp. 18–19 for my dating of the *Rejoinder* on other than historical grounds.

[2] This is far from decisive, since the association of Lollardy with artisans was a continuing one. It is perhaps implied a hundred years later by an Act of Henry VIII (34 and 35 Henry VIII c. 1) 'for the advancement of true religion' which forbade women, artificers, husbandmen, and the like to read the Bible in English, whereas (with a nice sense of social and political discrimination) noblemen and gentlemen were permitted to read it quietly to their families, and merchants might read it privately.

Sathanas pistile is the *Epistola Luciferi*, an anti-clerical satire widely current in the later Middle Ages, a letter purporting to come from the devil himself to popes and bishops, his ministers on earth, sardonically commending their way of life and their efficiency in recruiting souls for hell. A work beginning as it does 'Lucifer princeps tenebrarum, tristicie profunde sublunorum, regens Acherontis imperia, dux Erebi, rex inferni rectorque Jehenne, universis sociis nostri regni, superbie filiis, etc.'[1] would, for the fifteenth-century mind, have affiliations with misery and magic which make it an obvious antithesis to the gospels. By the orthodox, as one might expect, it was further associated with Lollardy; in the version of it in the Register of John Trefnant, Bishop of Hereford (1389–1404), it is inserted (as Foxe says in a headnote to his translation) 'among the tractations of Walter Brute'—the notorious Lollard who was tried before Trefnant in 1391–3; and the Register itself declares by way of introduction 'Sequitur littera per Lollardos contra viros ecclesiasticos'.[2]

Lollardy ceased to be a serious reform movement quite early in the fifteenth century, and its decline is not so much a matter of loss of political effectiveness (which it never possessed) as of intellectual respectability. It is not the failure of Oldcastle's revolt in 1414,[3] but the flight to Bohemia in 1413 to escape martyrdom of Peter Payne, Lollard Principal of St. Edmund Hall, that symbolizes its collapse. It is not an accident that Lollardy's greatest monument—the translation of the Bible into the vernacular—was a purely academic enterprise, nor that its most momentous political action (next to Oldcastle's abortive rising) was the nailing of a manifesto to the doors of Westminster Hall during the parliament of 1395.

---

[1] I quote from the version in Trefnant's Register, for which see next note.

[2] The Latin text in Trefnant's Register is printed by W. W. Capes, Canterbury and York Society, xx (1916), 401–5; Foxe's translation is in *Actes* (1570), i. 599–600. For evidence of contemporary vernacular versions and further references, see *FDR 899 n.*

[3] This was a ragged affair with no hope of success, as McFarlane has shown: see *Wycliffe*, pp. 167 f.

After 1400 Lollardy rapidly became a private religion, on the one hand of the devout, on the other of cranks and enthusiasts. Of the devout we know little; presumably most of them stayed at home and quietly read their Bibles. The cranks and enthusiasts provide us with a catalogue of extravagances in the records of the period, and in so far as Lollardy was publicly practised, its doctrines provided a portmanteau in which nothing was too wild to find a place.[1] Persecution led to recantation, and many submitted; those whose consciences refused to be bridled either went to the stake or, like Payne, fled.[2]

In the records identifiable Lollard heresies are often found associated with a wide variety of the occult arts;[3] Daw's imputation of sorcery is therefore not in itself remarkable. But if a date late in 1419 is allowed as probable for the *Reply*, his remark is given a context which may be held both to confirm my conjecture *sorcerie* for *snowcrie*, and support the tentative dating of the piece arrived at on other grounds.

The context is provided by three episodes, all occurring within a space of two months in the autumn of 1419. First, in the middle of his last campaign in France, Henry V requested the Archbishop of Canterbury to command the offering of prayers and processions 'pro statu, prosperitate, et felici expeditione domini regis, et sui exercitus contra necromanticorum operationes', and this he did in a decree dated 25 September

---

[1] For some examples taken from the register of a single diocesan in the middle of the century, see McFarlane, pp. 184–5.

[2] He was still alive and still recalcitrant in 1433: see *FDR 575 n.* He died at Prague in 1455.

[3] It is often impossible to tell whether any given case involves a Lollard dabbling in the occult, or an occultist dabbling in Lollardy; it is the common association that matters. Cp. the mandate of 24 August 1431, issued by John Stafford, Bishop of Bath and Wells, against sortileges, perjuries, Lollards, Lollard books, or any others written in the vernacular. It is cited by J. A. F. Thomson, *The Later Lollards, 1414–1520* (Oxford, 1965), p. 30, who remarks, 'It is hard to say how far the conjunction of heresy and the practice of magic in this was merely an accidental combination by the church authorities of two threats to orthodox belief, both of which they were trying to combat, or whether they believed that some of the Lollard beliefs were affected by a belief in magic' (pp. 30–31).

1419.[1] An explanation for this mandate may be seen in the second episode: the extraordinary prosecution of his stepmother, Joan of Navarre, by Henry V in October 1419 for attempting to kill him by means of sorcery and necromancy; her accomplice in this was her confessor, John Randolf, a Franciscan, who admitted his guilt.[2]

Third, on 8 November 1419 there was presented to Convocation in St. Paul's a chaplain Richard Walker, who was charged with practising magic arts and telling fortunes, and the books and instruments of his art were displayed for all to see.[3] Walker publicly confessed, recanted, did penance (17 Nov.), and was released:

Quo die Veneris coram praefatis reverendissimis patribus, archiepiscopo, et confratribus suis, caeterisque praelatis, ac clero et populo in multitudine numerosa ad altam crucem in coemeterio ecclesiae S. Pauli London. congregatis . . . ostendit ibidem in publico venerabilis pater [sc. John de la Zouch, Bishop of Llandaff] coram toto populo praefatum dominum Richardum Walker, capellanum et sortilegum supradictum, tunc ibidem personaliter praesentem, et etiam libros suos, ac pixidem, et instrumenta supradicta, tunc vulgariter exposuit toti populo causam adductionis ejusdem domini Richardi. Qua quidem causa sic per venerabilem patrem Landaven. episcopum exposita, statim idem dominus Richardus Walker publice coram populo recognovit, et dixit, quod hujusmodi ars magica et sortilegium fuerunt et sunt falsa . . . et tunc in poenam peccati in exercitio ejusdem artis superius confessatae commissi, praefati duo libri suspensi fuerunt circa collum praedicti domini Richardi, unus sc. ad pectus, et alter ad ejus dorsum, aperti; sic quod totus populus ante et retro posset inspicere et videre characteres, et figuras in eisdem libris factas et depictas. Et in tali apparatu idem Richardus capite disco operto statim de illo loco recessit, et perrexit

[1] Wilkins, Concilia, iii. 392–3.
[2] G. L. Kittredge, Witchcraft in Old and New England (Cambridge, Mass., 1929), pp. 79–80.
[3] 'ostendit . . . in publico coram omnibus ibidem praesentibus duos libros, in quibus scriptae et depictae fuerunt nonnullae conjurationes, et figurae, artem magicam, ut dicebatur, et sortilegium sapientes; ac etiam unam pixidem, in qua contenti erant unus lapis de birillo, artificialiter in corio nigro suspensus, tres parvae schedulae, et duae parvae imagines de cera crocea' (Wilkins, Concilia, iii. 394).

ante totum clerum et populum processionaliter more solito incedentes per altum vicum vulgariter dictum 'le Chepe'; et cum reversus esset idem dominus Richardus, ante processionem hujusmodi ad australem partem extra ecclesiam S. Pauli praedict. capti fuerunt ab ipso duo libri praedicti, et ibidem in uno igne propter hoc ordinato, fuerunt iidem libri, una cum pixide et imaginibus ac instrumentis supradictis, publice coram toto populo combusti; et sic idem dominus Richardus a custodia carcerali extitit liberatus.[1]

This account shows the medieval Church at its most impressive. It was everything a provincial synod should be, and it can hardly have been soon forgotten.

My argument will be clear: that Daw, probably a member of the London Blackfriars (see p. 9), had every reason to know in the autumn of 1419 that sorcery was much in the air. The plot of Joan of Navarre against the king was common knowledge, and it must have especially scandalized the mendicants that a friar was involved in it. Daw himself may well have offered up prayers for the protection of Henry V and his armies against necromancers;[2] and, even if he was not himself a witness, he could hardly have been ignorant of the episode of Richard Walker whose books were burned in the very shadow of the walls of his own house. Finally, the three episodes would be fresh in the mind of one who could speak of the taxation of the exempt imposed on 20 November 1419 (by the same convocation before which Walker was arraigned) as 'now late'.[3] Daw's imputation

---

[1] *Concilia*, iii. 394.

[2] It seems safe to assume that they would account the treason more scandalous than the necromancy. Apparently the occult arts were tolerated by the friars both as a personal taste and a corporate interest. It is difficult to explain otherwise the very heavy representation of works on the subject in the library of the Austin Friars at York. Under the heading 'Prophecie et supersticiosa' sixty-four items are listed. Such titles as 'tractatus ad habendum loquelam cum spiritu et effectum eternum', 'theorica artis magice in 56 capitulis', and 'liber rubeus qui aliter dicitur sapientia Nigromancie', leave no doubt about their unsavoury nature. All were originally part of the private library of Master John Erghome, a member of the society at the end of the fourteenth century (M. R. James, 'The Catalogue of the Library of the Augustinian Friars at York', *Fasciculus Ioanni Willis Clark dicatus* (Cambridge, 1909), pp. 53–55).

[3] The levy was of one noble from chaplains of parochial chantries (Daw's *annuellers*) of seven marks annual value and upwards. See Jacob, *Reg.*

of sorcery to Upland is not only explicable, it is, in the circumstances, almost predictable. For these reasons, and with moderate confidence, I would date Daw's *Reply* late 1419 or early 1420.

There is very little evidence of any kind for *Upland*, and none firm enough to encourage an attempt to date it exactly. An earliest date is fixed by Upland's familiarity with Wyclif's sacramental heresies (390 f.).[1] Wyclif's frontal attack on the orthodox theory of the Eucharist dates from 1379; it seems first to have been propounded in lectures, and within two years was given permanent form in a treatise *De Eucharistia*. Condemnation followed quickly; first during the winter of 1380-1 by a commission of doctors of his own university, and again in the summer of 1382 by a council summoned by William Courtenay, Archbishop of Canterbury. The dissemination of the Eucharistic heresies, their translation from Latin into the vernacular, and their vulgarizing and misinterpretation at the hands of an Upland, can hardly have taken less than a decade, and it seems reasonable to date *Upland* not earlier than about 1390.[2]

If 1419-20 is accepted as the probable date of Daw's *Reply*, it constitutes a *terminus ad quem*. On balance, a date later rather than earlier in the period 1390 to 1420 seems likely. It allows for the intellectual debilitation that already characterized Lollardy by the end of the fourteenth century. The condemnation

Chichele, iii. 523. For the general concern at this time at the proliferation of unbeneficed stipendiary clergy (of which chantry chaplains were the most numerous) see Jacob, *The Fifteenth Century, 1399–1485* (Oxford, 1961), pp. 283-4.

There is no evidence that friars were taxed in 1419. But it does no violence to Daw's syntax (loose here as elsewhere) to translate 'Neither friars nor (until recently) chantry chaplains'. His testiness stems not from an affection for chantry chaplains, but from his awareness of the encroachment on traditional privilege that the levy represented.

[1] In fact, Upland characteristically confuses the issue: he imputes to the friars the Wyclifian position that after consecration the bread remains both in accidents and substance, while reserving for himself the orthodox belief. Hence Daw's complaint, 'þou drawist a þorn out of þin hele & puttist it in oure' (841).

[2] But cp. Mrs. Aston, 'the heretical missionaries who began to vulgarize his views were already active during the last two years or so of his life' (*Past and Present*, xxx (1965), 41).

engineered by Courtenay at the 'Earthquake Council' of May 1382, by cutting off Wyclif's support at Oxford and denying him the university as a recruiting ground, virtually destroyed any hopes of the success of Lollardy as a reform movement.[1] No amount of populist enthusiasm or ignorant sincerity could make up for the loss of the professionalism of the schools, with their polemical and pedagogical skills. *Upland* must be among the earliest (and perhaps not quite the worst) of the stream of tracts that poured from semi-literate pens at the end of the fourteenth and throughout the fifteenth century.[2] Their connexion with Wyclif is slender; the shibboleths are his, but little else.

I set out below (pp. 41–4) my reasons for believing that the *Rejoinder* is a holograph, and if my argument is accepted the hand affords evidence of the date of composition. Mr. N. R. Ker is of the opinion that it is to be dated shortly after 1450.[3] The extensive corruption of Daw's text argues for a distance of at least two, and possibly three or more, mediate copies from the original;[4] and in a text which, because of the official disapproval of vernacular replies to Lollard polemics,[5] was probably not much copied, it does not seem unreasonable to assume a period of transmission of thirty years or so.

[1] In this condemnation Wyclif himself was not mentioned by name, and only twenty-four propositions from his works were cited. Of these, ten were declared heretical and the rest erroneous. Wyclif himself remained unmolested, probably for the same reason that earlier attempts to discipline him—by Courtenay, then Bishop of London, in 1377, and by the Pope in 1378—had failed: he enjoyed the political protection of John of Gaunt. Wyclif's personal authority seems to have remained more or less intact, at least until his condemnation by the Southern Convocation in 1407, and arguably until he was finally proscribed at Constance in 1415. In 1382 Courtenay succeeded by striking at him through his pupils.

[2] *JU* 247–50 may refer to the Statute of Heresy which made burning at the stake the penalty for an obstinate heretic. If so, *Upland* must be dated 1401 or later. But see Arnold i. viii–xii, and Skeat, *Piers Plowman*, ii. xiii–xiv (where he discusses an allusion to burning in B. xv. 80–81).

[3] I am grateful to Mr. Ker for his help in dating the hands of this and the other MSS.

[4] See *FDR* 767 n.

[5] In the middle of the fifteenth century Reynold Pecock, Bishop of Chichester, was condemned and imprisoned for writing theological argument in English. Yet even he takes the precaution, in an English work, of writing

Thus the allusion 'And þe kyng by his juges trwe execute his lawe / As he did now late when he hangid ȝou traytoures' (*UR* 271–2), used by Wright and Skeat to date the *Rejoinder* to 1402, may refer to some such episode as the condemnation of eight of Jack Cade's accomplices by a royal commission which sat at Canterbury in August 1450, or perhaps to the so-called 'Harvest of Heads', the bloody assize held in February 1451 by which the last traces of the popular movement in Kent were extinguished. It is unnecessary to follow Wright and Skeat in assuming that *ȝou traytoures* refers to friars; it is quite as likely to refer to the enemies of the established order, of King and Church. The latinity of the author of the *Rejoinder* is enough to set him apart from the ignorant and extravagant Lollardy of the mid fifteenth century; he may well have been a secular who did not like friars. Without attempting an exact identification of the allusion, it seems reasonable to place it in the period which the hand suggests.

LANGUAGE

Linguistically the texts have few distinctive features, and all but *UR* show many inconsistencies. I therefore do not attempt a full description, but point out those features which may help to localize the manuscripts. MS. C is so late that firm dialectal criteria can hardly be hoped for, and even the others are late enough for much doubt to surround the traditional treatment of spellings as representative of sounds.

MS. Harley 6641

The spelling is conservative and exhibits few irregularities. For the palatal and velar spirant, ȝ appears in all positions: medially after front and back vowels before *t*, as 4 *almyȝti*, 69 *brouȝte*; finally as 66 *þouȝ*; for later *y* in initial position ȝ is regular in the second person plural pronoun, as *ȝe, ȝou,*

in Latin passages where the subject-matter is too lofty and difficult to be expressed in the vernacular. See E. F. Jacob, 'Reynold Pecock, Bishop of Chichester', *PBA*, xxxvii (1951), 135.

ȝoure, also 23 *ȝit* 'yet', 105 *ȝeere* 'years'. For the dental spirant, *th* appears initially (beginning a new paragraph) in 79 *thei*, 83 *thes*; elsewhere *þ* is invariable in all positions. The group *sch* is regular initially, as 37 *schal*, 156 *schulde*, 366 *schame*; is usual in the middle of a word, as 181 *bischopis* (4x, but cp. 72 *bisshopis*, 51 *schepisshenesse*), and finally, as 387 *fleisch*. Next to minim letters *y* is written for *i*, as 5 *ymage*, 85 *matrymonye*, 168 *ynne* (but usually *in*), 212 *lyuynge*, and occasionally where no minim is present, as 336 *meryt* beside 339 *merit*. Letters are often doubled when vowels are long, as 10 *goost*, 13 *lijf*, 210 *heeste*, 351 *apostataas*; in words of French origin initial *h* is usually omitted, as 60 *oost*, 82 *eiris* 'heirs', 125 *abite*, 254 *erise* (but 52 *heryse*), 394 *eritikis*. Initially *c* appears before *e* in such words as 190 *certeyne* but also once before *a* in 67 *cauce* 'sauce', and once (for usual *sc*) in 320 *claunderers* 'slanderers'; *ff* is regularly written for capital *f*.

The North is excluded by regular *o(o)* for OE. *ā*; 10 *holi*, 20 *more*, 345 *goostli*, 399 *oold*. The West Midlands are excluded by the appearance of OE. *a* before a nasal (except before lengthening groups, where *o* is not restricted to the West Midlands) as *a*: 3 *many*, 5 *man*, 282 *names*, 409 *answere*. The South-east and South-west are excluded by regular change of OE. *ў* to *i/y*: 225 *birie*, 243 *myrþis*, 338 *synnes*, 384 *bisien*.

The most striking feature of the language is the very great preponderance of forms with *i* (occasionally *y*) in inflexional syllables other than *-en*. Thus, in the plural and genitive of nouns *-is* is regular except in words ending in a nasal or a liquid (which have *-s*). It is regular in the second and third singular present indicative, as 99 *þenkist*, 109 *rulist*, 146 *owiþ*, 215 *techiþ* (only occasionally with *e*, as 21 *ȝeueþ*); usual in weak past participles, as 25 *dowid*, 42 *professid* (the exceptions are chiefly after stems ending in a minim letter); also in the comparative of adjectives, as 132 *bettir* (but more usually *e*, as 132 *better*), and superlatives, as 69 *fellist*; also in 64 *sikir*, 65 *aftir* (regularly), 70 *wondir*, 276 *vttirli*, 343 *vndir*, etc.

This could appear in the North or the Midlands, but the

morphological evidence is decisive for the Midlands: *-ist* and *-eþ/-iþ* (with no syncopated forms) are regular in the second and third singular present indicative; in the present plural *-en* predominates; in the past participle of strong verbs forms with and without *-n* appear in approximately equal numbers, and there is no example of a *y-* prefix.

In such a late MS. the North Midlands seem excluded by the evidence of the pronominal forms: only the nominative plural *þei* (which is invariable) is established, except for an isolated case of possessive plural *þer* in 331, against nearly two dozen examples of *her*; in the accusative and dative *hem* is regular. These forms are supported by the regular appearance of *ȝ* initially in such words as 95 *ȝifte*, 96 *ȝeue*, and by the non-northern form *axe(n)* 'ask' in 99, 187, 189.

Beside the predominant *i* of unstressed syllables noticed above, there are frequent spellings with *u* especially in the past participle of strong verbs, as 20 *ȝouun* (also 34, 40, 55), 23 *takun*, 56 *chosun*, 72 *knowun* (also 256), in the noun *lustus* at 387 and the adjective *rotun* at 406. Such spellings are usually associated with the West but occur also in MSS. of the Central Midlands.[1] The form *ȝouun* 'given' is, according to Professor Samuels, especially characteristic of Central Midland MSS., and is one of the indicators for which he traces isoglosses to support his contention that the Central Midland dialect has the best claim to be considered the 'standard literary language' of the early fifteenth century. Of the other typical forms for which he plots the distribution (maps 4–10), *myche*, *ony*, and *silf* beside *ȝouun* are invariable in H; *sich* is not found, but H *such* appears (map 4) adjacent to, and slightly to the north and west of, the *sich* area of the Central Midlands; two others—the words 'stead' and 'saw'—do not occur in H in any form. In view of this coincidence of typical forms, and since there is nothing in the other linguistic evidence to forbid it, it seems admissible to conclude that the language of H is that of the Central

---

[1] See M. L. Samuels, 'Some Applications of Middle English Dialectology', *English Studies*, xliv (1963), 81–94.

Midlands. This is encouraged by Professor Samuels's identification of the language as that of the majority of Wyclifite MSS. (although by no means limited to them), and H is, of course, such a MS.

Professor Samuels argues persuasively for acceptance of this type of language as that with most claim to the title of 'literary standard' before 1430, but he also points out that it is found in MSS. known to have been copied in areas far from the Central Midlands (as Somerset and Dorset, for example), and that it survived in written form largely unchanged until the later fifteenth century. It seems best to describe the dialect of H as basically that of the Central Midlands, while attempting no precise geographical localization.

C.U.L. MS. Ff. vi. 2

The spelling displays much variety. This is most marked in the representation of the palatal and velar spirant, where the same word often appears with different spellings; thus 44 *neyghtbus* 'neighbours' is found beside 91 *neybur*, 159 *thrugh* 'through' beside 203 *throwe*; also 34 *fyȝt*, 175 *nyght*, 69 *browȝt*, before *t*; 174 *wellnye*, 211 *galhows* 'gallows', 355 *ynowe*, and without historical justification in 282 *wryghtest* 'writest'. In the second person plural pronoun *y* appears invariably, as *ye*, *yow*, *yower*, as also in 20 *yere* 'years', 178 *yett*, 'yet', etc. In the hand of the scribe *þ* has the form of *y*; *th* and this *y* (=*þ*) are interchangeable initially, as 1 *the*, 159 *thrugh* beside 8 *ye*, 55 *yem*, and *y* is found in this position especially in abbreviated words, as 23 *y^r* = 'their', 36 *y^t* = 'that'. In the middle of a word the scribe shows a marked preference for *th* (although *y* does occur, usually with the following syllable abbreviated, as 21 *a noyer*, 187 *boyerhede* [*sic*] 'brotherhood'); in final position only *th* is written.[1] The group *sch* is regular in all positions, as 26 *schall*, 51 *schepyschenes*, 147 *flesche*. There is a heavy preponderance of *y* over *i* without noticeable limitation to parti-

---

[1] In the citation of variants from C (in the apparatus of *Upland* and elsewhere) I substitute *þ* for this *y* of the scribe's orthography.

cular contexts (e.g. next to minim letters) where ambiguity might result; thus, 12 *minyster* (vb.) but also 17 *ministers*; 32 *lyvyng* where some ambiguity is possible, but 347 *begyle* and *chyldern* where none is. In words of French origin initial *h* is usually found, as 60 *hoste* (but 89 *oost*), 82 *hoyers* 'heirs', 377 *heresie*, 394 *heretyckes*, while original *abyttys* 'habits' and *abite* at 130, 136 have *h* inserted later; *ff* appears for capital *f* and occasionally elsewhere, as 64 *lyff*, 126 *wyffe*.

The MS. is late and the phonological evidence difficult to interpret. The North is excluded by regular *o(o)* for OE. *ā*: 10 *gooste*, 52 *old*, 114 *moo* 'more'. The West Midlands are excluded by the appearance of OE. *a* before a nasal as *a*: 3 *many*, 5 *man*, 282 *namys*, and (before a lengthening group) 362 *hand*. The South-east and South-west are excluded by regular change of OE. *ȳ* to *i/y*: 154 *fyrst*, 243 *myrthes*, 280 *synnith*. The appearance of *u* beside *i/y*, as 204 *buried*, 220 *bury* and regularly in *church(e)* hardly points to the South-west or West at this date.

The loss of the spirant before *t* in pronunciation, confirmed by the spelling of 282 *wryghtest*, points to the East, and so does 64 *xall* 'shall', a characteristic East Anglian feature which is very old-fashioned at this date. Assimilation of *rl* in *wordly* 'worldly' (in 7, 30, 161, 370) against 360, 387 *world* is probably a Midland feature, and, on the evidence of original *word(e)* at 61, 62 (and possibly at 172) later corrected by the scribe to *world(e)*, and *wold* in 173 corrected by insertion of *r*, a feature present in the MS. the scribe was copying. A difficult group of spellings is that in which *i/y* may appear as the diacritic of length often found in Northern texts: this explanation would fit 3 *waist* 'waste' (vb.) and 66 *waist* (adj.), 48 *wraith* 'wrath', 134 *apostatais* 'apostates' and 135 *apostatai*, 201 *truyth*, 237 *hait*, and (frequently) *haith(e)*, *haist* 'hath', 'hast'.[1] But 205 *cloithis* is not satisfactorily explained in this way. The expected Northern form would be *claith-*; *cloysse*, however, appears in the Towneley plays. The association seems in any case to be

---

[1] It is possible that the *ai* spellings represent [æ:] or [ε:].

Northern, perhaps (on the basis of the Towneley form) with Yorkshire. The stop *g* appears regularly in such words as 13 *gyve*, 95 *gyft*, 121 *agayn*.

Pronominal and (with one exception) verbal forms are un-remarkable. The forms *þei*, *þem*, *þer* (written *yei*, *yem*, *yer*) are regular, as one would expect at this date; in the second person plural pronoun the objective form *yow* has replaced the nomina-tive in at least a dozen places. In the second and third singular present indicative *-est*, *-eth* forms are regular; the present plural indicative appears with and without *-e*, but there is one striking example of a Southern form in 370 *passith*, and in a strongly plural context where an erroneous third singular present indica-tive is very unlikely: 'in tresorye & jewylles & r(i)che ornamentes fryers passith lordes & oþer riche wordly men' (369–70).

From all this no definite pattern emerges; the mixture of forms can perhaps best be explained by the assumption that the MS. was copied in London, with regional forms—possibly North-east Midlands—from earlier copies showing through.

MS. *Digby 41*

(*a*) *Friar Daw's Reply*

The spelling is irregular. One of the more stable features is the representation of the palatal and velar spirant: with a single exception (151 *litht*) *ȝ* appears in all positions. In the second person plural pronoun *ȝ* is invariable, as *ȝe*, *ȝou*, *ȝoure*, also in such words as 141 *ȝere*, 799 *ȝonge*. Usage of *þ/th* is more various; *þ* heavily predominates in all positions, but there is a scattering of *th* forms: initially, as 9 *throwun*, 235 *thrift* and 922, 932 *thryue*, with a single instance of definite article 159 *the*; in the middle of a word only in 95 *sothli*, and in 624 *pathes*; finally, in a few third singular present indicatives, as 20 *fadith*, 505 *worchipeth*, 648 *amountith*, in 533 *cloith* (against *cloiþ* 3 times), in the adjective *soth* (at 6, 598, 671) beside the noun *soþ(e)* (4x), and also in *with* (180, 628) against usual *wiþ*. Usage is evenly divided in the *s(c)h* group: *shal*, etc. is invariable and *shulde* regular, but also *schulde(n)* (4x); so too 590 *shryuen* but 593 *schryue*, 73 *shendship* but 95 *schenden*; medially, 82 *parischens* but 594 *parishens* (MS. *paishens*), in other words usually *sh* as 51 *bishopes*, 763 *worship* (but 505 *worchipeth*); in final position *sh* is usual, as 266 *fleish*, 896 *freishe*, but also 232 *Englis*. Next to minim letters *y* is usually preferred to *i*, as 18 *pursuynge*, 151 *begynnynge*, 477 *lymytours* (but also 693 *ministren*), and occasionally in words where no minims are present, as 319 *byhold*. Usage with *u/o* next to minims varies, as 33 *vnboxom* against 378 *boxumnesse*, 130 *trompes* beside 205 *trumpe*, 269 *ponishid* beside 269 *punishid*, and *somme* regularly beside *summe*. Letters are often doubled when vowels are long, as 106 *oold*, 283 *maad*, 368 *wijd*; in words of French origin only *abite* is usually without initial *h* (but 531 *habite*), others, as 12 *heresie*, 636 *heretike*, with it. For capital *f* (usually at the beginning of a line) *ff* is normally written, as 21 *ffoxes*; occasionally *ff* also appears in words which stand first in the line but in which no capital is intended, as 238 *off* 'of', 239 *iff*. For OE. *hw-*, *wh-* is regular; forms without *h*, 674 *wen*, 688 *wich*, both result from correction.

The North is excluded by regular *oo* for OE. *ā*: 90 *goost*, 158 *woo* 'woe', 361 *hoot* 'hot', 798 *hooli*, 848 *stoon*. The West Midlands are excluded by the appearance of OE. *a* before a nasal as *a*: 41 *man*, 64 *many*, 71 *name*, 234 *answer*. The Southeast and South-west are excluded by change of OE. *ȳ* to *i/y*: 12 *chirche*, 134 *first*, 375 *bisynesse*; in some words there is alternation between *i/y* and *e*: 578 *biryynge*, 591 *birien* beside 525 *beried*, 584 *beriynge*; 403 *myry* beside 301 *merie*.

Such forms as 152 *mykil* against 65 *michel*, 232 *Englis* against usual *-s(c)h*, 362 *cloiþ* (4x) are (despite regularity of *oo* for OE. *ā*) northerly, and these are supported by some third singular present indicative forms: while *-eþ/-iþ* is usual, forms with *-s* appear in 201 *preamblis*, 231 *suposis* (emendation), 869 *susteynes*.

There is little else to support such a localization. The other morphological evidence is unremarkable: second singular present indicative is regularly *-est/-ist*, but there are eight places where forms without -*t* occur—seven of them (which I let stand) probably from simplification of a group of dental consonants (see 64 n.). It is possible that 575 MS. *hauep* and 879 MS. *delith* are Southern plurals, but it seems to me more likely that they result from corruption (see the notes to these lines). Strong past participle without *y*- and with -*n* is regular, but forms without -*n* occur in 74 *growe*, 589 *take*; a weak past participle with *y*- appears twice in the same word *yfourmed* at 36 and 256. Of pronominal forms *pei* is regular in the nominative, *hem* in the accusative and dative (but *pem* occurs once at 517); genitive *her* is regular with one doubtful *pere* form (which may be adverbial) at 130.

Perhaps the most significant feature is the frequent appearance in verb plurals and strong past participles of -*un* endings beside -*en*: thus, 449, 658 *foundun* beside 116 *founden*, 31, 339 *growun* beside 156 *growen*, *holdun* (4x), *holden* (3x), *knowun* (2x), *knowen* (1x), *ȝouun* (2x), *ȝeuen* (3x). These (and in particular *ȝouun*) may point to the Central Midlands. Of the other indicators listed by Professor Samuels (see p. 21) the following usually occur: *silf(e)*, *sich(e)* (but also 588, 792 *suche*), *ony* (but also 338 *eny*); also *myche* (twice, but *moche* 5x) as well as *ȝouun*. Such forms as 311 *puple* beside *peple* (10x), 209, 623 *eende* beside 625 *ende*, *axe* 'ask' (4x) beside *ask* (8x), 932 *wers* beside 417 *worse*, and (of the morphological indicators) 217 *ar* 'are' beside regular *ben*, and preterite plural 397 *chesen* 'chose' with the vowel of the preterite singular 436, 776 *chees*, are also found in Wyclifite MSS. of the period, written in a language based on the Central Midland dialects.

In view of the conclusions reached about H (p. 22) it seems best to attempt no exact geographical localization for the MS. on the basis of the Central Midland characteristics of its language. But it is worth remarking that if, as I argue, the author of the *Reply* was a resident of London writing in about 1420, the admixture of forms in the MS. does not exclude the possibility that subsequent copying of the text may have been largely confined to the same area.

(b) Upland's Rejoinder

The spelling is generally conservative. For the palatal and velar spirant ʒ appears in all positions. In the second person plural pronoun ʒ is regular for later *y*, as also in *ʒit*. Usage of þ/*th* is divided: þ appears initially in personal pronouns, demonstratives, adverbs, relatives, etc., as *þou, þis, þer(e), þat*, while *th* appears in the same position in nouns, adjectives, adverbs formed from nouns, and verbs, as 26 *theft*, 132 *thre*, 125 *thefly*, 189 *thynkiþ*; elsewhere þ is invariable except in the preposition *with* (abbreviated *wᵗ* in every case). Except for 129 *wirchipiþ*, 384 *wirchip*, *sh* is regular, as 94 *shal*, 200 *fleshe*, 283 *bisshopes*; *y* is usual for *i* next to a minim letter, as 47 *symonye*. Vowel length is shown by doubling the letter only occasionally with *o* as 97 *woo* 'woe', 114 *noo*. In words of French origin initial *h* is regular, as 176 *habit*, 308 *heritikes*, as also is *ff* for capital *f*; at 107 *we* is spelt *whe*.

The North is excluded by regular *o(o)* for OE. *ā*: 140 *holichirche*, 196 *oo* 'one', 258 *more*. The West Midlands are excluded by the appearance of OE. *a* before a nasal as *a*: 1 *answere*, 6 *name*, 16 *man*, 43 *many*. The South-east and South-west are excluded by regular change of OE. *ȳ* to *i/y*: 39 *synne*, 45 *chirche*, 49 *gilty*.

There are very few dialectal features and no significant pattern emerges. Such forms as *meche* 'much' (5x), *werse* (4x), 352 *wedowes* with lowering of *i* to *e*, may at this date be associated with the East Midlands, as also the Norse-derived form 62 *hundriþ* and the stop *g* instead of initial ʒ once in 348 *gif* 'give', while the form *puple*, 'people' (9x), originally Western, was not restricted to this area by the middle of the fifteenth century. Verbal and pronominal forms are stable: *-ist/-est*, *-iþ/-eþ* are regular in the second and third singular present indicative, as is strong past participle with *-en* (but once 45 *cropun*); *þai* in the nominative, accusative and dative *hem*, genitive *her(e)* are invariable.

The striking feature of the language is its consistency: its freedom from dialectal contamination, the regularity of its verbal and pronominal forms, and the stability of its spelling conventions. If, as I believe, the *Rejoinder* is holograph, and the dialect East Midland, it shows how settled could be the usage of a man writing in a dialect which represents the emergent 'standard' and, as early as the middle of the fifteenth century, how strong were its characteristics and conventions over a wide range of linguistic usage.

VERSIFICATION

Upland has suffered from Wright's conviction that it is in alliterative verse, and from his curious printing of it as a succession of half-lines. Hence, presumably, Oakden's opinion that it is 'entirely lacking in poetic form and inspiration. . . . The poem is entirely formless.'[1] Only three passages can lay any claim to verse form—69–74, 79–89, 401 to the end;[2] the rest is prose and unequivocally prosaic. The verse passages do not fall inadvertently; they are used to contrive rhetorical climaxes at two important places in the text. They contribute their vigour to the first identification and description of the friars ('þe fellist folk þat euer Antecrist foond') in 69 f., 79 f. at the end of the prologue to Upland's catechism proper, and to the hortatory imperatives ('take hede to my tale & to myn entent'; 'Go now forþ frere & fraiste ʒoure clerkis') of the concluding lines of the piece. These passages apart, *Upland*'s debt to the alliterative tradition is indirect and amounts to no more than a handful of alliterative phrases.

The *Reply* and *Rejoinder* are recognizably alliterative verse, though of a very late and debased variety. The scribe of *FDR* writes 1–248, 258–346 (except 267, 277) in verse lines; the rest he writes continuously as prose with a double virgule to show line-division. The same method of line-division is used by UR,

---

[1] J. P. Oakden, *Alliterative Poetry in Middle English: A Survey of the Traditions* (Manchester, 1935), p. 60.
[2] I print these as prose; they are written thus in the MSS.

who also writes continuously as prose. None of the verse in the
three pieces merits detailed analysis; it displays every licence to
be found in fifteenth-century alliterative practice.[1] The most
striking fact to emerge from an examination of *FDR* and *UR* is
the evidence the texts afford of the persistence of the regular
four-beat line when the systematic alliterative technique with
which it was originally linked had decayed so completely. But
by the time that the Cambridge MS. of *Upland* came to be
copied half a century later, the whole system had perished; the
scribe's occasional modifications of the verse passages in H
often destroy both alliteration and rhythm.[2]

<h3 style="text-align:center">THE TEXT</h3>

There is no doubt that the Harley (H) and Cambridge (C)
MSS. represent a version of the text different from the black-
letter print (1536).[3] Skeat, ignorant as he was of the MSS., was
able to infer the existence of two versions from his comparison
of 1536 and the text of Daw's *Reply*. From the discrepancies
between the questions *Upland* asks and Daw's answers, he con-
cluded that originally *Upland* existed in two 'editions', and
that 1536 is a print of the later, and on the whole fuller,
version.[4]

The MSS. confirm Skeat's conjecture: H and C stand together against 1536, which adds some passages and omits others,
transposes, varies, and conflates, expands and contracts. The
argument in favour of 1536 being an independent version rests

[1] Cp. Oakden, 'The metre of these poems is so corrupt and crude that the
usual investigation is quite impossible', *Alliterative Poetry in Middle English:
The Dialectal and Metrical Survey* (Manchester, 1930), p. 180. Emendation
on metrical grounds is hazardous as a result, but cp. *FDR* 103 n., 408–9 n.,
836 n.

[2] See *JU* 402 n.

[3] I ignore the later prints of Foxe and Speght; Foxe probably took his
text from 1536, and Speght certainly took his from Foxe. It is possible that
Foxe took his text from the edition of Day referred to by Bale; if so, it must
have been so close to the text of 1536 as to be hardly worth distinguishing for
textual purposes.

[4] *Chaucerian and Other Pieces*, pp. xxxv–xxxvii.

upon the considerable differences that distinguish it from HC. The most important of these are as follows:[1]

Additions

A short headnote (Ai^v beg. *These ben the*) before *JU* 1; a paragraph (Aii^r–v beg. *SAynt Paul*) after *JU* 100; a paragraph (Aiii^v beg. *If ye saye*) after *JU* 144; followed by a paragraph (Aiii^v beg. *Why maye not*); a paragraph (Av^v–vi^r beg. *why couette you*) after *JU* 229; a paragraph (Avi^r beg. *why be ye*) after *JU* 236; a long paragraph (Avii^r–v beg. *If thou sayest*) after *JU* 287; a long passage (Aviii^v beg. *& yf ye sayne*) after *JU* 306; a passage (Bi^r beg. *And but this*) after *JU* 321; a paragraph (Bi^v beg. *Why haue ye*) after *JU* 329;[2] a passage (Bii^r–v beg. *and all were*) after *JU* 341; followed by a paragraph (Bii^v beg. *what tokeneth that*); a long paragraph (Biiii^r–v beg. *Frere what charyte*) after *JU* 378;[3] followed by a long paragraph (Biiii^v–v^r beg. *Frere what charyte*);[4] a paragraph (Bv^v beg. *why name ye*) after *JU* 389; followed by a long paragraph (Bvi^r beg. *Frere wheter was*);[5] followed by a long paragraph (Bvi^r–vii^r beg. *Frere which of*); followed by a long paragraph (Bvii^r beg. *Frere is there*);[6] followed by a long paragraph (Bvii^r–v beg. *For yf he*); followed by a long paragraph (Bvii^v–viii^r beg. *Frere canst thou*); a paragraph (Bviii^v beg. *If freres cunne*) after *JU* 411.

Omissions

JU 4–68;[7] *JU* 79–97 (end. *ordre nede be*); *JU* 117 (beg. *For Cristis rule*)–21; *JU* 141 (beg. *þat ʒe maken*)–3; *JU* 155

---

[1] I do not attempt to list every variation. I supply in brackets references to the text of 1536.

[2] This is an expanded version of *JU* 180–1, found in HC and 1536 at that place.

[3] This is an expanded version of *JU* 204–8, found in HC and 1536 at that place.

[4] This is an expanded version of *JU* 335–41, found in HC and 1536 at that place.

[5] This is another version of *JU* 148–59, found in HC and 1536 at that place.

[6] This and the following paragraph are very much expanded versions of *JU* 114–15, found in HC and 1536 at that place.

[7] Except for 46–47, which follows *JU* 1–3.

(beg. *for þan ʒe*)–59; *JU* 169 (beg. *ne hise apostlis*)–72 (end. *make gay housis*); *JU* 182–6; *JU* 191–2 (end. *most perfiʒt loue*); *JU* 244–56; *JU* 269 (beg. *Where is a*)–71; *JU* 277 (beg. *& nameli of*)–81; *JU* 390–407.

Transpositions

JU 257–62 (much abbreviated) inserted after *JU* 232 (Avi^r); *JU* 282–4 (slightly expanded) inserted after *JU* 269 (Avi^v); *JU* 291–4 (much abbreviated) inserted before *JU* 287 (Avii^v).

1536 has also been heavily edited. Passages that are substantially the same as the equivalent passages in *JU* are modified in the following ways:

by abbreviation, as 233–6:

JU: Frere, whi preche ʒe fals fablis of freris & feined myraclys, and leuen þe gospel þat Crist bade preche & is moost holsum lore to bodi & to soule, & so also oure bileue bi whiche oonli we moste be saued?

1536 (Avi^r): what cause hast thou that thou wylte not preache the gospell? as God sayeth that thou shuldest, syth it is the best lore and also oure beleue?

by omission, as 187–90:

JU: Frere, whi axe ʒe not lettris of briþered of oþer pore mennes preieris, good & cristen leuers, ne of preestis, ne of monkis, ne of bischopis, as ʒe desire þat oþer riche men axen ʒou letteris for a certeyne summe bi ʒeer?

1536 (Aiiii^v): Why axe ye no letters of bretherhedes of other mens prayers, as ye desire that other men shulde aske letters of you?

by substitution, as 282–4:

JU: Frere, whi writist þou mennes names in þi tablis? Wenest þou þat God is suche a fool þat he wot not of mennes dedis but if þou telle hym bi þi tablis?

1536 (Avi^v): Why wrytest thou her names in thy tables that yeueth the money? Sith God knoweth all thynge, for it semyth by thy wryting, that God wolde not rewarde hym, but thou wryte him in thy tables, god wolde els forgetten it.

and by expansion, as *JU* 379–82:

JU: What power haue ȝe to asoile lordis & ladies þat ȝe ben confessouris to, of synnes þat þei leuen not, as pilinge of her tenauntis & lyuinge in leccherie & glotony & oþere heed synnes, of whiche þei cecen not but ben counfortid bi ȝoure suffraunce?

1536 (Bv^r–v): Frere what charyte is this to be confessoures of lordes and laydes, and to other myghty men, and not amend hem in her lyuing, but rather as it semeth to be the bolder to pyl her poore tenauntes, and to lyue in lechery, & there to dwel in your offyce of confessour for winning of worldly goodes, & to be holden greate by coloure of suche goostly offyces, thys semeth rather pryde of freres than charite of God.

A comparison of HC and *FDR* raises the question whether there were not, in fact, three versions of *Upland*: that represented by HC, that printed as 1536, and that used by Daw as his text in controverting Upland's charges.[1] It is curious that after the first sixty-eight lines of *Upland* Daw takes up in the order in which they occur in HC every one of Upland's charges (with the exception of the two referred to in n. 2 below) as far as *JU* 284, while from 285 to the end he ignores more charges than he replies to.[2] An argument from silence is hazardous, since Daw may simply have chosen to pass over these charges (as the

---

[1] Daw quotes and paraphrases *Upland* freely and must have had a copy beside him to refer to.

[2] Daw does not reply to the following passages in *JU*: 1–68, 122–4, 180–1, 285–94, 307–8, 312–34, 342–53, 366–89. His ignoring of *JU* 1–68 is not necessarily significant, since it is an introductory section that says much about the religious in general but nothing about mendicants in particular. Upland's attack on the friars begins at 69 and Daw starts his reply at that point. Daw's silence at the charges in *JU* 122–4 and 180–1 is also explicable: 122–4 deals with the apostasy a friar was guilty of if he abandoned the habit of his order for that of another, and the next section (125–36) goes on to deal generally with the question of mendicant dress. Daw replies to 125–36 in *FDR* 330–50, and this passage is probably intended also to answer *JU* 122–4. *JU* 180–1 accuses the friars of being 'not lege men to kyngis ne obediente to bischopis'; this repeats almost verbatim an accusation made in *JU* 72–73, which Daw replies to in *FDR* 49–52. There is no reason why he should repeat himself.

Thus, in *JU* 285–411 Daw ignores thirteen charges, viz. 285–90, 291–4, 307–8, 312–14, 315–21, 322–9, 330–4, 342–6, 347–53, 366–72, 373–8, 379–82, 383–9. He replies (in the order in which they occur in HC) to eight, viz. 295–7, 298–306, 309–11, 335–41, 354–65, 390–400, 401–7, 408–11.

author of the *Rejoinder* certainly passes over much in *FDR*), or it may be that the copy he used was defective and lacked several leaves towards the end. But the possibility must remain that the copy of *Upland* used by Daw in composing his *Reply* was, as compared with HC, so truncated that it constituted another 'version'.

Even if we allow Daw's copy of *Upland* the benefit of the doubt and assume that it represents the same version as HC, a comparison of Daw's citations from it and the text of HC suggests that it provides very treacherous ground from which to assail the authority of HC's particular readings. Thus, in the case of *JU* 125–9 cited at *FDR* 330–2:

JU 125–9: Whi be ȝe faster weddid to ȝoure abite bi mannes mariage þanne a man is weddid to his wijf bi Goddis mariage? A man may leue his wijf a moneþ eþer a ȝeer as many men doen, and if ȝe leuen ȝoure abite a wike eþer a quartere of a ȝeer, ȝe ben holden apostataas.

FDR 330–2: Whi bi mannes mariage ȝe ben weddid to ȝour abitis Wele harder þan worldly men ben weddid to her wyues,
Which þei mowe leeue & lete go as longe as hem [MS. him] list?

For H's singulars 125 *abite*, 126 *man, wijf, man*, Daw has plurals 330 *abitis*, 331 *men, wyues* and 332 *þei*. Only MS. *him* in 332 suggests that Daw's readings are probably editorial and not original in the text of *Upland* he is paraphrasing.[1] Elsewhere, as *JU* 233–43 cited at *FDR* 600–3, and *JU* 354–65 cited at *FDR* 809–15, there is not a scrap of evidence on which to base conclusions about the relationship between the two passages.

JU 233–43 · Frere, whi preche ȝe fals fablis of freris & feined myraclys, and leuen þe gospel þat Crist bade preche & is moost holsum lore to bodi & to soule, & so also oure bileue bi whiche oonli we moste be saued? Frere, whi hate ȝe þat þe gospel schulde be prechid to þe trewe vndirstondinge of holi doctouris &, ȝe

---

[1] I assume that MS. *him* is not an authentic plural form; there is no evidence in the text to suggest that it might be. At 125 C reads *habytys*.

clepen it þe newe doctrine in sclaundringe of Crist? & ȝe ben
more holden þerto þan to alle þe rulis þat euer ȝoure patroun
made, & ȝe winnen more wiþ In principio þan Crist & hise
apostlis & alle þe seintis of heuene; & in þis mynistrallis ben
bettre þanne ȝe, for þei contrarien not her myrþis as ȝe don.

FDR 600–3 : þou seist þat we prechen fallace & fables
     & not Goddis gospel to good vndirstondinge,
     & we ben more holdun þerto þan to alle oþer reulis,
     For we wynnen more þerwith þan Crist & his apostlis.

JU 354–65 : Frere, what charite is it to charge þe puple wiþ so
many freris, siþen persouns, vikers, & prestis were jnowȝ to
serue þe puple of preestis office wiþ bischopis—ȝhe, monkis,
chanouns wiþ out mo. & þus for to encrese with so many freris is
greet cumbraunce to þe puple & aȝens Goddis wille þat made
al þingis in mesoure, noumbre, & weiȝt; & Crist ordeyned
twelue apostlis wiþ fewe oþere prestis to do seruyce to alle
þe world, & þanne was it best don. And riȝt as foure fingris & a
þombe on a man helpiþ hym to worche, & double so many on
oon hond schuld lette hym, & treble schuld lette hym more; & so
to many freris & oþere ordris passynge þe ordinaunce of God,
lettiþ Cristis chirche to growe to heuene.

FDR 809–15 : More ouer þou mouest multipliyng of so many
     freris,
     Whiche encresen combrouseli aȝens Goddis wille,
     Siþ preestis wiþ oþer religious myȝte serue þe peple;
     For twelue apostlis & fewe moo serueden al þe world,
     And mo fyngris on myn hond þan foure & þe þombe
     Amenusiþ my worching more þan it acresiþ.
     And so þou seist þat freris letten Cristis growinge in
     to heuen.

These are excellent paraphrases, but such skilful condensation
makes any assumptions about the faithfulness with which Daw
reproduces his text very dangerous indeed.

Further, to take only a few places where the text of HC is in
doubt because of disagreement between the MSS., when H
at 141–3 reads 'copis þat ȝe maken ȝou of so dere cloþe, siþ
lesse cloþis & of lesse prijs is more token of pouert' and C

reads *clothe* for *clopis*, *FDR* replying to this reads at 351 'Iak, of oure presciouse clopis fast þou carpist', but at 356 'if my cloþ be ouer presciouse, Iakke, blame þe werer'. At 177 H reads 'whi sette ȝe al þe kyngis londe to ferme', C reads *lett* for *sette*, *FDR* at 477 'we leten, þou seist . . . þis rewme to ferme' but at 479 'vnsikir þing soþly it were to sette to ferme'; and at 248: H 'to prisonynge & to fire', C 'prisonyng & burnyng', *FDR* at 631 'to prisoun & to fire' and at 636 'to fire or to prisoun'. To the editor in search of security such evidence affords neither help nor comfort.

There is another and a very disturbing piece of evidence relevant here, and its importance goes beyond any immediate decision about editorial method: the occurrence of a version of *JU* 46–53 in the Wyclifite tract *Vae Octuplex*.[1] The two passages are as follows:

Upland: and þus bi Anticrist and hise clerkis ben uertues transposid to vicis: as mekenes to cowardise, felnes and pride to wisdom and talnes, wraþþe to manhode, enuye to iustificacioun of wrong slouþe to lordlynes, coueytis to wisdom & wise puruyaunce, glotonye to largynes, leccherie to kindeli solace, mildenes to schepisshenesse, holines to jpocrisie, heryse to pleyne sadnes of feyþ and oolde vsage, & holy chirche to synagoge of Satanas.[2]

Vae: and herto vertues ben transposid to vices; as mekenes is cowardise, and felnesse of pride is clepid riȝtwisnesse for to maynteyne Goddis riȝt, and wraþþe is clepid manhede, and myldenesse is shepenesse, and envye is condicioun of Goddis child to venge him, and slouþe is lordlynesse, as God restiþ evermore; coveitise is prudence to be riche and myȝti, as glotonie is largenesse, and leccherie is myry play; Goddis servaunt is an ypocrite, and an eretike is sad in feiþ. And þus

---

[1] *Vae* accompanies all the complete copies of Wyclif's sermons except Douce 321, and seems to have been regarded as a pendant to them. It is printed by Arnold (ii. 379–89) from what is thought to be the earliest extant MS. of Wyclif's sermons, Bodley 788, dated by Dr. Richard Hunt as early fifteenth century, possibly as late as 1425 (Arnold, 'last decade of the fourteenth century'), but on internal evidence (see E. W. Talbert, *Speculum*, xii (1937), 464–74) not earlier than 1411. The passage quoted is on p. 387.

[2] This is the text of H; C reads *cowardnes* for *cowardise, prudence & polytike* for *wisdom & wise*, and omits the phrase *felnes and pride to wisdom and talnes*.

alle vertues ben transposid to vicis, and so holy Chirche to synagoge of Saþanas.[1]

These represent versions of the same original, and there can be little doubt that the *Upland* version is the earlier of the two. The *Vae* passage has all the characteristics of a late and corrupt copy: repetition (*vertues ben transposid to vices* at beginning and end); editing of a difficult reading (*ȝU felnes and pride to wisdom and talnes*);[2] and nonsense (*envye is condicioun of Goddis child to venge him*). There is, on the other hand, no suggestion of corruption in the *Upland* version;[3] it must represent, as near as can be, the actual text of its original.[4]

Whatever the source of this passage, it suggests the possibility that the text in which it appears may have resulted from compilation rather than from composition, and it implies a tradition in which casual plagiarism is an accredited principle of authorship. In relation to such a work the idea of 'original authorship' is a questionable one, and the reconstruction of 'the text' of a piece which has its genesis in such conditions must be very difficult indeed.[5]

---

[1] A version of the opening words of the passage ('where through by Antichrist & his, many vertues bene transposed to vyces') occurs in the 1536 black-letter in isolation, sandwiched between *ȝU* 1–3 and 69 f., with all the intervening text (4–46, 47–68) omitted.

[2] C's omission testifies to its difficulty. See *ȝU* 48 n.

[3] The only doubtful phrase is *enuye to iustificacioun of wrong*. Taking *iustificacioun* in the sense 'punishment' suggested by the context, this presumably means that envy is disguised as the high-minded disapprobation one sometimes enjoys at the expense of wrong-doers. But this is hardly a 'virtue'.

[4] It is of some interest that a tract (*Upland*), a product of the semi-literate fringe of Lollardy, extant in a MS. (H) possibly to be dated as late as the end of the fifteenth century, should preserve a passage of text also found in a piece closely associated with Wyclif himself, which exists in a MS. (Bodley 788) of the early fifteenth century, and preserves it in a version markedly superior to that found in the earlier Wyclifite copy.

[5] These remarks probably hold good for many of the so-called Wyclifite tracts. I quote extensively from some of them (including *Vae*) in the commentary to *Upland* to illustrate not only the dull repetitiveness of the anticlerical, and especially anti-mendicant, clichés of Lollardy, but also to show how the same or very similar verbal formulas recur again and again. They testify to a pool of material into which a writer could dip according to his particular prejudices and his immediate purpose.

There is no lack of evidence to confirm the medieval appetite for (and indifference to) plagiarism,[1] and it raises serious problems for the critic. But it does not result in a completely desperate situation. Where there is evidence (as there is in the case of *Upland*) that a version gained some measure of popularity and was transmitted in a form which escaped substantial revision or augmentation, the normal techniques of textual criticism can be used to achieve a less corrupt state of that version than exists in any of the extant copies of it. Discretion must be exercised in admitting emendations based wholly or in part on stylistic considerations, but they need not be totally excluded; it is a reasonable assumption that the style of an author-compiler or adapter will, to some extent, impress itself on the work he adapts.[2] Yet no claim can be made for a text reconstructed from such materials except the modest one that it represents one version in a text probably less corrupt than that of any surviving copy. It can be accorded no special authority or dignity in the textual tradition and it will not do to argue that it is superior or inferior to any other version.

I attempt to provide a critical text of the version represented by HC, and use 1536 and the version underlying *FDR* only as guides to conjecture in places where H and C seem to be

---

[1] From force of circumstance the Lollards seem to have developed a special facility in it. A sermon cycle in Sidney Sussex, Cambridge, MS. 74 regularly uses the Sunday Gospel sermons of Wyclif (as found in Bodley 788) as prothemes—prologues to the sermons proper—for the Sunday sermons (E. W. Talbert, 'A Fifteenth-Century Lollard Sermon Cycle', *Texas Studies in English* (1939), 5–30). Talbert suggests (pp. 20–21) that this practice may represent an attempt to evade restrictions on preaching of heretical and seditious doctrines by introducing Wyclifite ideas in the protheme under cover of otherwise innocuous and orthodox sermons of a perfectly legitimate sort. It is interesting that in the Sidney Sussex cycle, f. 127, a discussion of the Eucharist present in the Wyclif sermon here used, is torn out. See also Talbert, 'A Lollard Chronicle of the Papacy', *JEGP*, xli (1942), 163–75 for an account of a skilful adaptation of Higden's *Polychronicon* which results in an historical narrative supporting the Wyclifian doctrine (developed in Wyclif's *De Dominio Divino* and *De Civili Dominio*, and condemned by Gregory XI in 1377) that all jurisdiction depends on righteousness.

[2] I use 'style' here of those habits of grammatical and syntactical usage in a writer that are insistent, mechanical, and unconscious. For examples see the notes to *JU* 61, 118–19, 137, 148, 208, 226, 235.

corrupt.[1] H is probably the earlier of the two MSS., although not by very much; Mr. N. R. Ker will say only that its hand is probably fifteenth century, Wanley dates it boldly as 'about Hen. 7[th's] time'.[2] If Wanley is right the scribe of H must have been very faithful to his copy, since the language is that of the early rather than the late fifteenth century.

If H conscientiously reproduces his exemplar, C does not. C's forms and spellings seem to have been introduced by him in the course of copying. This is suggested by his original writing of *on* (H *oo*) at 123, with subsequent cancellation and substitution of *one*; the same correction appears at 144 (H *o*), 145 (H *oon*), 179 (H *o*), and in a passage substituted in C for H 255–6. The addition of initial *h* to original *abyt(t)ys* (125, 130) and *abite* (136) points in the same direction, and so, perhaps, does 17 *them syf* corrected to *them self*. C is also careful to eliminate archaic vocabulary. Thus, 105 H *stiӡe* is in C *ascendyd*; 112 H *heestis*, C *commandmentys*; 381 H *heed*, C *deadly*; 392 H *sacrid*, C *consecrate*; 408 H *fraiste*, C *sek owt*; H *siþ* (invariably) C *seyng* (invariably); and where H has *ne* fifteen times, C has no example—he alters to *nor* eleven times, to *&* twice, and omits twice.

In other ways C modifies the text represented by H so consistently that a marked pattern of scribal variation is noticeable. Where H usually has a simple verbal construction, C often weakens it by the use of some form of periphrastic *do*, as 114 H *Approueþ crist*, C *dothe crist alowe* (so also at 130, 137, 145, 149, 187, etc.). H frequently displays emphatic syntactical parallelism which C edits away, as 118–19 H *to pore feble men and pore blynd and pore lame*, C *to poore febyll men blynd & lame* (so also at 208, 266, 390). But C has an appetite for doublets not shared by H, as 17 H *prestis*, C *ministers or preastys*; 23 H *hire*,

[1] I have recourse to *FDR* for 83 *falsli*, 406 *ritis*; to 1536 for 210 *þefte*. I also quote *FDR* or 1536 in the commentary in places where their readings seem to be of some interest.

[2] Reported in a note in W. Thomas's hand on the MS. title-page (f. 279) of his transcript of H in B.M. Addit. MS. 38180. The labelling-piece on the spine of Harley 6641 reads 'Cod. Sec. XV'. Mr. Ker dates the hand of C early sixteenth century.

C *stipendys or wagys*; 29 H *wynnynge*, C *lucre & avawntage* etc. Where H regularly uses the conjunction *and*, C often substitutes other parts of speech.[1] C also modifies the negatives of H, as at 65, 105, 169.

Generally H has a succinctness that C lacks; C expands and occasionally paraphrases to bring out more clearly the sense sometimes obscured by the economy of H, its obsolete forms or constructions. But C often expands where H presents no difficulty, as in the following cases:

15–16 H: to defende Goddis seruauntis from letters of her office

C: to defend godys saruantys frome thos that will lett them to minister ther holy offyces

336–7 H: part & meryt of alle ȝoure massis & oþere good dedis & ȝe witen not

C: part of þe meritys of all yower massys fastyngys watchyngys & prayers & yet ye wot not

C sometimes omits corrupt or difficult phrases found in H (as at 48, 267), but occasionally he expands by way of a gloss and is led into nonsense. Thus, at 252–3 H has *whi be ȝe so wode þat prestis prechen of*, C *why be ȝe so farr owt of þe way þat ye will not suffer þat preastis may preach agaynst*, where *farr owt of þe way* must be a gloss on an original *wode*, misread as *wide*. A similar but more sophisticated confusion is seen at 363–4, where original *treble* and *ordris* have in C been corrupted to *trubyll* and *lordys* and C edits the whole passage to accommodate the corruptions.

Since H preserves the text in an older form than C, and is less corrupt and more sincere, I take it as my base MS. But C corrects H in more than two dozen places and is my chief source of emendations.[2] I resort to conjectural emendation at 65, 67, 74, 172, 218, and 289.

The text of Daw's *Reply* is dependent upon the unique copy in MS. Digby 41. The hand is to be dated a little before 1450

---

[1] See *JU* 61 n.

[2] When I emend on the authority of C, I adjust the spelling to conform to that of H.

and the hands of the several correctors are of about the same period.[1] If my conjectural dating of the *Reply* as late 1419 or early 1420 is accepted, the MS. is therefore not more than about thirty years after the date of original composition. In view of the official policy of discouraging the orthodox from replying to Lollard attacks one might expect a text in an early copy reasonably free from corruption. This is not the case. The text is very corrupt and stands at a distance of at least two, and possibly three or more, copies from the original.[2]

The dependence of the text upon a single witness means that where it is defective the editor must resort for the most part to conjectural emendation. Exceptions are those places where Daw's use of scriptural texts makes possible fairly obvious corrections to citations corrupted in the course of transmission. Thus, *Achan* for MS. *Achor* at 23, *at þe sixt* for MS. *in þe siȝt of* at 192, and *þridde* for *ferþe* at 194; less certainly, the variety and weight of scriptural evidence persuades me that the MS. is corrupt at *FDR* 9.

I use *Upland* as a guide to conjecture in passages where Daw paraphrases *Upland* and where the MS. reading is unsatisfactory. Thus, I supply with some confidence *yee* (supported by *JU* 114–16) for MS. *þee* at 273, and *lettris* (on the authority of *JU* 187–90) to fill a lacuna at 508. I let stand at 34, 55, and 454 readings rejected in the text of *JU* (at 74, 172): the evidence (for *FDR* 34 see n.) suggests that Daw there quoted accurately from the text of *Upland* that he had before him; in such cases correction seems to me to be beyond the authority of an editor.

Upland's *Rejoinder* also survives in a unique copy, written in the margins of the *Reply* in MS. Digby 41. As it stands in the MS., it is not the work of a single hand but of two: one hand (UR) accounts for 393 lines of the 440 in the MS., the other (T) for 47 lines.[3] The two hands are quite different. In general

---

[1] See pp. 47–49.

[2] This is implied by the corruption at *FDR* 767; see 767 n.

[3] T is responsible for three passages omitted in my text: (1) eight lines after *UR* 349; f. 13ʳ (upper margin) to f. 13ᵛ (upper margin); (2) eleven lines after *UR* 374; f. 14ᵛ (lower margin); (3) twenty-eight lines after *UR* 393;

effect T is less bold and less careful than UR. In detail, many letters are differently formed: this is especially noticeable in *y*, *f*, the *sp* ligature, and the sigma form of *s*. Orthography confirms the distinction. Although T is responsible for only forty-seven lines there is a sufficient number of words common to both to make this clear. Thus, UR has *ȝour* forty times, no *ȝoure* forms; T *ȝoure* 12x, no *ȝour* forms. For the verb 'say' UR has twenty-eight examples with *a* as root vowel, only one (193 *seggist*) with *e*; T seven *e* forms, no *a* forms. UR *þi* (25x), *þin* (10x), no forms with *y*; T *þy* (6x), *þyn* (1x), no forms with *i*. UR *meche* (5x); T *much* (1x). Most striking of all, UR *bot* (66x);[1] T *but* (13x), *bot* (1x), with one doubtful form.

I am convinced that T's passages are interpolations originating with himself rather than passages imported from a fuller copy of the *Rejoinder*. The most immediately striking evidence is the absence, in what I believe to be the interpolated passages, of Latin quotations. UR regularly introduces quotations from the scriptures and occasionally from the Fathers to buttress his argument. In fewer than 400 lines of text he introduces such quotations thirty-four times; in forty-seven lines of text T finds room only for one—and that a quotation from Ps. cviii. 10 borrowed directly from UR, who has employed it two lines previously.[2] Beyond this, the first and third interpolated passages are variations of arguments already present in *UR*, dealing with the favourite Lollard topics of the friars' abuse of begging and their heretical sacramental doctrines.

The weightiest argument against the authenticity of the interpolations is the probability that the *Rejoinder* is a holograph. The chief evidence is the remarkable freedom (interpolated passages apart) of the text of *UR* from corruption. I can find

f. 15[v] (lower), f. 16[r] (lower) to f. 16[r] (upper). They are transcribed in *UR* 349 n., 374 n., 393 n. See frontispiece.

[1] At 357 T inserts *but*.

[2] T also repeats (slightly modified) *UR* 349 at l. 4 of his first interpolation. It is worth noting that this interpolation complains of Daw's tendentious use of texts in support of the practice of begging. This may account for the interpolator's reluctance to resort to them; a reluctance that UR, at least, does not share.

reason for emendation in only eight places. Three emendations
are made necessary by the meddling of the interpolator: at 357
and 385 I omit single words (*but, oste*) inserted by him; at 296
I am obliged to emend a phrase that he has attempted to alter.
One, *ȝee* for MS. *ȝe* at 308 is merely the correction of a spelling
error; 269 and 343 are simple grammatical errors resulting from
confusion, so common in late ME., between personal and impersonal constructions.[1] At 59 preterite for present in MS. *spake*
may be explained by the pull of the vowel of past participle in
the preceding line; at 84 MS. *þo* for *þe* probably results from
anticipation of the next word *mo*, and perhaps of 87 *þo*. There is
no hint of radical corruption that would point to a history of
transmission. The five errors for which UR can be held responsible are as likely to be an author's as a scribe's.

This absence of casual scribal corruption is matched by the
text's singular freedom from dialectal contamination and the
general mixture of linguistic usage invariably found in texts
with a history of transmission. Phonological, morphological,
and orthographical features are unusually regular, and this in
itself argues for acceptance of the MS. as an autograph.

There is no certain evidence that the corrections in the text
are the work of anyone but UR himself; those made by erasure
and overwriting, or erasure and penwork, all seem to be in the
hand of UR, and the commonest kind of corrections, those which
result from insertion of a letter or word, are, with one possible
exception, certainly in his hand.[2] Some of these insertions (as
25, 117, 131, 233, 273, 293) are strictly necessary to the sense;
others (as 27, 51, 80, 128, 219, 263) are not; and while the
former may show a scribe repairing his omissions, the latter

[1] Cp. UR's divided usage in the verb 'marvel': impersonal at 31, 85,
personal at 245, 305.
[2] These number about three dozen. It is interesting that twenty-nine are
monosyllabic—the insertion into a word, or the addition to it, of a letter or
letters (as *re* of 10 *blaberest*); the introduction of a common word, as *þe* (def. art.)
(4x), *&* (3x), *a, not, þat, with, while, here*; of pronouns *ȝe* (4x), *þou* (2x),
I, we, his, hem. The only corrections certainly not monosyllabic are *Cristis,
marriþ*, and *allegyng*. I do not account the interpolator's alteration at 296,
or his insertions at 357 and 385 corrections; only the insertion of 59 *here*
may, in my opinion, be in another hand.

(together with the alterations of syntax in 36 and 69) may be held to suggest an author polishing his style. None of them seriously modifies the sense of the passage into which it is introduced.[1]

Also suggestive is UR's regular use of conventional signs to link his arguments to the passages in *FDR* that he is refuting. Thus, at 114 *UR* reads 'þou saist þou knowist no lettre here, as if þou wer noo clerke'; immediately before the line in the MS. stands the letter A, corresponding to a similar A in the inside margin of Daw's text, opposite *FDR* 213. This practice shows a solicitousness for his opponent's argument that is hardly to be expected from a mechanical copyist;[2] and UR's use of *here* in the line just quoted gives to it a sense of immediacy that is very marked.[3]

There are also two pieces of negative evidence. First, there is nothing in *UR* to suggest that its author used a text of *FDR* different from that in the Digby MS. Yet, given the corrupt state of the Digby text and the casualness of transmission that it argues for, it would be surprising if any other text used by the author of *UR* were not different from Digby, and that discrepancies resulting from its dependence upon a different version of *FDR* should not appear in the *Rejoinder*. Second, if the *Rejoinder* is not holograph, it is a curious and happy chance that the author of the *Rejoinder* should have been so conveniently selective in those parts of Daw's *Reply* that he chooses to confute, and so economical in his argument, that in only six MS. pages out of twenty-six on which he writes does the copyist have to use the upper margin (on the other twenty his text fits very comfortably into the lower margin alone, often with room to spare), and nowhere does he have to carry over an argument from one page to the next; and so it is that the scribe should have had in

---

[1] With the possible exception of that at 69, where inversion of original *saiþ he* removes a serious ambiguity.

[2] UR was solicitous about his opponent's text as well as his argument; see p. 47 for his corrections of *FDR*.

[3] Cp. a similar use of *here*, in conjunction with a conventional sign in the margin of *FDR*, at *UR* 106, and without the sign at *UR* 219, 293.

his hands at the same time a MS. of the *Rejoinder*, and the MS. of the *Reply* into which he could copy it.

The evidence seems to me to favour acceptance of the *Rejoinder* as a holograph, a piece tailored to fit the exiguous accommodation that the margins of the *Reply* afforded the author, hence carefully planned and rigorously edited. The text as it stands in the Digby MS. probably derives from a fair copy, and in its extensive and careful corrections incorporates the author's final revisions.[1]

EDITORIAL METHOD

Manuscript abbreviations except ampersand are expanded and given their common value, and printed in italic. In the case of corrections and elsewhere, I try to show by the use of question marks places where in my opinion the evidence is in any way doubtful.

Jack Upland

In H only superior ^{9} is difficult. It occurs four times: 45 *religiou*^{9} with value *s*,[2] 210 genitive *godd*^{9}, plurals 205 *clop*^{9}, 327 *hond*^{9}. Expansion *clopis*, *goddis* is confirmed by every other example of the forms (six and twenty-nine unsuspended plurals). The plural of *hond* occurs elsewhere only at 328 with a doubtful suspension mark, but probably an ill-formed *is* suspension.[3] I expand *hondis* in 327 because of the great preponderance of *-is* plurals and genitives in H and the fact that *is* is certain in 205, 210.[4]

---

[1] See further '*Jack Upland's Rejoinder*, a Lollard Interpolator and *Piers Plowman* B.x. 249 f', *MÆ*, xxxvi (1967), 242–8.

[2] N. Denholm-Young says that ^{9} for *s* alone seems to be a French trick (*Handwriting in England and Wales* (Cardiff, 1954), p. 67 n.). F. P. Magoun (*Anglia*, lxi (1937), 129–30) points to its occurrence in fourteenth-century West Midland texts (beside more usual *us*) and wonders whether it 'geographisch auf das westliche Mittelland beschränkt ist, oder ob sie im 14 Jahrhundert allgemein verbreitet war' (p. 130).

[3] What may be the same mark in 284 *tablis*, I take to be a cramped long *s*.

[4] It is possible that the mark represents *us*: a plural in *-us* occurs once (387 *lustus*) and *-un* often in past participle for more usual *-en*. Denholm-Young (*Handwriting*, p. 70) declares that the mark frequently means *es*

H has been extensively corrected and I think that I can
identify at least two correcting hands, neither demonstrably
later in date than H. If I am right in identifying the hand of the
interlined *art* in the interpolated passage added to the text in H
(see *JU* 411 n.) as that of the first corrector (C¹), it is possible
that C¹ actually compared H with the MS. it was copied from,
and this would account for his numerous and convincing corrections. The second corrector (C²), on the other hand, is certainly seen only at 58, 68, 71, and 174, and possibly also in
241 *money*.¹

I record in the apparatus all the changes for which I think that
either C¹ or C² is responsible; I also draw attention to corrections, cancellations, erasures and the like (presumably the work
of H himself) whenever they are of interest (as at 216, 219) and
often when they are not.

In the apparatus I record C's every substantive and syntactical
variation, but generally ignore morphological and orthographical variants. Exceptions are usually to be explained by special
circumstances, as at 177, 193, 385 or 155, 169, where in emendation spelling variants of *ʒour* and *his* are important. Occasionally I admit a variant which has no importance for the text but
is of some interest, as at 282, where both H and C result from
corrections.

in Anglo-Norman. But in *MÆ*, xxxi (1962), 77, M. Mills cites evidence
which corroborates the value I allow MS. ⁹ here: he points to readings in
Sir Launfal 469, 1036, where MS *þ⁹* must mean *þys*, and he remarks that the
expansion is 'unusual'.

¹ It is possible that one or other of the two correctors is the original
scribe adapting his hand to the special conditions imposed by correcting.
But if I am right in identifying the corrections at 177, 193, 385 as the work
of the same hand, the hand of C¹, I am convinced that C¹ is not the scribe.
It is otherwise difficult to account for the fact that the three *ʒour* forms resulting from these corrections are the only three in the MS. (in a total of more
than sixty) without final *e*. In correcting, a man might modify his handwriting;
but he would surely not abandon a deeply rooted spelling habit such as the
sixty or more *ʒoure* forms witness to.

My use of 'first' and 'second' implies no priority in time; C¹ is 'first'
because the number and importance of his corrections supports the assumption that his correcting was systematic and was intended to be authoritative.
At any rate, H as corrected by C¹ is a remarkably sound text and largely
free from casual error.

The apparatus does not attempt a full description of C; information about corrections, etc., is admitted only if it is relevant to a variant quoted for other reasons; there are occasional exceptions, as at 17, 144, 179, where the scribe's correction may suggest the forms of the MS. he was copying. In expanding abbreviations there are some doubtful cases, and in these I have tried to be governed by the scribe's usage elsewhere; but his spelling is irregular and I have tried to avoid imposing on him a false consistency. Thus, the terminal flourish used frequently to represent noun plurals and genitives I generally reproduce as *ys*, since this is the predominant form in unsuspended endings; but I occasionally and arbitrarily allow *is* or *es* since a few scattered examples (66 *clopis*, 289 *cloithis*; 2 *disciples*, 24 *tythes*, 29 *devoweres*) testify to the scribe's occasional irregularity.[1] Capital letters are retained where they occur in the MS.; word-division of the MS. is also followed, except at the end of a MS. line where it is treated arbitrarily.

Friar Daw's Reply

Of the abbreviations only an occasional flourish on -*r* in *ʒour/our* forms (and once in 229 *afer*) is difficult. Although forms without *e* predominate, there are two certain cases of uncontracted *ʒoure* (32, 165); on the basis of these I expand the flourish as *e* at 125, 127, 220; in the case of *our*, forms with *e* predominate (*our* only at 666, 675 (twice), 681), and I expand the flourish as *e* where it occurs,[2] as also in 229 *afere*.

At 280 I read *sheep* for what in the MS. is quite distinctly *shoep*. If authentic the form is very odd, standing as it does against 456 *sheep*, 401 *shipun*, 456 *shepen*.[3] I attribute the MS.

---

[1] I ignore a stroke through *ll*, and a flourish over final *s*; but a similar backward flourish over final *c* I reproduce as the *e* that C's orthography seems to demand. The horizontal flourish on 2-shaped *r* and other consonants, I sometimes, but not invariably, expand as *e*, both medially and finally.

[2] It is curious that of nine contracted *oure/ʒoure* forms, six occur in the space of twenty-two lines (110–31), only three elsewhere in the text.

[3] Daw's erroneous association of *shippen* with 'sheep' in 456 (see 456 n.) and presumably also in 401, makes valid the introduction of these forms as evidence.

form to the scribe's occasional miswriting (in words with doubled medial vowel) of *e* so that it can be read as *o* (cp. 777 *seed*), and of *o* so that it can be read as *e* (cp. 457 *noon*, 829 *toon*).[1]

FDR has been extensively corrected, and there is no doubt that some of the corrections are the work of UR. I identify UR's hand with moderate confidence in the following places: 169, 222, 249, 343, 458, 545, 625, 633, 727, 734, 746, 783, 807, 854, 898; it may perhaps also be seen in 405, 434, 590, 676, 858. The evidence of the hand is supported by the consistent nature of the corrections which, with two exceptions, are all modest: the insertion or alteration of a single letter or abbreviation mark (405, 434, 545, 590, 625, 676, 727, 746, 854); of two letters (458, 633, 783, 858); of three letters (807); or the introduction of a monosyllabic word—*þe* (222, 734), *is* (249), *we* (343). The two exceptions are the introduction of 169 *Enuye*, 898 *grace*, to fill blank spaces left by the scribe of *FDR* in the middle of a line; both are satisfactory fillers.

None of these corrections involves violent alteration of the text; they are of a kind that might occur to any intelligent and interested reader. But they have no authority beyond their own intrinsic probability and must be judged by the ordinary canons of textual criticism. By any standard UR does well: of the twenty corrections I associate with him I feel obliged to admit fourteen (169, 405, 434, 590, 625, 633, 676, 727, 746, 783, 807, 854, 858, 898) and to reject only six (222, 249, 343, 458, 545, 734). While most of his readings adopted in the text are obvious enough, the emendation of probably original *maistrie* to *mysterie* at 783, and of *se* to *sesse* at 807, show a nice critical sense; and his provision of *Enuye* and *grace* to fill lacunae at 169, 898 I am especially grateful for.

It is possible to identify at least one other corrector of *FDR*. He is responsible for a group of corrections which are linked (1) by a characteristic method of cancellation by underlining,

---

[1] So too 704 *manheed*, where the MS. reads *manhoed*; *-hood*, *-heed* are both current forms, but cp. 702 *godhede*. Other obvious miswritings I ignore. But for difficulty caused in one case (misplacing of the horizontal stroke generally put over vowel letters to represent following *m*, *n*), see 151 n.

with substitution indicated by a caret before the cancelled reading, the new reading in the margin; this links the corrections at 128, 140, 162, 274, 466, 500, 625; (2) by an *e* form quite distinctive in this MS., made by writing the normal semicircular bowl, but with a tick flying off from its upper lip. It is quite different from the *e* form regularly used by either FDR or UR[1] and links, in my opinion, corrections at 54, 81, 162, 460, 625, 674. To this group (established by the appearance of the corrections at 162, 625 in both categories) I would add the corrections at 225, 271, 373 not on the basis of consonance in particular details, but because of the general impression they give of having been written by the same hand.

The alterations I associate with this corrector (M) are very different from the intelligent tinkering of UR: they are violent and substantive and are characterized by a bold decisiveness. Scrutiny of his corrections argues against accounting M a mere 'improver': without his marginal *take hede*, 460 would be nonsense; *holilicch* for *holy chirche* at 225 is a very convincing emendation, *honyed* for *heued* at 128 a brilliant one. And why, if merely 'improving' the text, does he alter 162 *we* to *ve* while letting the next word in the MS., nonsensical *westheth*, remain? If M is the official corrector the explanation is simple: the text he was comparing the MS. with (presumably the text actually copied by the scribe of the *Reply*) read *ve westheth*. Finally, it is doubtful whether an improver as impetuous as these alterations suggest he was would have allowed the lacunae at 169, 508, and 898 to remain, two of them later to be filled by UR.[2] But if he was the official corrector he lets them stand for the same reason as he does *westheth*: because they were present in the copy text.

[1] It occurs also in *e* (2) of *pouerte* in *UR* 134, possibly in *e* (2) of *couetise* in *UR* 369, and in *e* of *lawe* at l. 27 of the third interpolation in *UR* (see *UR* 393 n.). A similar form appears in *e* (2) of *ese* in *FDR* 35. But these are isolated forms, and they do not persuade me that UR, T, or FDR is responsible for the group of corrections listed here. Most hands are liable to occasional aberrations from normal usage; cp. FDR, who in 652 *contrarious* and 661 *arrians* uses a long-tailed *r*-form found nowhere else in the text.

[2] I assume that UR is later than M. If 373 MS. *sothely hit scheweth* is the work of M, M is certainly the earlier of the two: the reading is added in the lower margin where the *Rejoinder* stands, and UR is obliged to write round it.

The author of these corrections is the only one that I am prepared to identify with any confidence, and only in the places noted; but it is possible that his hand may also be seen elsewhere, viz. 125, 146 (both), 187 (both), 391 (*absque*), 464, 498 (both), 502, 514–15 (all), 623, 688 (both). In each of these there is evidence, either in individual letter-forms, or in the hand generally, to suggest the ascription, and there is support in the nature of the corrections: they are nearly all violent and substantive and, with one or two exceptions, declare themselves to be inevitable. And if M is not responsible for the careful and complicated correction of 514–15, it is difficult to avoid the conclusion that there must have been at least two 'official' correctors.[1]

Upland's Rejoinder

Abbreviation of plurals presents some difficulty. Only plurals which in the singular end in *r* are abbreviated, and then not the full inflexional ending is suspended but only the vowel; this is represented by a flourish on the *r*, and I expand this as *e* on the basis of the great preponderance of unsuspended *es* forms.[2]

UR's usage with final *e* in *her(e)* (adv.), *her(e)* (pron.), *wer(e)*, *wher(e)*, *per(e)* (advs.) is inconsistent. He has, for example, 369 *where*, 156 *wher*, uncontracted; but at 148, 243 final *r* has a flourish which I take to be a suspension and expand *where*, *whare* accordingly. Again, although 368 *pere*, 392 *per*, at 122, 380 forms with flourished *r*, and I expand *pere*.[3]

There is some uncertainty about the significance of a stroke through the ascenders of *ll* in MS. *all* (22, 384) and *allgates* (273). The word appears elsewhere only without the stroke and with following -*e*, simplex *alle* twenty-three times, in compound

---

[1] Where correctors' forms differ from the scribe's usage (as 225 *holilicch*, 336 *hey*, 373 *hit*, etc.) I emend them to conform to the spelling of the text.

[2] In words ending in a consonant the unsuspended plural inflexion is -*es* in all but two cases—112 *lordis*, 174 *tateris*. Genitives preserve what appears to be a traditional -*is* inflexion in *Goddis* (7x, none suspended), *Cristis* and *Anticristis* (13x, 5 suspended), and in 299 *Dominikis*. In other words (8, none suspended) with the exception of 372 *Pharaouse*, the genitive has -*es*.

[3] A terminal flourish (but it may be the letter *e*) on 235 *bot*, I ignore: in more than sixty examples in *UR* there is no case of *bot* with final *e*.

(80 *allemost*) once. I assume therefore that at 22, 384, 273 the stroke represents suspension of *e*.

Possible *cc/tc* spellings are difficult to distinguish in UR's hand. The collocation occurs in five places.[1] The evidence of letter-forms (extension of the bow of the letter above the flat top = *t*) would argue for *tc* in every case except one (205), where the evidence is indecisive; but the criterion is called into question by the form of initial *c* in 256 *cacche* which has such an extension and consequent *t* shape, yet *c* cannot be in doubt. In every case (but with no great conviction) I admit the *cc* spelling. In certain other collocations (between some consonants, as *k/þ*, *d/r*—both usually in final syllables) *i* is often graphically so reduced that it virtually disappears; this is the case in the apparent MS. form 361 *spekþ*, but the full form is confirmed by 93, 198 *spekiþ*.[2]

The corrections to *UR* are discussed on pp. 42–43. With the exception of those for which T is responsible (296, 357, 385), and possibly that at 59, there is no evidence that they are the work of anyone but UR himself, and it is unnecessary to treat them further here.

Capitalization and punctuation are editorial. I generally preserve the word-divisions of the MSS., since the scribes are on the whole careful and consistent in their practice. Where there is variation in the treatment of a word, I adopt the majority form.[3] For isolated forms I generally follow the modern con-

---

[1] In 150 *smacchiþ*, 205 *strecche*, 256 *cacche*, 221, 364 *grucche*.

[2] As well as obvious miswritings I ignore the marginal *Iak* regularly inserted by the scribe, presumably as an indication of authorship. This leads Wright into error at l. 10 where marginal *Iak* stands before initial *dawe* and is easily read as part of the line, as it is by Wright.

[3] Consistent treatment of words that might be expected to follow the same pattern of division is not always possible: in *FDR* the separation of *sum þing* (818, 820) and *no þing* (501, 830, 858 (twice), and probably 441) stands against joining of *sumtyme* (629, 807), *sumwhat* (460), *noman* (352, 802, 806 (twice), 904), and 930 *nomore*. But wherever a pattern of scribal variation emerges in such cases I adjust minority forms to agree with majority usage. Hence, in *FDR* where *holi chirche* is separated nine times, joined once (62), and twice (633, 798) line-division makes the scribe's intention uncertain, and *holigo(o)st* is joined at 241, 663, and probably joined at 776, 781, I allow *holi chirche* to stand as two words everywhere, *holigo(o)st* as one.

vention.[1] I do not follow the MSS. in joining variously article, preposition, or pronoun to a following noun, nor pronoun to verb.

The following conventional signs are employed:

(1) half brackets enclose emendations.
(2) superior angled ticks show interlinear and marginal insertions, without differentiation of authorship.
(3) an obelus shows places where MS. readings are omitted.
(4) angled brackets enclose letters which are illegible for any reason, where reconstruction is not seriously in doubt; ⟨. . . .⟩ represents letters which cannot be confidently identified.[2]

Since I do not attempt to construct a critical text for the Latin quotations introduced by Daw and UR, I have chosen to avoid adding to the conventional signs and to the apparatus. I therefore expand abbreviations silently, generally ignore corrections, and supply without notice letters or words in obvious cases, and emendations where necessary.

Biblical references are to the Vulgate. In the Commentary, New Testament references are generally to the edition of Wordsworth and White (edit. min. Oxford, repr. 1957), Old Testament references to the Marietti edition (Rome [1959]). In the Commentary quotations from the Wyclifite version (ed. Forshall and Madden (Oxford, 1850)) are from the earlier or later version depending upon which offers the closer parallel to the text. Occasional slight discrepancies in verse-numbering between Biblical versions I ignore. For evidence of 'conflation' in identifying sources for Vulgate quotations in *FDR* and *UR* I go by the Wordsworth and White and Marietti texts; but I am fully aware that some MSS. of the Vulgate in some places

---

[1] But *UR* 9 *in dede*, 29 *a waye*, 97 *in to*, 180 *an oper*, I allow to stand: UR's extreme consistency in other forms, and the fact that he chooses to separate these elements despite the encouragement exigency of space gave him to join them, both argue against modifying MS. usage.

[2] Occasionally letters difficult or impossible to read in the MS. are legible in photographs of the MS.; when I admit readings on the basis of photographic evidence this is made clear in the palaeographical notes.

where I have suggested 'conflation' read the actual text quoted by Daw or the author of the *Rejoinder*.

In quoting illustrative material for *JU* and *UR* I have intentionally restricted myself to a very few Lollard works. There are two reasons for this. First, most of the charges made by Upland and UR are commonplaces of Lollard polemic, and full documentation would run to many hundreds of pages. Second, there is some value in showing how characteristic *Upland* and the *Rejoinder* are, and this can best be done by illustrating extensively from a limited number of texts. I have generally avoided quoting parallels from obvious sources such as Langland, Chaucer, and the *Romance of the Rose*; it seems to me better to sacrifice the well-known to the less well-known source. I am also moved by sympathy for Upland; I suspect that in his narrow way he would have resented being contaminated by literature. For historical reasons I quote only from vernacular Lollard texts: there is strong evidence to suggest that Wyclif's Latin works had little appeal for his English followers. Out of nearly a hundred authentic and spurious Latin works of Wyclif listed in Loserth's revision of Shirley's *Catalogue*, some sixty are not represented by a single MS. in English libraries, while, on the other hand, there appear to be no MSS. of his English writings in libraries abroad.[1]

In the Commentary and elsewhere critical notes are distinguished by line-references in roman, exegetical notes by line-references in italic; thus *JU* 48 refers to the critical note on that line, *FDR 865-7* to the exegetical note on those lines. In the Appendix I supply a table of parallel passages in the form of a continuous series of references to the appropriate passages in *Upland* as Daw answers them, and to those in *FDR* as UR answers them.

It remains to be said that the modest interest of these texts is that of a footnote to an historical controversy. In five hundred years they have received barely a dozen pages of desultory

---

[1] E. M. Thompson, *British Museum. Wycliffe Exhibition in the King's Library* (1884), p. xv.

academic discussion scattered over as many books, and it is to their credit that they cannot claim a single learned article to themselves. They have earned their neglect. If I tidy them away to an honest grave it is not with any claim to 'definitiveness', but because there is no good reason why they should ever be disinterred again.

JACK UPLAND

f. 1ʳ To veri God & to alle trewe in Crist, I Iacke Vplond make my
moone, þat Anticrist and hise disciplis bi coloure of holynes
wasten & disceiuen Cristis chirche bi many fals signes.

For God þat is almy3ti, alwitti, algoodli, & alwilful, as he haþ
5 made man in soule to his ymage, as in mynde, resoun & wille,
& to his liknesse bi werkis of bileue, tristi hope, & lastinge
charite, so he sette mannes state: in lordis to represente þe |

f. 1ᵛ power of þe Fadir; preestis to represente þe wisdom of þe
Sone; and þe comouns to presente þe good lastinge wille of þe
10 Holi Goost.

Preestis office to preche þe gospel truli and to preye in herte
deuoutli, to mynistre þe sacramentis freli, to studie in Goddis
lawe oonli, and to be trewe ensaumpleris of ⌈holi⌉ mennes lijf
continuli, in doynge and in suffringe. Lordis office to iustifie

f. 2ʳ mysdoers in ward & to defende Goddis seruauntis from | letters
16 of her office. Comouns office to truli laboure for þe sustinaunce
of hem silf, & for prestis and for lordis doynge wel her office.

And þus haþ Crist tau3t boþe bi dede and bi word, as holi
writ beriþ witnes in many placis, and þus was Cristis chirche

1 veri] the lorde.   trewe . . . Crist] the congregacion of cristys churche.
Vplond] vpon londe.   3 chirche] congregation.   4 God] þat congregation.   þat] *om.*   alwitti] all full of wysdome.   algoodli] & godlines.
5 ymage] pure ymage.   as . . . his (6)] *om.*   6 liknesse] and lyknes.
bi . . . charite (7)] by faith hope and contynuall charite.   7 he] is: *from*
his.   in] fyrst in.   lordis] lordys wordly.   represente] present.
8 represente] present.   9 lastinge] contynuall.   11 Preestis] The
preastys.   to (1)] is to.   and] *om.*   12 Goddis lawe (13)] godlines.
13 and . . . continuli (14)] to gyve good exampill contynually in holy liuyng.
holi] alle H.   14 doynge] doyng teachyng.   in (2)] *om.*   Lordis]
The lordys.   to] is to.   iustifie] chastyse.   15 in ward] *om.*   letters . . .
office (1) (16)] thos that will lett them to ministerther holy offyces.   16
Comouns] The comons.   to . . . laboure] is truly to labor.   sustinaunce]
mantenance.   17 hem silf] them 'self': self *for cancelled* syf.   for prestis]
of the ministers or preastys in cristys gospell.   for (2)] of.   office] offycys.
18 þus] this: -i- *from* u.   haþ] *om.*   Crist] *ower* savior crist.   boþe . . .
word] diligently not alonly in worde but also in dede.   19 writ . . .
witnes] scriptur maketh mencion.   many] diuerse.

gouerned a þousand ȝeer and more. But Anticrist haþ ȝouun 20
leue to leue al þis and to do anoþer maner. For he ȝeueþ leue
to preestis of parischis boþe hiȝe & lowe to leue prechinge and
to do lewid mennes office; and ȝit þei takun hire of her parischis
neuer | þe lasse—as offringis and tiþis and oþere possessiouns   f. 2ᵛ
dowid for almes.† þei marren many matins and massis wiþ out 25
deuossioun, & herto sacramen`t´is schulen be soolde or els gete
no man noon; and lest þei schulden studie in Goddis lawe he
haþ ordeyned hem to studie in oþere dyuers lawis for þe more
wynnynge. And as anentis ensaumple of prestis lijf in doynge,
who doiþ more worldli werkis þanne þei, or more couytous, 30
& suffre mai þei no wronge | but if þei plete anoon, & of alle f. 3ʳ
men þei mai worst suffre to be repreued of her defautis, be þei
neuer so many.

To lordis haþ Anticrist ȝouun leue to fiȝte for rewmes &
oþere lordschips, and sle her briþeren and brenne her housis, 35
& þerwiþ wynne perdoun; and he þat is vnable of vertues to
gouerne o lordschip schal haue leue to fiȝte for tweyne. And þis
power ordeined bi God to meyntene and defende men in charite
is ordeined bi Anticrist to distrye charite.

To þe comoun peple haþ Anticrist ȝouun leue | to leue her f. 3ᵛ

20 þousand] mˡ.   But . . . maner (21)] But whan anticrist came he gave
a new licence to euery man that wolde purchase it of hym to lyve after a
noþer maner.   21 ȝeueþ leue] gaue lycence.   22 parischis] parysche.
prechinge] preachyng of the holy gospell.   23 do . . . office] take vpon
them lay menys offycys.   þei . . . parischis] to resayve ther stipendys
or wagys of þer parischners.   25 dowid] gyven.   almes] H adds and
as for worldli bisines.   marren] murmur.   26 herto] þer to.
sacramentis . . . soolde] þei sell sacramentis.   els . . . noon (27)] ell non
schall be goten of them.   27 Goddis lawe] holy scriptur.   he] þer
father antecrist.   29 wynnynge] lucre & avawntage.   And . . . doynge]
C substitutes & hath ordenyd & made þe lyff of preastys to be devoweres.
30 who] for who.   þanne þei] om.   more couytous] who is more
covetus than þei be.   31 suffre . . . no] þei in no wyse may suffer ony.
but if . . . anoon] but anon þei wyll go to þe lawe & plett.   alle] all
oþer.   32 defautis] vngracius lyvyng.   þei (2)] it.   33 many] many
fold open & knowen.   34 To . . . leue] Secondly þis anticrist haith
gevyn lycence to þe lordys.   36 wynne perdoun] ‘wene’ to bye perdons:
wene for cancelled wyne.   vnable . . . vertues] not abyll in vertuusnes
& good conuersacion.   37 o] ? ‘whon’: for cancelled on.   39 charite]
charite among cristys congregation.   40 To] Thyrdly to.   comoun
peple] comons.   leue (1)] lycens.

41 trewe laboure and bicome idil men ful of disceitis to bigile eche
oþere, as summe bicome men of crafte & marchauntis professid
to falsnes, and summe men of lawe to distroye Goddis lawe &
loue amonge neiȝboris, and summe crepen into feyned ordris
45 and clepen hem religious, to lyue idilli bi ipocrisie and disceiue
alle þe statis ordeyned bi God, and þus bi Anticrist and hise
clerkis ben uertues transposid to vicis: as mekenes to cowardise,

f. 4ʳ felnes and pride to wisdom and tal | nes, wraþþe to manhode,
enuye to iustificacioun of wrong, slouþe to lordlynes, coueytis
50 to wisdom & wise puruyaunce, glotonye to l⟨ar⟩gynes, leccherie
to kindeli ⟨so⟩lace, mildenes to schepisshenesse, holines to
jpocrisie, heryse to pleyne sadnes of feyþ and oolde vsage,
& holy chirche to synagoge of Satanas. & lest þat þis greete
abhomynacioun of Antecrist were aspied & lettid, he haþ sus-
55 pendid prestis fro her office and ȝouun hem greete wagis of

f. 4ᵛ possessiouns & dignytees aȝens Cristis lawe, & chosun | suche
þerto þat kunnen not ne moun not grucche aȝens his lordschip, & þes lordis ben in þe rerewarde of Antecristis
bateile.

60   And herto haþ he made anoþer oost aȝens Cristis ordinaunce,
& closid hem as fro þe world in wallis of stoon, cloistris & sellis;
& þereas þei schulden haue labourid in þe world in help of alle
þre partis of Cristis chirche, wiþ meke loue & leue lijflode, now
þei schulen lyue in idil lijf & sikir fro al pouert, & al men

41 bicome] to be come. disceitis] dissay⟨t⟩. to] redy to. 42 bicome]
om. marchauntis] merchandyse 'be'. 43 falsnes] falshod. and]
om. men] be come men. 44 loue] in conclusion 'love'. neiȝboris]
neyghtbus. 45 hem religious] them self holy religius men. to] & all
is to. idilli] slouthfully. ipocrisie] false ypocrysye. and] *om.*
disceiue] dyssayvyng. 46 þe] *om.* statis] maner of staatys. God]
allmyghty god. 47 ben uertues] all vertuis be. cowardise] cowardnes.
48 felnes . . . talnes] *om.* 50 wisdom & wise] prudence & polytike.
53 & (1)] *om.* to] turnyd in to. synagoge] the sinagog. 54 were]
schulde be. lettid] in conclusion lettyd. 55 office] offycis. hem
. . . aȝens (56)] great wagis & possessions & dignites to þem contrary to.
56 chosun] haith chosen. 57 kunnen . . . grucche] dare not grudge nor say.
58 in þe rere-: C² *over erasure.* 60 herto] to them. made] annectyd.
61 as] *om.* cloistris & sellis] in cloysters in cellys & suche oþer.
62 & þereas] for wher. help] helpyng. 63 þre] þe iij. meke
. . . lijflode] lefull lyvelode & meke love. 64 schulen] xall þer. sikir]
sure. fro] of.

schulen help hem & þei neuer no man aftir, but lyue in ⌐mam | 65
elynge⌐ of mete and many wast cloþis, & þou3 þei weren þe f. 5ʳ
'h'eire & þe hood, † euer enuy ⌐is⌐ her cauce at eueri melis mete.
& þes hidde jpocritis ben in þe myddilward of Antecristis bateil.

But þe fellist folk þat euer Antecrist foond ben last brou3te
into þe chirche & in a wondir w'i'se, & for þei ben of diuers 70
settis of Antecristis sowinge, of dyuers cuntreis & kynredis, and
alle men þei knowun. þei ben not obediente to bisshopis ne lege
men to kyngis, neþer þei tilien ne sowen, weden ne | repen, f. 5ᵛ
neþer ⌐whete⌐, cor'n' ne gras, ne ⌐good⌐ þat men schal help but
oonli hem silf. & þes men han al maner power of God, as þei 75
seien, in heuen and in erþe, a mannes lijf to saue—3he, to sille
heuene or helle to whom þat hem likiþ—and 3it þes wrecchis
witen not where to be hem silf.†

Thei ben confessouris & confundouris of lordis & ladies, of
prelatis and persouns, & pilers of þe chirche; & also þei ben 80
parteneris of alle sacramentis þat schulen be soold as Simon-
undis eiris, for þei preien for no mo | þan paien wele þerfore. f. 6ʳ

Thes ben þe flateringe freris of al þe ⌐fyue⌐ ordris, ⌐falsli⌐
founden in oure feiþ & first schulen be distried. þes ben cockers

---

65 neuer . . . aftir] schall neuer helpe on man.   mamelynge] murþringe H;
murmuryng & grudgyng C.   66 of mete] om.   þou3] þan.   weren . . .
hood (67)] weren þe heire & þe hood ouer þe i3en H; vary in þer hartis
when þer hode hangyth ouer þer eyn C.   67 heire: h- margin? corrector.
& þe: over erasure?   euer] for euer.   enuy: e cancelled after -n-.
is] C; his H.   melis] malyce.   68 myddilward: C² over erasure.
69 fellist] most wrechid.   70 & (1)] om.   wondir] meruelus.   & (2)]
om.   71 settis . . . dyuers] om.   cuntreis: C² over erasure.   72 alle
. . . knowun] thei know all men.   bisshopis] þe byschopys.   73 kyngis]
þe kyngis.   neþer . . . tilien] þei do not tyll.   74 whete corn] wode
corn H; corne wode C.   ne (2)] nor do oþer.   good] C; godd H: -d-
from o?   men . . . help] schall helpe any man.   75 hem silf . . . saue (76)]
hem silf a mannes lijf to saue & þes men han al maner power of god as þei
seien in heuen and in erþe H; þem self & þes men haue all maner of
gouernance & power of god (as þei say) in hevyn & also in hell C.   76 saue:
-a- from e.   3he . . . likiþ (77)] to as many as it pleaseth þem.   sille:
si- from h?   77 hem: he- alteration?   78 hem silf] þemself C;
hem silf saued or dampned H.   81 parteneris] executors.   Simon-
undis] trew symons.   82 eiris: ?C¹ over erasure.   þerfore]
om.   83 Thes] Therfor to be breffe þes.   þe (2)] om.   fyue]
v C; foure H.   falsli] falsist H; last C.   84 first] sonest.   cockers]
cok croweres.

85 in couentis and coueitous in markettis, marrers of matrymonye
& Caymes castel-makers, Pharesies fagynge þe folk & profetis
fals, vnsikir soudiouris sette al bifore, vayne men & voide in
Antecristis vowarde—God scheeld vs from þis capteyne and his
oost.

f. 6ᵛ   Wel I woot bi my bileue þat Crist wole þat | eueri cristen
91 man loue his God moost & siþ his neiȝbore as hym silf, &
herynne, as Crist seiþ, al þe lawe hangiþ & þe profetis. But
hou loueþ he his neiȝbore þat loueþ his good more þan his
soule hele or bodeli heele, and Cristis ordre, as Seynte Iame seiþ,
95 is to refreische nedi helples men wiþ þi ȝifte. But what ordre
is þat þat wole haue of alle men & ȝeue hem not at her nede?
þis moost Antecristis ordre nede be. And þerfor frere if þin
⌜ordre⌝ and þi rulis ben groundid in Goddis lawe, telle þou
f. 7ʳ now | Iacke Vponlond þat I axe þee, and if þou be or þenkist to
100 be on Cristis side, kepe þi pacience.

Frere, hou many ordris ben in erþe, & whiche is moost perfiȝt
ordre?

Frere, of what ordre art þou and who made þin ordre? What
ben þi rulis & who made þi 'cloutid' rulis, siþ Crist made hem
105 not ne noon oþer a þousende ȝeere aftir þat Crist stiȝe into
heuene?

Frere, is þer ony ordre more perfiȝte þan Crist hym silf
made?

---

85 coueitous] cuvytyse.   86 Caymes] cain.   Pharesies fagynge] faynyd
pharyseis dyssayvyng.   & (2)] *om.*   profetis fals] false prophettis.   87 vnsikir]
& sure.   88 vowarde] forwarde.   scheeld] kepe.   capteyne] cumpeny.
his] þis.   89 oost] false oost.   90 Crist . . . man (91)] euery man
after *cristis* will schuld.   91 moost] most & above all thyngys.   siþ]
next.   92 herynne . . . seiþ] hys enmy as crist byddeth In þes ij.
94 and] *om.*   95 nedi] oþer nedy.   helples] & comfortles.   96 haue]
haue crave & pill.   of] from.   hem . . . nede] nothyng to ony nedy
97 Þis . . . be] must not þis nedys be anticristis order.   frere] C *transposes*
of what order art þou & who mad þi ordre what be þi rulys *from* 103–4.
þin] þi.   98 ordre] C; ordris H.   þi] *om.*   99 Iacke] to jack.
Vponlond] C *adds* & mak answere to thyngys.   axe] will ask.   100
side] partye.   101 &: *over erasure.*   whiche: whi- *over erasure.*
103 and . . . ordre] *om.*   104 cloutid: *margin* C¹.   siþ] seyng.
105 ne] &.   stiȝe] ascendyd.   into] vp to.   107 Crist] þat þat crist.

Frere, if Cristis rule is moost perfi3t, whi rulist ⌐þou⌐ þee not
þeraftir?   110

Whi schal a frere be more punyschid | if he breke þe rulis   f. 7ᵛ
þat his patroun made, þan if he breke þe heestis þat God
hym silf made? For brekynge of 3oure rulis 3e ben prisonyd ofte.

Approueþ Crist ony mo religiouns þan oon þat Synt Iame
techiþ vs? If þou seist 3he, tel þou now in Cristis lawe where   115
it is; and siþ þou canst not finde where, whi hast þou left his
rule and take þee anoþer contrarie þerto? For Cristis rule
⌐biddiþ⌐ þee 3eue to pore feble men and pore blynd and pore
lame, vpon peyne of dampnacioun; | and þi rule biddiþ þee pike   f. 8ʳ
fro pore and riche al þat þou mayst, & 3eue hem no þing   120
a3en, haue þei neuer so myche nede.

Whi is a frere apostata þat leueþ his ordre and takiþ þe cloþis
& rulis of anoþer ordre, siþ Crist haþ made but oo religioun
good and esie & comun for alle men & wymmen?

Whi be 3e faster weddid to 3oure abite bi mannes mariage   125
þanne a man is weddid to his wijf bi Goddis mariage? A man
may leue his wijf a moneþ eþer a 3eer as many men doen, and
if 3e | leuen 3oure abite a wike eþer a quartere of a 3eer, 3e ben   f. 8ᵛ
holden ⌐apostataas⌐.

Frere, makiþ 3oure abite 3ou men of religioun or no?   130
If it doiþ, euer as it wereþ 3oure relegioun wereþ, and

109 is] be.   rulist . . . not] rulist þee not H; dost þou not rewle
þi self C.   111 rulis] rule.   112 heestis] commandmentys.   113 hym
silf made] mad hym self.   ofte] om.   114 Approueþ Crist] ffryer
dothe crist alowe.   115 tel þou] it is reson þat þou schuld tell us.   now]
om.   in . . . is (116)] in what place of cristys lawe it is writen.   116 and
. . . where] C substitutes but 'it' where for þe to long to studie ffor of suche
þer is no mention.   left] than left.   his] þis.   117 rule (1)] C adds þat saynt
jamys taw3t us in þe spret of crist.   take] takyn.   anoþer] to a noþer.   con-
trarie] contrarius.   118 biddiþ] bidiþ H; byddythe C.   3eue] to gyve
goodys.   and (1) . . . lame (119)] blynd & lame.   119 pike] to pyk.   120
fro] a way fro.   riche] C adds with beggyng & lyeng.   mayst: e cancelled
after -y-.   123 rulis] þe rulys.   siþ] seyng.   oo] 'one': for cancelled
on.   125 faster] surer (?).   abite] habytys of ypocrisie: habytys, h- added.
126 A man] for aweddyd man.   127 may] om.   a] for a.   eþer] or.   and]
but.   128 eþer] or.   a quartere] half a quarter.   129 holden] holden &
taken for.   apostataas] apostatais C; apostaas H.   130 makiþ . . . abite]
doth yower habyttys make: habyttys, h- added.   131 it (1)] þi.   euer]
than even.   it (2)] þei.   3oure . . . wereþ] so do yower religion on yere.

aftir þat it is better ȝoure relegioun is bettir; & whanne ȝe leyen
ȝoure abite bisidis ȝou ȝe leyn ȝoure religioun bisidis ȝou, & þanne
ȝe ben ⌜apostataas⌝. & ȝif ȝe seie, Iacke nay oure relegioun is not
135 in oure abite, frere, whi art þou prisoned and clepid apostata |
f. 9ʳ for leuynge þin ordre & weringe a blewe gowne & a reede hood?

  Seye frere, whi bie ȝe ⌜ȝou⌝ so preciouse cloþis & so fyne to
were, siþ no man vsiþ suche but for veyn glorie, as Seynt Gregori seyþ, & ȝit ȝe seien ȝe ben pore begers?

140 Frere, what bitokeneþ ȝoure greet hood, ȝoure scapalarie, &
ȝoure knottid girdel, & ȝoure side & wide copis þat ȝe maken
ȝou of so dere cloþe, siþ lesse cloþis & of lesse prijs is more
token of pouert? |

f. 9ᵛ Whi vse ȝe al o coloure more þanne oþer cristen men doen?
145 '&' whi holde ȝe silens more in oon hous þanne in anoþer, siþ
man owiþ ouer al to speke þe good and leue þe yuel? And whi
ete ȝe fleische more in oon hous þanne in anoþer?

  Frere, if ȝoure ⌜ordre⌝ & rulis ben perfiȝte and ȝoure patrun
þat made hem, whi gete ȝe ȝou dispensacioun of court to haue
150 hem more esi? Certis, eþer it semeþ þat ȝoure patroun was
f. 10ʳ vnperfiȝte eþer a fool to make an ordre so hard þat | ȝe may not
holde it, or ellis ȝe ben vnperfiȝte to take suche an ordre &
bynde ȝou þerto and siþ leue it & ⌜take ȝou⌝ anoþer bi dis-

132 aftir . . . bettir (2)] þe better þat þei be þe better is yower religion.
ȝe . . . ȝou (133)] om. 133 leyn] leve. &] om. þanne] C adds yow know
ryȝt well. 134 apostataas] apostatais C; apostaas H. & . . . ȝe] para-
ventur ye will. 135 frere] Tell me than fryer. 136 þin] of þi.
ordre] habite: h- added. 137 Seye] Syr. bie ȝe] do 'ye' bye.
ȝou] yow C; om. H. 138 siþ] seyng. 139 ȝe (1)] illegible word for
cancelled ye. pore: -e over partial erasure. 140 scapalarie: sc- over
three-letter erasure. 142 siþ] seyng. cloþis] clothe. prijs: -j-
rubricator over i. 144 ȝe] yow. o] 'one': for cancelled on. 145 &:
?C¹. &] om. holde ȝe] do ye kepe. silens] yowerys (?) sylence. more . . .
hous] in 'one' howse more: one for cancelled on. siþ] seyng.
146 man] a man. owiþ] owȝt. ouer al] specially. 147 ȝe] yow.
oon hous] þe hall. anoþer] þe fratur. 148 ordre] order C; ordris H.
rulis] rule. 149 gete . . . ȝou] do ye purchase. dispensacioun] dys-
pensacions. of] in. court] anticristys cowrt. 150 esi] easier.
Certis] truly. eþer] om. þat] om. 151 eþer . . . fool] & vndyscret.
make] begyn. hard] harde & strayt. ȝe . . . holde (152)] no man
can kepe. 152 ȝe] yow. 153 siþ] om. take ȝou] make H; gett
yow C. anoþer . . . dispensacioun] a dyspensacion.

pensacioun, & þanne ȝe lien on ȝoure patroun first '&' on ȝou
silf, to clepe ȝou ⌐hise⌐ freres and forsake his ordre, for þan ȝe   155
schulde be clepid þe popis freris for he is patroun of ȝoure ordre;
& ȝit ȝe seien ȝoure first fundacioun was bi reuelacioun of
þe Holy Goost, whom ȝe han forsaken in leuynge of þat
ordynaunce bi dispensacioun. |

Frere, whi make ȝe ȝou as deed men whanne ȝe ben professid f. 10ᵛ
in ȝoure ordre, & aftirward ȝe ben more quicke to begge worldli 161
goodis & ⌐do⌐ pursue men þat displesen ȝou þan ony oþere
men ben? & ȝit it is vnsemeli to se deed men to go so fast
on beggynge.

Frere, whi wole ȝe not suffre ȝoure nouycis to here ȝoure 165
counseile in ȝoure chapitre hous or þanne þei ben professid, if
ȝoure counseilis ben trewe & aftir Goddis lawe?

Whi make ȝe so costli | housis to dwelle ynne, siþ Crist dide f. 11ʳ
not so, ne ⌐hise⌐ apostlis, ne noon holi men þat ȝe reden of?
And alle is pilage of pore men & lordis almes, for more almes 170
it were to help men at her nede þanne leue þat & make gay
housis. Also men fro þe world schulde haue but† housis of
mornynge & not to flatere þe world; for ȝe maken ȝou courtis
passinge lordis so þat ȝe 'mai' wel nyȝ pas þoruȝ þe rewme

---

154 þanne] if.   lien] leye.   on] of.   ȝoure . . . first] 'yower fyrst' patrone.
& (2): margin ?C¹.   ȝou silf (155)] yower self.   155 to] and.   hise]
his HC.   and] and than.   for . . . clepid (156)] þen 'we' must nedys
call yow.   156 is: i- alteration?   patroun] þe ?true patrone.   157
ȝit: ȝ- over erasure?   was] came.   bi] by þe.   158 han] haue vtterly.
leuynge: -e- from i.   of þat] his.   159 ordynaunce: -y- from ?r.
ordynaunce] ordynances.   bi] thrugh yower.   dispensacioun] dyspensacons.
160 make ȝe] do ye make.   ben professid] do professe yow.   161 in]
in to.   162 goodis] C adds with false dyssymulation.   do] also do C; to H.
163 after ben: is cancelled.   & . . . vnsemeli] is not þis a seamly syȝt.
to (2)] om.   164 on beggynge] a beggyng.   165 whi . . . ȝe] what meanith
it þat ye do.   166 counseile] cowncellis.   þanne] euer.   167
counseilis] cowncell.   aftir] stond with.   168 siþ] seyng.   Crist . . .
apostlis (169)] crist & his apostles ded not so.   169 hise] his HC.   ne (2)]
nor.   170 is] is of.   171 leue] to leve.   172 fro] owt of.   housis] grauis
'or' housis HC: or ?C¹ over erasure and margin.   173 for ȝe maken:
C¹ over erasure.   ȝe] yow.   ȝou] yower.   174 passinge] broder than.
lordis] lordys cowrtys.   mai: margin C².   wel nyȝ pas þoruȝ þe r-: C² over
erasure.   wel . . . ligge (175)] passe thrugh þe realme wellnye euery
nyght lyeng.

175 and eche ny3t ligge *in* a court of 30ure owne, & so may not |
f. 11ᵛ lordis.

Whi sette 3e al þe kyngis lo*n*de to ferme to ⌐3ou'r'e⌐ lymytouris as 3e were*n* lordis of alle me*n*nes goodis, & 3e wole not
suffre o frere to begge *in* ano þeres lymytacio*un* v*n*punyschid?

180   Frere, whi be 3e not lege men to ky*n*gis ne obedie*n*te to
bischopis ne v*n*dir her visitacio*un*?

Frere, si þ 3e be*n* so ryche þat 3e pey*n*ten 30ure wallis wi þ
golde & fyne clo þis, & ha*n* many iewilis & myche tresoure,
whi pay 3e not taliagis to oure ky*n*g in help of þe rewme &
12ʳ supportyn*ge* of pore | men,† si þ Crist paied tribute to þe
186 he þen emperour?

Frere, whi axe 3e not lettris of bri þered of o þer pore me*n*nes
preieris, good & criste*n* leuers, ne of preestis, ne of mo*n*kis, ne
of bischopis, as 3e desire þat o þer riche me*n* axe*n* 30u letteris
190 for a certeyne su*m*me bi 3eer?

Frere, if 3e presume þat 3e haue most holinesse aboue al o þer
lyuers, & þat ⌐3e⌐ most sto*n*de in most perfi3t loue, whi ⌐graunte⌐
3e not to alle me*n* ⌐30ure⌐ lettris & preiers for charite, & nameli
f. 12ᵛ to pore | criste*n* puple?

195   Frere, may 3e make ony ma*n* more perfi3te bi 30ure feyned
lettris e þer 30ure soold preiers þa*n*ne God ha'þ bi' bileue of
baptem & his owne gra*n*te? If 3e seie 3he, þa*n*ne be 3e goddis
aboue oure God.

Whi make 3e me*n* bileue þat 30ure golde*n* tre*n*tale, soold for
200 a certeyne su*m*me of money—as fyue schylingis or more—may

176 lordis] lord*ys* do.   177 sette 3e] do ye lett.   30ure] 30u'r' H: -r
?*C*ᴵ; yo*w*er C.   178 3e (1)] yow.   3e (2)] yett ye.   179 o] 'one':
for cancelled on.   ano þeres] ano þer.   180 lege . . . ne] *om.*   181 ne] &.
182 si þ] seyng.   3e (2): -e *over two-letter erasure.*   183 clo þis] color*is.*
myche] great.   184 not] no.   oure] yo*w*er.   ky*n*g] criste*n* kyng.   in] &.
þe] yo*w*er.   185 supportynge: -o- *from* r?   men] H *adds* þat 3e p'i'le*n.*
si þ] seyng.   187 axe . . . not] do ye not ask.   bri þered] bo þerhede.
188 good] þat be good.   &] *om.*   ne (1)] nor.   ne (2)] nor.   ne (3)] nor.
189 3e] yow   axe*n*] schall aske & tak of.   192 3e] ye C; *om.* H.   most
(1)] *om.*   in most] most in.   graunte] graau*n*te H.   193 -le men
30ur le- H: *C*ᴵ *over erasure.*   30ure] 30ur H; yo*w*er C.   nameli] specially.
196 e þer] or elly*s* with.   soold] sowll.   bileue] faith.   197 grante]
promyse.   þa*n*ne] 'now' tha*n*.   be 3e] ye be.   200 money] syluer.
fyue . . . more] xᴵ & nolesse.

bry*n*ge a soule out of helle or of purgatorie? If þis be sooþ, what
schal bifalle of ȝou þat may saue so liȝtli al soulis & suffre*n*
hem to be | da*m*pned or peyned i*n* ȝoure defaute?   f. 13ʳ

Whi make ȝe me*n* bileue þat he þat ⌐is¬ biriede i*n* ȝoure
abite schal neuer come i*n* helle? Þis vertu was not i*n* cloþis of 205
Crist ne þe apostlis, & ȝit wite*n* ȝe not where to be ȝou silf. & if
it were sooþ, as it is a b'l'asfemy, ȝe schulde*n* selle ȝoure hiȝ
housis & make cotis for many me*n* to saue many soulis.

Frere, whi stele ȝe me*n*nes childre*n* to make he*m* of ȝoure
settis siþ ⌐þefte¬ is aȝe*n*s Goddi*s* ⌐heeste¬, & for lesse prise 210
men be*n* | hangid on galowis? And ȝoure ordre is v*n*perfiȝte,   f. 13ᵛ
& ȝe wite not where þat maner of lyuy*n*ge is worst for þat child
& may be cause of his da*m*pnaciou*n*.

Frere, where fy*n*de ȝe bi Goddis lawe þat preestis schulde*n*
prisou*n* her briþere*n* & so distroie he*m*, siþ þe gospel techiþ 215
to v*n*dirnyme he*m* in charite & so to wy*n*ne he*m*? & if he wole
not be wo*n*ne bi ȝou, ne bi þe chirche, Goddis lawe & Sei*n*t
Austi*n*s rule techiþ† to putte hy*m* from þee as an heþe*n* ma*n*;
þis is not to priso*n* | ⌐hym¬.   f. 14ʳ

Frere, whi coueite ȝe schrift & biriy*n*ge of oþer me*n*nes 220
parische*n*s, & not to do oþere sacrame*n*tis þat falle*n* to criste*n*

201 of (2)] owt of.   purgatorie] þi faynid p*u*rgatory.   sooþ] truyth.
202 bifalle] be come.   saue . . . liȝtli] so easly save.   203 i*n*]
throwe.   204 is] C; his H.   205 not] neu*er*.   cloþis] þe
cloithis.   206 ne þe] nor yet of no*n* of his.   wite*n* ȝe] ye know.   where...
silf] yo*w*er self where ye schalbe come.   207 it . . . sooþ] so be
þat it were true.   a blasfemy] C *substitutes* þe most blaspheme agaynst
crist*ys* blode.   selle . . . housis (208)] pull downe yo*w*er howsys & sell þem.
208 many (1)] *om.*   to . . . soulis] þat þer sowll*ys* may be savyd.   210
siþ] seyng.   þefte] þeste H; it C.   heeste] heestis H; *com*mandment
C.   for . . . galowis (211)] also men be hangyd on þe galhows for stealyng
of a lesse valowr.   212 wite] wote.   þat (1) . . . & (213)] C *substitutes* a
man 'can' fynd an v*n*p*ar*fytter lyvyng & more vngodly þen yo*w*eris is and to
bry*n*g a childe to þis nowȝty lyff it.   215 distroie] to dystroy.   siþ]
seyng.   216 hem (1): -e- *from* i.   to (1) . . . in] C *substitutes* alonly to rebuk
& þat in all pacience &.   hem (2): -e- *from* i.   hem (2)] hyn.   217 be] so
be.   ne . . . chirche] *om.*   Goddis] bothe god*ys*.   &] & also yo*w*er.   218
techiþ] techiþ vs H; teachith yow C.   from . . . hym (219)] not in p*r*ison.
219 hym] C; he*m* H: -e- *from* i.   220 schrift . . . of] to schryve & to
bury.   221 p*a*rische*n*s] parischeners.   do] minist*er*.   falle*n*] longyth.
criste*n*] oþer.

folkis? & whi coueite ȝe not schrift of pore men, siþ lordis &
riche men mai haue prestis more plente ⌜þanne⌝ pore men? &
siþen pore men, as ȝe seien, ben moost holi, whi coueite ȝe not
225 to birie hem at ȝoure housis as ȝe doen riche men?

Whi wole ȝe not seie ⌜þe gospel⌝ at pore bedrede mennes
housis þat may not go to chirche, as ȝe doen at riche mennes
f. 14ᵛ housis | and schoppis þat mai go to chirche & here þe gospel
þere?

230 Whi wolen ȝe not go on a longe route to diriges of pore deed
men þat sumtime visitiden ȝou wiþ almes as ȝe don to riche men,
siþ God preisiþ þe pore more þanne þe riche?

Frere, whi preche ȝe fals fablis of freris & feined myraclys, and
leuen þe gospel þat Crist bade preche & is moost holsum
235 lore to bodi & to soule, & so also oure bileue bi whiche oonli we
moste be saued? |

f. 15ʳ   Frere, whi hate ȝe þat þe gospel schulde be prechid to þe
trewe vndirstondinge of holi doctouris, & ȝe clepen it þe newe
doctrine in sclaundringe of Crist? & ȝe ben more holden þerto
240 þan to alle þe rulis þat euer ȝoure patroun made, & ȝe winnen
moreϯ wiþ In principio ⌜þan⌝ Crist & hise apostlis & alle þe
seintis of heuene; & in þis mynistrallis ben bettre þanne ȝe, for
þei contrarien not her myrþis as ȝe don.

222 whi: *twice, first cancelled.*   coueite . . . of] do ye not covite to schryve.
siþ] seyng.   223 men mai: ? *C¹ over erasure.* mai] *om.* þanne] þane
H; than C. men] men haue. &] *om.*   224 siþen] seyng. pore . . . as]
om. ben] ye be.   225 as] as well as. *after* doen (*and margin*): carets,
no insertion.   226 seie] patter. þe gospel] gospels H; yower gospell C.
227 may] can. chirche] þe churche. as . . . chirche (228)] *om.*   230 on]
of. route] rowe.   231 to: *over erasure.* men: -n *over erasure.* riche
men] þe rich mens dirig*is.*   232 siþ] seyng. preisiþ: -siþ *over erasure.*
preisiþ] praysed. þe . . . more] more þe poore.   233 myraclys and: *C¹ over
erasure.*   234 leuen . . . preche] þe gospell þat crist bade 'to' preache 'is
le⟨ft⟩'. &] which. moost] þe most.   235 lore] lawe. to (2)] *om.* so also]
C *substitutes* þe pure way to. whiche] þe which.   237 ȝe] you.
schulde be] schalbe. to] after.   238 ȝe] *om.*   239 doctrine]
lernyng. Crist] ower savior crist. &] seyng. holden] beholden. þerto:
-to *over erasure.*   240 &] for.   241 more] C; more money H:
money ? *C² over erasure.* wiþ: *C¹ over erasure.* In prin-: *margin C¹.*
In principio] clatteryng of in principio. þan] then C; þat H.   242
seintis: -eit- *over erasure.* bettre: -e- *over erasure.*   243 ȝe] yow.

Frere, siþ Crist & hise apostlis ordeyneden preestis to |
preche, & preie, & sacramentis to mynystre to þe puple—ȝhe, f. 15ᵛ
a þousande ⌈ȝeer⌉ bifore ȝoure capteyns & prestis han suffrid 246
ȝou as foolis to come in among þe puple—whi ben ȝe so vnkynde
as bastard braunchis to pursue prestis to prisonynge & to fire
for ⌈prechinge⌉ of Cristis lawe freli, with outen sillinge of þe
gospel? 250

Frere, siþ ȝe wolen opinli preche aȝen þe defautis of prelatis,
of prestis, lordis, lawiers & marchauntis & comouns, whi be ȝe
so wode | þat prestis prechen of ȝoure defautis in amendement f. 16ʳ
of ȝoure lijf in charite, & ȝe falsli sclaundren hem of erise? & þe
more part of ȝou woot not what an eresie is for to seye—but 255
ȝe knowun þe dede bi experiens.

Frere, siþ God takiþ a mannes preier aftir þat þe persones
ben worþi of her good lyuynge þat preien & ben preied fore,
& þou wost not hou þou art worþi bifore God, whi wolt þou
take hire for þi preier and ⌈sillen⌉ þou wost neuer what? Of alle | 260
chaffaris þis is moste perelous, & next to Balams boost & f. 16ᵛ
Gizies lepre.

Frere, siþ þou proferist to so manye men a masse for a penye,

244 siþ] om.   245 preie] to pray.   sacramentis . . . puple] to minister to
þe pepill sacramentys.   ȝhe: -e over two-letter erasure.   ȝhe] om.   246
ȝeer] yere C; ȝeris H.   ȝoure capteyns] yower sect was inventyd but now
captans.   han] haith.   247 as foolis] om.   in] om.   248 to (2)] om.
to fire] burnyng þem.   249 prechinge] prechge H; preachyng C. of (1)] om.
251 siþ] seyng þat.   defautis] fawtys & abusions.   252 of prestis] om.
marchauntis] merchandys.   & (2)] & also.   253 wode] farr owt of
þe way.   prestis] ye will not suffer þat preastis.   prechen of] may preach
agaynst.   defautis] fawtys & abusions.   in . . . charite (254)] with charite
trustyng of amendment of yower lyfe.   254 in: ? C¹ over erasure.   & (1)]
but.   255 more] greatest.   for . . . seye] om.   but . . . experiens (256)] C
substitutes but þat ye here þe comon voyce say so þat þis is an heresie to
say þat crist hath preparyd to all his congregation but 'one' religion to beleue
& put all þer confydence in hym with such oþer rulys: one for cancelled on.
257 siþ] seyng.   takiþ] alowith.   a] om.   þat] om.   persones . . .
fore (258)] purenes of þe persons faith & his good lyvyng þerin both of þem
þat be prayd for & also of þem þat pray.   259 & . . . God] as þis j know
for a suerte fryer þat þou wotist not how þou art alowid befor god.   whi]
j pray þe than tell me why.   wolt þou] þou wilt.   260 hire] wagys.   and
sillist þou: C¹ over erasure.   sillen] sillist H; so to sell C.   Of] surely of.
261 moste] þe most.   262 Gizies] iesis (?).   263 siþ] seyng.   to]
om.   penye] peny j pray þe tell me.

what sillist þou for þat penye, wheþer þi preier or Cristis bodi
265 or þi traueil? If þou woldiste not seie a masse but for a penye,
þanne þou louest coueitousli more a penye þanne þin owen
soule, & alle Holi Chirche quicke & dede; & if þou sillist Cristis
bodi for a penye, þanne art þou worse þanne Iudas þat soolde
f. 17ʳ it for þritti pens. | Where is a falser symonyent if þou wolt not
270 preie for a man but for a penye? Hou hast þou lerned Cristis
gospel þat biddiþ þe'e' preie freli for frende & fo?

Frere, whi sclaundre ȝe falsli Crist lord of alle creaturis, þat
he beggid his owne good as ȝe don oþer mennes good, siþ he
had no nede þerto on þat wise?

275 Frere, siþ in Goddis lawe suche clamerous beggeynge is
vttirli forfendid, on what lawe groundist þou þee þus for to
begge, & nameli of porer þan þou art þi silf? For soþ it is þat
f. 17ᵛ no man schulde þus begge; for if a man suffice to hym | silf bi
goodis or bi strengþe, he synneþ for to begge; & so if he be
280 pore & vnmyȝty, þanne þe peple synneþ but þei visite hym or
þat he begge.

Frere, whi writist þo'u' mennes names in þi tablis? Wenest
þou þat God is suche a fool þat he wot not of mennes dedis
but if þou telle hym bi þi tablis?

285 Frere, if þou þinkist it a good dede to begge for þin idil
briþeren at hoom, þere eche oon of ȝou haþ an annuel salarie
eþer two, whi wolt þou not begge for pore bedrede men—porer

---

264 sillist þou] þou saidist.   þat] þi.   þi] þou sellist þi.   265 traueil]
labur.   woldiste] wilt.   266 coueitousli] cuvitusnes.   a penye] om.
owen: -we- *over erasure.*   267 quicke & dede] om.   269 þritti] xxx.
Where is] which was.   falser] false.   symonyent] symoniack.   if] &
if.   270 hast] haith.   271 þee: -e *margin ?C¹.*   272 lord] þe
lord.   þat] sayng þat.   273 ȝe] yow.   good (2)] goodys.   siþ] seyng.
274 þerto] to gett good.   wise] maner.   275 siþ] seyng.   276
forfendid] forbyde.   groundist þou] dost þou grownd.   277 nameli]
specially.   porer] power (?).   it . . . þat] om.   278 þus begge]
begge on þis maner of wyse.   suffice . . . goodis (279)] haith of his sufficient
goodys.   279 bi strengþe] be strong & abyll to gett his lyvyng.   synneþ]
'synneth': *for cancelled* ?semith.   for] greatly in þe syȝt of god for.
& . . . he] lykwyse if a man.   280 vnmyȝty] C *substitutes* vnabyll to gett his
lyvyng.   but] grevusly except.   282 þou: -u *corrector;* 'þou' C.
283 wot] knowith.   mennes] mans.   286 hoom: -om *over erasure.*
þere] þer as.   haþ] haue.   salarie] service.   287 eþer] or.

þan ȝe, febeler þan ȝe, þat moun not go aboute? Knowe ȝe no
men for ȝoure briþeren but if | ⌐þei⌐ haue on moornynge cloþis   f. 18ʳ
& be of ȝoure sett, here ȝou lackiþ charite.   290

Frere, siþ ȝe seie þat it is so medeful a þing to ȝeue almes,
whi wolen ȝe neuer gete ȝou þat mede on pore sike men
& pore prisoned men in her myscheef, ne visite þe pore
laborers in dere somers þat ȝe han pilid in wynteris?

Frere, whi make ȝe so many maistris among ȝou aȝens Cristis 295
biddynge in þe gospel, seiynge þat oon is maister oon is lord, &
þis ȝe contrarien bi many waste & costli meenes?

Frere, whos ben alle ȝoure riche coortis & ȝoure | riche f. 18ᵛ
iewels þat ȝe han, siþ ȝe 'seien' ȝe han no þyng in propre ne in
comoun bi vertu of ȝoure ordre? If ȝe seien þei ben þe popis 300
ȝoure holiest fadir, whi gadere ȝe so many goodis of pore men
& lordis of þe rewme to make þe pope so riche? And ȝe han
chosun for moost perfeccioun to haue no suche in propre ne
in comoun bi vertu of ȝoure ordre, & þe pope schulde be
moost per⟨fi⟩ȝte. Ȝe ben cursid children to sclaundre so ȝoure 305
fadir & putte on hym so moche vnperfeccioun.

Frere, whi make ȝe not ȝoure feestis to pore men & | ȝeue f. 19ʳ
hem ȝiftis, as ȝe doen to riche men?

Frere, siþ Crist sente hise apostlis whanne þei weren perfiȝt
oon to o cuntre, anoþer to anoþer, whi go ȝe two to gedre & ȝe 310
seien ȝe ben perfiȝte as þe apostlis weren?

Frere, siþ ȝe taken salaries—ȝhe, sum double & treble—whi
begge ȝe þerto more þanne oþer prestis don? Wite ȝe not wel
þat þe more þat ȝe han þe more is ȝoure charge?

288 moun] may.   *after* aboute: *caret, no insertion.*   289 but if] except.
þei] he H; ye C.   290 here] þer.   ȝou] ye.   lackiþ] lack.   291
siþ] seing.   292 neuer] not.   ȝou] *om.*   293 myscheef] miserie.
ne] nor.   þe] *om.*   295 ȝe] yow.   maistris: -tris *C*¹ *over erasure?*
ȝou: ȝ- *alteration ?C*¹.   296 þat] *om.*   297 þis] þes.   299 siþ]
seyng.   seien: *margin ?C*¹.   ȝe seien] *om.*   ne] nor.   301 whi:
w- *over erasure.*   302 lordis: *after* -r- *letter erased.*   303 no]
non.   ne] nor.   305 perfiȝte: -fi- *alteration.*   sclaundre: -r- *over*
erasure.   306 so] *om.*   307 ȝe] *om.*   309 siþ] seyng.   310
anoþer (1)] & one to.   two] *om.*   312 siþ] seyng.   salaries]
seruycys.   &] some.   313 þerto more] more þer to.   314 þat (2)]
om.

315   Frere, siþ ʒoure patrouns han seide þat þei hadden þe
makynge of ʒoure rulis bi schewynge of God & his ordynaunce,
f. 19ᵛ whi holde ʒe not þe ordynaunce of Goddis | makynge? Forsoþe,
if God haþ ordeyned it þe pope mai not fordo it leuefuli; & if
it were not of Goddis ⌐ordynaunce⌐, þan bi ʒoure seiynge ʒoure
320 patrouns weren liers on God, & ʒe her claunderers as cursid
children.

Frere, whi wole not summe of ʒoure ordre touche siluer wiþ
þe crosse & þe kyngis heed, as ʒe wolen touche a silueren spone
& oþere siluer? Certis, if ʒe dispisen þe cros & þe kyngis heed,
325 ʒe ben worþi to be dispisid of God & of þe kynge, & so of alle
f. 20ʳ her trewe seruauntis; | & siþen ʒe wolen resceyue þe money in
ʒoure hertis & not in ʒoure hondis, it semeþ ʒe holden more
holines in ʒoure hondis þanne in ʒoure hertis. þanne ben ʒe
false to God þat knowiþ ʒoure coueitous hertis.

330   Frere, whi paien summe of ʒoure ordris eche ʒeere a certeyne
to þer prouinciale or to summe oþere souereyne, til þat he haþ
stoole a certeine summe of children to make hem freres? & þus
ʒe ben construyned bi ʒoure ordre to breke Goddis comaunde-
f. 20ᵛ mentis in doyng | of þeefte passynge þeefte of hors & maris.

335   Frere, whi ben ʒe so foole hardi to graunte to eche man
þat wole paie ʒou þerfore, bi lettris of fraternyte, part & meryt
of alle ʒoure massis & oþere good dedis? & ʒe witen not where
ʒoure dedis displesen God for ʒoure synnes, and also wheþer þat

315 siþ] seing. þei: -e- *alteration.*   316 rulis: *twice, first cancelled.*
ordynaunce] ordynancys.   318 haþ] haue.   mai] can.   fordo] vndo.
leuefuli] lawfully.   if: -f *from* ?t.   319 ordynaunce] ordynauce H;
ordynance C.   320 ʒe] ye be.   322 wole] 'will' ye.   ordre] orders.
324 siluer] syluer knackys.   Certis] *om.*   325 of (2)] *om.*   326 her]
his.   siþen] seyng.   327 holden] haue.   328 ben ʒe] ye be.   329
coueitous] covityse.   330 eche] euery.   331 þer] þe.   þat] *om.*   he] þe
tyme he.   332 certeine: -ei- *? corrector over erasure.*   summe] nomber.
þus . . . ordre (333)] þus by þe statute of yower ordyr ye be constraynid.
333 Goddis] cristys.   334 in . . . of] 'commyt'tyng.   passynge] which theft
passith.   þeefte] stealyng.   hors] horsys.   &] or.   maris] maers (?).
335 foole hardi] foolische hardy.   eche] euery.   336 þat . . . fraternyte]
by letters of fraternyte þat will pay þerfor.   part . . . meryt] þat
he schall haue part of þe merityas.   337 massis . . . dedis] C *substitutes*
massys fastyngys watchyngys & prayers.   ʒe] yet ye.   338 displesen]
be acceptabyll to.   for] or.

man be worþi to resceyue merit for his owne lyuynge. For if he
schal be dampned, hise owne dedis ne ȝouris schulen neuer 340
availe hym to blisse.

Frere, what charite is it to ouere | charge þe puple bi beggynge f. 21ʳ
of so many myȝti men vndir coloure of prechynge & preiynge
& massis syngeynge, siþen holi writ biddiþ not þis but þe contrarie? For alle suche goostli dedis schulden be freeli don as God 345
ȝyueþ freeli, & ellis it were cursid symony.

Frere, what charite is it to bigile ynnocent children or þei
kunne discrescioun, & bynde hem to ȝoure ordris þat ben not
groundid in Goddis lawe, aȝens her frendis wille & from helpynge
of fadris & modris, 'where'as Goddis lawe biddiþ 'þe con- 350
tra⟨rie⟩'? For bi þis foli | ben many apostataas in herte & wille al f. 21ᵛ
her lijf, þat wolden go out in dede but for drede of deeþ if þei
weren taken aȝen.

Frere, what charite is it to charge þe puple wiþ so many
freris, siþen persouns, vikers, & prestis were jnowȝ to serue þe 355
puple of preestis office wiþ bischopis—ȝhe, monkis, chanouns
wiþ out mo. & þus for to encrese with so many freris is greet
cumbraunce to þe puple & aȝens Goddis wille þat made al

339 merit] ony merit*ys*.   340 hise] neþer his.   owne] *om.*   ne] nor.
schulen . . . blisse (341)] schalbryng hym to þe blys euerlastyng.
343 so] *om.*   prechynge: e *cancelled after* -h-.   preiynge] long prayng.
344 siþen] seyng þat.   writ] scriptur.   biddiþ . . . contrarie] *com*mand
us not so to do but *com*mandyth us in ony wise þe contrary.   345
dedis] act*ys*.   God] god hym self.   346 ȝyueþ freeli] frely dyd redeme
us.   &] or.   it were] all is but.   347 ynnocent] poore innocent.   or] or
euer.   348 kunne discrescioun] come to yerys of dyscrescion.   þat]
which.   349 in] on.   wille] will*ys*.   from . . . modris (350)] also
byndyng þem þat þei schal not helpe faþers nor moþers.   350–1 whereas:
where- *margin* ?Cᴵ, þe contrarie: *margin (cropped)* ?Cᴵ.   whereas . . .
contrarie (351)] C *substitutes* whiche is plane agaynst þe lawe of god & his
*com*mandment.   351 For] and.   foli] subtyll meanys.   in] amongst
yow in.   herte] þer hart*ys*.   & . . . lijf (352)] *om.*   352 go . . . dede]
C *substitutes* gladly be delyueryd from yower wikyd religious.   drede] fere.
deeþ] C *substitutes* cruell dethe & tyranny persecution þat ye wold mynister
vnto þem.   þei . . . aȝen (353)] ye myȝt tak þem agayn.   354 charge]
burden & charge.   þe puple] crist*ys* congregation.   355 siþen]
seyng.   persouns] þer be persons.   were] *om.*   serue] mynister to.   356
of . . . office] þe offic*ys* of preast*ys*.   wiþ] besyd.   monkis] & monck*ys*
&.   chanouns] *om.*   357 wiþ out mo] many oþer mo.   þus] yow þus.
for] *om.*   greet] a great.   358 cumbraunce] combrance & hurt.   aȝens]
playne agaynst.

f. 22ʳ þingis in mesoure, noumbre, & wei3t; & Crist ordeyned twel | ue
360 apostlis wiþ fewe oþere prestis to do seruyce to alle þe world,
& þanne was it best don. And ri3t as foure fingris & a þombe on
a man helpiþ hym to worche, & double so many on oon hond
schuld lette hym, & treble schuld lette hym more; & so to many
freris & oþere ordris passynge þe ordinaunce of God, lettiþ
365 Cristis chirche to growe to heuene.

Frere, whi may 3e for schame lye to þe puple, and seye þat
3e folowe þe apostlis in pouerte more þanne oþere men don;
f. 22ᵛ & 3it in | curious & costlew housis, & fyne & precious cloþinge,
delicious & lusti fedynge, in tresorie & iewels & riche ourne-
370 mentis, freris passen lordis & oþere riche worldli men; & sun-
nest 3e bringen aboute 3oure causis, be þei neuer so costlew or
a3ens Goddis lawe.

Frere, what charite is it to gadere vp þe bokis of Goddis
lawe, many mo þanne nediþ 3ou, & putte hem in tresorie, & do
375 prisone hem fro seculer preestis & curatis, wher bi þei ben lettid
f. 23ʳ of kunnynge of Goddis | lawe to preche þe gospel freli? And
ouer þat, 3e defamen trewe preestis of erisie & letten þe sowynge
of Goddis word.

What power haue 3e to asoile lordis & ladies þat 3e ben con-
380 fessouris to, of synnes† þat þei leuen not, as pilinge of her
tenauntis & lyuinge in leccherie & glotony & oþere heed synnes,
of whiche þei cecen not but ben counfortid bi 3oure suffraunce?

---

359 Crist] ower sauior crist.   twelue] xij.   361 ri3t] like.   foure] iiij.
362 man] hand.   hym] a man.   worche] work well.   &] om.   double] so þe
contrary wise dubbyll.   oon] a.   363 schuld lette] & þei schall lett.   hym]
hym more.   treble] trubyll hym then do hym good.   schuld ... more]
om.   364 &] & also.   ordris] lordys.   of God] C substitutes
which he left in his churche schall trubill greatly.   lettiþ] & let.   365
Cristis chirche] his congregation.   heuene] hevynward.   367 þe
apostlis] crist.   don] om.   368 & (4)] om.   369 in] & in.   370 passen]
passith.   371 costlew] vngracius.   373 vp] togeþer.   374 nediþ
3ou] yow nede.   in] vp in.   tresorie] yower tresory.   do] om.
376 of kunnynge of] to conne.   to] & so to.   þe gospel] it.   freli]
to þe pepill frely.   377 ouer ... preestis] trew preastys þat sow godys
sede among þe pepill ye defame þem.   letten] so ye lett.   380
to] vnto.   synnes] H repeats of whiche þei cesen not but ben counfortid
from 382.   pilinge] spoylyng.   381 heed] deadly.   382 whiche] þe
which.   cecen] descrase.

Frere, siþ ȝoure ordris ben moost perfiȝt, as ȝe seien, for
ȝoure pouert, chastite, & obediens, | whi bisien ȝe ȝou fast, & f. 23ᵛ
nameli ⌜ȝou'r'e⌝ grettist clerkis, to be bischopis & prelatis & 385
popis chapleins, & to be asoilid fro pouert & fro obedience,
'&' euer to lyue in lustus of fleisch & of þe world, þat is goostli
leccherie? Ȝe ben verri Fariseis þat don oon & seien anoþer
contrarie þerto.

Frere, whi sclaundre ȝe trewe preestis & oþere trewe meke 390
men of þe sacrament of Goddis bodi, for þei seien þat þe holi
breed duli sacrid is Goddis bodi in foorme of breed, & ȝe seien
þat it | is an accident wiþ outen subiect, & not Goddis bodi. f. 24ʳ

Frere, who ben eritikis here & fer fro Cristis wordis, þat
took þe breed & blissid it & brak it & seide, þis is my bodi; & 395
Seint Poul seiþ, þe breed þat we breken is Goddis bodi; and
Seynt Austin seiþ, þat not eche breed is Goddis bodi, but þat
breed þat reseyueþ blissynge is Goddis bodi. & to þis acordiþ
þe oold doctouris & comoun bileue bifor þat freris camen in
ouer þe walle a þousande ȝeer & more. 400

Frere, take hede to my tale & to myn entent | also, for charite f. 24ᵛ
chasiþ me þerto to chalenge ȝoure defautis, þat ȝe moun
amende to God & to man þis mys or ȝe die, bi open know-
lechynge of ȝoure gilt, & go þerfro bityme. For hou schulde ȝe

---

383 siþ] seing.   ordris] order.   ben] is.   for] specially for.   384
ȝoure] yower iij vowys.   bisien . . . fast] be ye so dyligent & labur so
fast.   385 nameli] specially.   ȝoure] ȝou'r' H: -r ?C¹; yower C.
& (1)] om.   386 chapleins] om.   & (1)] & cuvite.   obedience] C
adds j will not say from chastite.   387 & (1): margin ?C¹.   & (1)] om.
euer] euery: -y cancelled?   lustus] þe lustys.   fleisch] yower flesche.
þat] which.   388 Ȝe ben] Thes be þe.   oon] on thyng.   390
sclaundre ȝe] do ye slawnder.   trewe (2)] om.   392 sacrid] consecrate.   ȝe] yow.   393 þat] om.   394 & . . . fro] but yow which
arre from.   þat] which.   396 þe . . . þat (1) (397)] om.   397 not . . .
is] euery brede is not.   but . . . bodi (398)] om.   399 þe] om.
comoun bileue] C substitutes specially a comon beleve of cristys
congregation.   þat] om.   400 þousande] m.   402 chasiþ] compellith.
þerto] om.   chalenge] declare vnto yow.   defautis] fawtys.   ȝe]
yow.   403 amende . . . man] call vnto crist for grace to ame⟨nd⟩ not only
before hyn but also before man.   þis mys] þat þou may.   or . . . die] om.
404 gilt] fawtys þat ye be gilty in.   &] om.   þerfro] from þem.   bityme] by
tymes.   404 ȝe: corrector?

405 endure vndampned to helle to leue Crist & his lawe for ȝoure
rotun ⌜ritis⌝, & seie þat Goddis lawe is fals to fourme or to lerne,
til ȝe hadden founden a glos feyned of ȝoure wittis?

Go now forþ frere & fraiste ȝoure clerkis, & grounde ȝou
in Goddis lawe, & ȝeue Iacke an answere, & whanne ȝe asoilen
f. 25ʳ þat I haue seide sadli in | truþe, I schal asoile þee of þin ordre &
411 saue þee to heuene.†

---

405 vndampned . . . helle] or skape þe depe & dangerus pitt of hell.
406 ritis] rutis H; roottys C.   & seie] & tradicions & say.   407 hadden]
haue.   a glos: a g- C¹ over erasure?   ȝoure] yower owne.   408
fraiste] sek owt.   409 in] on.   lawe: -w- first compartment wanting.
asoilen] haue assoiled.   410 þat] þat which.   seide . . . truþe] truly &
sadly spokyn 'vn'to yow.   411 saue þee] sett þe in þe ryght way.
heuene] C adds jack vpon lond lookith for an answer. See 411 n.

FRIAR DAW'S REPLY

Who shal graun*ten* to myn eye*n* a strong streme of teres
To waile*n* & to wepyn þe sorwyng of sy*nn*e,
For charite is chasid & flemed out of londe
And eu*er*y state stakerth vnstable in hi*m* silfe.
Now ⌜apperiþ⌝ þe ⌜prophecie⌝ þat Seint Ioon seide   5
To joyne þ*er*to Iohel in his soth sawis:
þe moone is al blodi & dymme on to lokyn,
þat signefieþ lordship forslokend in sy*nn*e;
þe sterres be*n* ⌜from heuen⌝ throwu*n* & falle*n* to þe erþe
& so is þe comou*n*te treuli opp*re*ssid;   10
þe su*n*ne is eclipsid wiþ al his twelue pointes
By errou*re* & heresie þat rengniþ i*n* þe chirche.
Now is oure bileue laft & Lollardi growiþ,
Envie is enhaunsid & ap*ro*ched to preestes
þat shulde*n* enforme her flok i*n* ⌜grou*n*ding of þis⌝ lawe: 15
To loue h*er* God souereynli & siþe*n* her broþir.
Bot not for þa*n*ne now is tauȝt ⌜sundri*ng*⌝ of states,
And p*ur*suynge of pou*er*te þat Crist haþ approued;
Now is þat seed of cisme sowe*n* in þe chirche,
þe whete fadith wiþ þe flo*ure*, oure fode is forto feche,   20
Foxes frettid in fere waste*n* þe cornes
And Cristes vine is vanishid to þe verray rote.
Now ⌜Achan⌝ spoiliþ Ierico & lyueþ of þe þefte
And so lyue*n* þis lollardis in her fals fablis.
Datan & Abiron & Chorees childre*n*   25
Wiþ newe senceres ensenc⟨e⟩*n* þe auters of sy*nn*e.
Baal preestes be*n* bolde sacrifice to make
And mortel maladi crepiþ i*n* as a canker,
And þus is Iak Vplond fodid wiþ folie,

---

5 apperiþ] apperid.   prophecie] pphecie.   9 from heuen] on erþe.
15 grou*n*ding of þis] grou*n*d i*n* godd*is*.   17 sundri*ng*] hindri*ng*.
23 Achan] achor.

30 And þourз formyng of his formerer þus freyneþ a frere:
On wounder wise, seiþ Iak, freres зe ben growun, |

f. 2ᵛ Sowen in зoure sectes of Anticristis hondes;
Vnboxom to bishopis not lege men to kynges;
Wede corn ne gras wil зe not hewen,

35 Ne lyuen wiþ Iakke in labour, but al to зour ese.

Iak, þi former is a fole þat þus þee haþ yfourmed
To make so lewid an argument aзens so many freres,
þat better knowen liзtles her doctours & her bible
þan he can rede his troper bi a long torche.

40 But Iak þouз þi questions semen to þee wyse,
Зit liзtly a lewid man maye leyen hem a water;
For ⌐summe¬ ben lewid, summe ben shrewid, summe falsly
supposid,
And þerfore shal no maistir ne no man of scole
Be vexid wiþ 'þy' maters but a lewid frere

45 þat men callen Frere Daw Topias, as lewid as a leke.
To medelin with þi malice as longe as þou wolt
þe sotil witt of wyse men shulde temte vs wel soone,
And fleme vs from felowship & done vs of dawe.

þat we ben not lege men Iak, lowde þou lyest,

50 For lenger þan we lyuen so, abide we not in londe;
We obeien to bishopes as boxomnesse askiþ—
Alþowз not so fer forþ as seculer preestes.

For Holy Chirche haþ vs hent & happid wiþ grace,
To were vs from wederes of wynteres stormes,

55 Wede corn ne gras haue we not to hewen,
Ne wiþ Iakke Uplond ferme þe dikes;
Alþouз Poul in his pistele laborers ⌐preisiþ¬,
⌐Displese¬ him not þe preestes þat syngen her masses.
For riзt as in þi bodi Iake, ben ordeyned þin hondis,

60 For þin heed, & for þi feet, & for þin eyen to wirken—

---

32 hondes: -es *over erasure.*   38 þat: -t *?corrector over erasure.*
39 þan: -n *?corrector over erasure.*   42 summe] summen.   44 þy]
margin ?corrector.   46 *After this line text occurs in MS. in sequence:*
49, 50, 47, 48, 51, 52, *etc.*   50 þan: -n *minim (2) over erasure.*
54 were: -e *M?*   57 preisiþ] preise.   58 Displese] displesiþ.

Riȝt so þe comoun peple God haþ disposid,
To laboren for Holi Chirche & lordshipis also.
A! forwriþen serpent, þi wyles ben aspied |
Wiþ a þousand wrynkels þou ⌜vexest⌝ many soules,   f. 3ʳ
þi malice is so michel þou maist not forhele,   65
But þi venym wiþ vehemens þou spittist al at ones.

    þou seist we ben confounders of prelates & of lordes:
But Iakke, bi my lewte, lowde þou lyest,
For telle me bi oure counseile what lord haþ ben confoundid,
Or what ⌜prelat⌝ of ony pepil put in ony peril?   70
But siþ þat wickide worme—Wiclyf be his name—
Began to sowe þe seed of cisme in þe erþe,
Sorowe & shendship haþ awaked wyde,
In lordship and prelacie haþ growe þe lasse grace.

    Iak, þou seist wiþ symonye þe seuen sacramentes we sellen   75
And preien for no men but ȝif þei ⌜wil⌝ paien.
God wote, Iakke, þou sparist here þe soþe,
And er we departen vs a soundre it shal wel be shewid.
But oon is þe sacrament þat we han to dispensen,
Off penaunce to þe peple whan nede askiþ.   80
I trowe it be þi paroche preest 'Iacke' þat þou meenest,
þat nyl not hosel his parischens til þe peny be paied,
Ne assoilen hem of her synne wiþouten schrift siluer.

    Iakke, of þi foli þou feynest fife ordres
And ȝit ben þer but foure foundid in þe lawe,   85
Falsly as þou seist, & soone shal be distroied.
Iakke, þi lewid prophecie y preise not at a peese—
Somme fantasie of Fiton haþ marrid þi mynde:
þow prophete of Baal, þi god is a slepe,
þe goodnesse of þe Goost may not liȝten vpon þee.   90
Whi presumyst þou so proudli to ⌜prophecie⌝ þese þingis,
And wost no more what þou blaberest þan Balames asse?

    þou mayntenist in þi mater þat matrimony þus we ⌜marren⌝,

---

64 vexest] vexes.   70 prelat] pralat.   76 wil] willen.   81 jacke:
margin M.   meenest: -st *corrector?*   91 prophecie] pphecie.
93 marren] marrer.

But þis arowe shal turne aȝen to him þat it sent: |

f. 3ᵛ For þou & þi secte sothli ȝe schenden,

96 In as moche as ȝe may, þe sacramentis seuen;
And reles of synne, & grauntyng of grace,
And Cristis bitter passioun, ȝe sette not at 'an' hawe.
Who marriþ more matrimonie, ȝe or þe freris?

100 Wiþ wrenchis & wiles wynnen mennes wyues
And maken hem scolers of þe newe scole,
And reden hem her forme in þe lowe chaier;
To maken hem perfit† þei rede ȝou'r' rounde rollis,
And ⌐call on men for þer⌐ lessouns with 'Sister, me nediþ!'

105   Iak, þou seist þat we bilden þe castels of Caym,
It is Goddis hous oold schrewe þat we ben aboute:
To mayntenen his seruauntis to singe & to reden,
And bidden for þe peple as we ben beholden.
Clerkes ⌐seien⌐ þat Salomon made a solempne temple,

110 And ȝit was it bot figure of oure newe chirche—
þat ech holi hous þat Crist him silf indwelliþ.
    Iak, þou seist ful serpentli and sowdiours vs þou callist,
Sette for oure sutilte in Anticristis vaunwarde.
Crist in þe gospel rehersiþ a rewle,

115 How ech man shal be knowun oonli bi his werkes;
And if we were founden on Anticristis side
Oure werkes shulden shewen, Iakke, ful soone.
þe werkes of Anticrist persuen oure bileue,
So do þe disciplis of ȝour sory secte,

120 Shending þe sacramentis, salue to oure soris;
W'h'o typiþ bot ȝe þe anet & þe mente,
Sterching ȝour faces to be holden holi,
Bla⟨un⟩chid graues ful of dede bones,
Wandrynge wedercokkes wiþ euery wynd waginge;

94 it: -t ?corrector over erasure.   98 an: corrector.   100 wrenchis:
-s alteration.   103 perfit: letter erased after -t.   perfit] perfit in ȝour
lawe.   ȝour: -r corrector.   104 call on men for þer] callen hem
forþ her.   108 we: w- from þ corrector? Letter erased after -e.
109 seien] sein.   111 him: letter erased before h-.   121 who: -h-, -o
(from e?) corrector.   typiþ: -y- corrector, -þi- corrector over three-letter erasure.

þe spiritis of þe de`u'el makyn ȝoure tokenys—   125
þourȝ quenching of torches in ⌐ȝour⌐ taylende ȝe resseyue ȝour
    wisdom; |

ȝoure preching is perilouse it poiseneþ sone,   f. 4ʳ
As 'honyed' venym it ⌐crepith⌐ in swot.

    Iak, in þe apocalypse ful pertli ȝe be peintid,
Whan þe seuen angels blowun þere seuen trompes,   130
To warne Anticristis meyne of oure lordes comyng;
Wiþ her sterne stormes astonye al þe erþe,
Reve men of her rest & ferli hem afese.

    þe first angel wiþ his blast† noieþ ful sore,
Hayl & fier† ⌐myngid⌐ wiþ blood he sendiþ to þe erþe.   135
By þe tokenyng þat ȝour preching, Iak, makith obstinat hertis,
ȝour daliaunce ⌐inducith⌐ jr & envie.
Who ben more Fariseis þan ⌐sunderers⌐ of soulis,
þe which in her interpretacion diuisioun ben callid?
& ȝour teching in an hour wil breke 'mo' loue daies,   140
þan ⌐we⌐ mowe brynge to gidere vij ȝere aftir.

    þe secounde aungel with his blast smytiþ with drede,
And an huge hill is sent adoun in to þe salt water.
þe þridde party of creaturis ben bitter þerof,
For Sathanas by ȝour sawes is sent in to soulis   145
þat ben ful vnsauery and saltti`d by' synne:
þe bitternesse of ȝour bacbityng brewiþ many bales.

    þe þridde angel sent doun a sterre from heuen,
Bremli brennynge as a bround, Wermode it was callid.
Wermode, Iak, moost verreli was Wiclif ȝour maistir: 150
⌐Wiþ men⌐ in his begynnynge litht lemed he by cunnynge,
But aftir, with wrong wrytyng, he wrouȝte mykil care,
And, presumynge perilously, foul fel from þe chirche,
Missauerynge of þe sacrament, infectyng many oþer.

125 þe deuel: þe de- *corrector over erasure*, -u- *corrector*   126 ȝour] ȝou.
128 honyed: *margin for cancelled* heued *M*.   crepith] crepit.   134 blast]
blast he.   135 myngid] he myngith.   137 inducith] inducit.
138 who: -h- *from* o *corrector*.   sunderers] hinderers.   140 mo: *inter-*
lined and margin for cancelled ȝour *M*.   141 we] ȝe.   146 salttid:
-tid *corrector*.   by: *margin for cancelled* be *corrector*.   150 *after* iak:
is *cancelled*.   151 Wiþ men] wiþinne?

155 þus brenneþ he ȝit as a bronde, consumyng many soulis,
  þat in her hard obstinacy growen schides of helle;
  Maximine ne Maniche neuere wrouȝten more wrake,
  þerfore from wele is he went & woo mote him wryng. |

f. 4ᵛ The iiijᵉ aungel wiþ his blast, smytiþ riȝt smerte:
160 þe iijᵉ party of þe sonne with dymmenes is dirked,
  Off þe moone and of þe sterres & of þe day also,
  And þe egle in þe eyre þries 've' ⌐scricheth⌐.
  þe sonne is Holy Chirche & lordship þe moone,
  þe sterres ben þe comuns, as y seid bifore,
165 And alle þese ben alured to ȝoure sory secte.
  And summe of ech of þese astates ben priuyly apoisond,
  þerfore þries ve is manassid vpon ȝou,
  For þree manere of synnes þat comunly ȝe vsen:
  Ve for enuye, ve for jpocrisie, & ve for ȝour leccherie.
170 Whan þe ⌐fift⌐ angel blew, þer was a pit opend,
  þer rose smoþeryng smoke & breses þerinne.
  Alle þei weren lich horsis araied in to bataile,
  þei stongen as scorpioun & hadden mannis face,
  Toþed as† lioun wiþ haburiouns of jren.
175 þis pitte is þe depnes, Iak, of ȝour malice,
  þe smorþering smoke is ȝour dymme doctrine,
  þat flieþ out from þe flawmes of þe deuelis malice,
  þat troubliþ & blindiþ þe jȝen of mannis resoun.
  þe breses ben not ellis but Anticristis menye,
180 With short legges bifore & longe bihinde;
  þe which pretenden first mekenesse of herte,
  And aftir rysyng to arrogaunce disdeynynge al oþer.
  þat ȝe ben lyke scorpions signefieþ not ellis,
  But þat ȝe flateren aforn & venym casten bihinde.
185 Ȝe ben also lich horses redy in to bateil,
  By woodnesse & foolhardinesse for heresie to dien.
  Ȝe ben toþed as lioun by stynkyng 'de'traccion.

---

158 wryng: wry- *over erasure.* 162 ve: *margin for cancelled we* M.
scricheth] westheth. 169 Enuye: *UR in lacuna.* 170 fift] first.
174 lioun] a lioun. 175 depnes: -p- *corrector over erasure.* 187 ȝe:
corrector over erasure. detraccion: det- *corrector.*

⌐þe⌐ haburions þat ȝe han vpon, ben cauteles & sleiȝtes,
Ech intrikid in oþer to snarre symple soules;
But þat þei ben of jren, obstinacie is schewid | 190
For þe which wiþ Farao in helle ȝe wil be dampned.   f. 5ʳ
  ⌐At⌐ þe ⌐sixt⌐† aungels blast, foure aungels þere were lousid,
þe whiche were redye, boþe day & nyȝte, men forto noien,
To sleen þe ⌐þridde⌐ part of men wiþ fiyr, smoke, and brymstone.
Foure angels singnefien foure general synnes,   195
Sett vp bi Sir Adam, Iakke, among ȝour maistris:
Cedeciouns, supersticions, þe glotouns, & þe proude,
To sleen þe þridde party of men wiþ þre deedly dartis
Off envie, pride, & leschry stynkynge.
For sum ben perfit, sum ben yuel, sum ben vnstable,   200
Poerte preamblis to ⌐preisen⌐ aforne Anticristis comyng:
þe perfit wole not ben hirt, þe yuel ben alredy,
But þei þat ben vnstable resseyuen þe strokes,
And þei ben clepid þe þridde part of hem þat ben dede.
  þe seuenþe angel blew his trumpe & ⌐voises⌐ in heuen†
  ⌐seide⌐   205
þat þe kyngdom of þis world shulde falle to Cristis hondis,
Betokenyng þat þouȝ Anticrist wiþ his myȝti meyne
Shulde for a short tyme bi tirantrie intrusyue
Ȝit shal God gader his flok to gider & rengne without eende.
  Iak, þus to dubby with scripture me þinkiþ grete folie,   210
For as lewid am I as þou, God wote þe soþe;
I know not an a from þe wynd mylne
Ne a b from a bole foot, I trowe ne þi silf noþir.
And ȝit, for al my lewidhed, I can wel vndirstonde,
þat þis priuy processe perteneþ to ȝour secte,   215
And we as giltles þerof as ȝe of Cristis blessyng.
It ar ȝe þat stonden bifore in Anticristis vanwarde,

---

188 þe] ȝour.   189 after snarre: inserted letter erased?   192 At
þe sixt] In þe siȝt of.   193 þe whiche: over erasure.   194 þridde]
ferþe.   199 leschry: l- from b?   201 preisen] presse: from
preise(n) corrector? In MS. this line stands after 197.   205 voises] noise.
seide] was made.   206 hondis: -d- from s.   207 Betokenyng: over
erasure.   215 perteneþ: letter erased before p-.

And in þe myddil, & in þe rerewarde, ful bigly enbatailid;
þe deuel is ȝour duke and pride beriþ þe baner,
220 Wraþþe is ȝoure gunner, envie is ȝour archer,
ȝour coueitise castiþ fer, ȝour leccherie brenniþ |
f. 5ᵛ Glotony gideriþ stickes þerto, & sleuþe myneþ† wallis,
Malice is ȝour men of armes & trecherie is ȝour aspie;
þus semiþ þat ȝe more þan we be Anticristis frendis.
225 Iak, of perfite paciens ⌐holily⌐ þou me prechist,
To kep it if 'I' will sitte on Cristis owne side.
But good Iak herdist þou euere how iudicare cam in to crede?
No more skil þou canst of paciens, Iak, so God me spede;
For þi schreude herte & he ben as afere a sundir
230 As Lucifer is from heuen & Gabriel from helle—
þe which as many man ⌐suposis⌐ shal neuere mete to gi'der'.
On old Englis it is seid vnkissid is vnknowun,
And many men speken of Robyn Hood & shotte neuere in his
     bowe.
Now Iak, to þi questions nedis me moste answer
235 Alþowȝ þei wanten sentence & god thrift boþe.
Which is þe moost perfit ordre, Iakke þou askist,
And how many ordres þer ben in erþe?
Off what ordre art þou, frere, & who made þin ordre?
Iff þow wolt haue þe hiȝest ordre seke it in heuen,
240 In þe blessid Trinite þat fourmed vs alle,
Where flowiþ þe Sunne from þe Fadir, þe Holigost from hem
     boþe,
Noon gretter in degre, no more perfite þan oþer.
But þe ordre þat þere is is in her proceding,
And if we comen lower þere finde we holy angels,
245 Stablid in iij jerarchies, diuidid in ordres nyne.
Seraphin he is þe souereynest, in charite he brenniþ,
And of al ordris in erþe y holde preesthood þe hiȝest,
þat han þe principal partis of men and kingis han þe bodies,

222 wallis] 'þe' wallis: þe *UR.*   225 holily] 'holilicch': *margin for cancelled* holy chirche *M.*   226 *after* kep: *letter erased.*   j: *margin for
cancelled* we *corrector?*   231 þe: þ- *corrector?*   suposis] suposer.

And þis† þe popes decre in comoun lawe.

But paraunter, Iak, þou menest of religious ordre—   250

Of templeres, hospitalers, | chanouns, monkes & freres?   f. 6ʳ

Iak, in þis mater, loke Seint Thomas bokes,

And þei shal þee techen & enfourme at þe fulle.

How many ordris þer ben can I not telle

But if y cowde calkyn al ⌜manniskynde⌝   255

Forto loken how many kyndes oure lord haþ yfourmed,

But euermore ⌜bi tweyne⌝† & two, Iak, þou shalt fynden ordre.

　　Off what ordre I am, & who made myn ordre,

Iakke, fast þou fraynest, & fayn woldist wite.

I am of Cristis ordre, Iak, & Crist made myn ordre—   260

Ensaumple in þe gospel in many sondry place;

For who tauȝte obedience, chastite, & pouerte,

Hopist þou not it was Crist, & fulfillid in him silf,

In which ech religion perfitli is groundid,

Reuersynge þe soorie synnes notid of þe postle—   265

Lust of fleish & lust of jȝe & pride in oure lyuynge;

On þis three Iak, bi my lewte, is groundid al ȝour colage.

Iff y breke myn ordre, I breke Goddis lawe,

And if I be punishid for þat oon, I am ponishid for þat oþer,

Bot þe contrarie of þis, Iak, þou falsly afermest.   270

　　'Iacke boy', jf ony religioun be more perfit þan techiþ Seint
　　　Iame,

Eiþer more appreued of God, fayne þou woldist witen.

Iff I seie ⌜yee⌝, þou askist where it is foundid,

And if y 'nayt' þat þou seist, þus þou procedist.

þou seist þat I contrarie Cristis owne rewlis,   275

Bidinge ȝeue to þe pore in peyne of dampnacion,

And we piken from þe pore & riche al þat we may geten.

Iak, þou shewist sikirli what scole þou hast ben inne,

Of sutiltee of arguyng me þinkiþ þi brayn ful þinne:

Go grees a sheep vndir þe taile, þat semeþ ⌜þee⌝ beter,   280

249 þis] þis is: 'is' UR.　　þe: -e clear photograph.　　decre: -c- corrector
over erasure.　　　255 manniskynde] manere kyndes.　　　257 bi tweyne]
betwene two.　　271 jacke boy: margin M.　　273 yee] þee.　　274 nayt:
margin for cancelled seie not M.　　280 þee] þe.

þan wiþ sotil sillogismes to perbrake þi witt. |

f. 6ᵛ   Iak, in Iames ⌜pistle⌝ al religioun is groundid,
For þere is maad mencion of two perfit lyues
þat actif & contemplatif comounli ben callid,
285 Fulli figurid bi Marie & Martha hir sistir,
By Peter & bi Ioon, bi Rachel & bi Lya.
þes lyues ben groundid in charite bi diuerse degrees,
By men of professiouns makyng sundri religiouns
And euident ensaumple moun techen vs þe waye.
290 For sum fleen from þe world & closen hem silf in wallis
And steken hem in stones, & litil wole þei speken,
To fleen sich occasiouns as foly wole fynden,
And þese we clepen ancres in þe comoun speche.
Also in contemplacion þere ben many oþer
295 þat drawen hem to disert & drye myche peyne,
By eerbis, rootis, & fruyte lyuen for her Goddis loue,
And þis manere of folk men callen heremytes.
þe þridde degree þere is, not forto be dispisid,
Off sich as ben gaderid in couentis to gidere,
300 Off þe which men spekiþ Dauid in his psalmis—
⌜Se⌝, he seiþ, how merie it is to dwelle to gider—
þe which for worldly combraunce kepen in cloistris,
On hert & oon soule hauyng wiþ þe apostlis,
And þis clepe we monasticale þat kendly is knowun.
305 Mo Iak, in contemplacion þer ben diuerse degrees,
And aftir þat charite growiþ in hem, þe more is her mede.
Off actif lyf y shulde þee tellen, yf þat y hadde tyme,
And shewen how men bi charite ben holden to helpe her
            breþeren—
Somm wiþ paynymes forto fiȝte, oure feiþ to defende,
310 Somm forto make puruyaunce for seke & for pore,
Somme forto preche to þe puple aftir her synne askiþ,
And somme in boþe lyues laboren full soore,

282 pistle] pistles.   286 lya: -a alteration.   291 þei: þ- corrector
over erasure, -i corrector.   301 Se] Siþ.   304 monasticale: -a- (1)
alteration.   311 aftir her synne: over erasure.

Liche vnto þe angels in Iacobis ladder. |
See now Iak þi silf, how þese boþe lyues
Opinli ben expressid in þe epistle of Iames: 315
Cleen religioun it is, he seiþ, to visite þe widewis,
þe fadirles & þe modirles—lo actif lyf expressid—
And vndefoulid, vs to kepen from al worldly werkes—
Byhold, of contemplacioun opinli he spekiþ,
So þis may be resonably þe conclusioun of my tale,   320
þat no religion more is þan techiþ Sent Iame.

    Iak, þou seist we piken from þe pore & from þe riche,
And not 3euen a3enward þou3 þat þei ben nedy.
þat almes is pykyng y fynde it in þi boke,
And I herde it neuere aforn in no maner scripture;   325
But if alwey pikers, Iak, þou wolt vs maken,
þer we piken but seely pans, þi secte pikiþ poundis.
What we 3euen to þe pore it nediþ not þee to telle,
For almesdede shul be hid & sweten in þin hondis.

    Whi bi mannes mariage 3e ben weddid to 3our abitis   330
Wele harder þan worldly men ben weddid to her wyues,
Which þei mowe leeue & lete go as longe as ⌐hem⌐ list?

    Iak, for siche manere scole 3e cacchen Cristis curse,
So freli to mayntenen Maniches errours,
To make men breke her matrimonye & leeue her wyues,   335
And whanne þe good man is oute, pleye ⌐þei⌐ god rode.
Iak, to oure abite be we not weddid
More þan eny preest is weddid to his coroun
þat is ouer growun wiþ heer & he preest neuere þe lesse,
Or ellis shulde euery barbour make newe preestes.   340
Ri3t so oure cloþis maken vs not men of religion,
But oonli oure profession byndiþ vs to þe stake,
And so apostasie mowe† maken in oure soule,
Liche men of religion abidinge in oure abitis. |
If Sathanas were transfigurid in to his forme† fairnesse,
Trowist þou he were ou3t ellis but a dampned aungel?   346

---

332 hem] him.   336 þei] hey: -y *corrector.*   343 mowe] mowe 'we':
we *UR.*   345 forme] forme'r': -r *corrector.*

And so not for þe leuynge of oure cloþis we be not punishid,
But bicause it bitokeneþ forsakyng of oure reule;
And, Iacke, no more þan þi sadil makiþ þin hors a mere,
350 No more makiþ oure abitis monkes ne freris.
    Iak, of oure presciouse cloþis fast þou carpist,
þe which ben so fyne þat noman weriþ better.
Euery man may perseyue apertli, Iakke, þat þou liest,
Were we no sendal, ne satyn, ne goldun cloþis,
355 And þese passen in presciousitee many foold ouris.
But if my cloþ be ouer presciouse, Iakke, blame þe werer,
For myn ordre haþ ordeyned al in good mesure.
    þou axist me, Iacke, of my grete hood, what þat it meeneþ,
My scapelarie, & my wide cope, & þe knottide girdil.
360 What meeneþ þi tipet, Iakke, as longe as a stremer,
þat hangiþ longe bihinde and kepiþ þee not hoot?
An hool cloiþ of scarlet may not make a gowne†
And þe cloiþ of oo man myȝte hele half a doseyne.
Why is þi gowne, Iakke, widder þan þi cote,
365 And þi cloke al aboue as round as a belle,
Siþ lasse myȝte serue to kepe þee from coold?
Iak, answere þou to þat oon, and I shal to þat oþer.
My grete coope þat is so wijd signefieþ charite
þat largeli longiþ to be sprad to sibbe & to ⌜fremde⌝,
370 Figurid in þe faire cloiþ of Salomons table,
And bi wedding garnement þat Crist hadde at his feeste.
My greet hood behynde, shapun as a sheeld,
Suffraunce in aduersitee 'sothely ⌜it⌝ scheweth' |
f. 8ʳ Herbi to reseyue repreef for oure Goddis sake,
375 Or ellis bisynesse of oure feiþ, it may wel bitokene,
Whiche þat ȝe lollardes constreyne ȝou to distroie.
þe scapelarie also, þat keueriþ þe schuldris,
It bitokeneþ boxumnesse dewe vnto oure prelatis,
And boxomly bere birþuns þat þey wole leyen vpon vs.

350 more: *twice, second cancelled.*   355 in: -n *alteration?*   356 cloþ:
letter erased after -o-.   362 *After 362 MS. adds*: þe pokes of purchace
hangen to þe erþe.   369 fremde] frende.   373 sothely hit scheweth:
margin M.   it] hit.

Off þe knottide girdil knowe I no mysterie,   380
þerfore what it meeneþ, axe Frere Menours.
　　But Iacke, amonge oure chateryng ȝit wolde I wite
Whi þat þe lollardis weren moost greye cloþis.
I trowe to shewe þe colour þat signefieþ symplenesse,
And wiþinne, seiþ Crist, ȝe ben rauenous wolues.   385
　　　Whi, seist þou, holde we more scilence in oon hous þan
　　　　anoþer,
Siþ ouer al a man is holden forto seie þe goode?
To þi lewide question Salomon þus answeriþ:
　　　Est tacens sciens tempus apti temporis, et homo sapiens
　　　tacet vsque ad tempus. Tempus tacendi, tempus loquendi.   390
　　　Et iterum. Sicut vrbs patens absque murorum ambitu, ita
　　　qui in loquendo non potest cohibere spiritum suum.
þus perfit scilens bi scripture is ⌈approued⌉.
Iakke, if þou vndirstonde no Latyn, go to þi paroche prest,
And ⌈blundir ȝe⌉ boþe wiþ Goddis grace, marren ȝe wolen ful
　　　yuele.   395
　　Whi also ete we no fleish in euery hous jliche,
But chesen þerto an hous and leeuen anoþer?
Iak, if euery hous were honest to ete fleish inne,
þan were it honest to ete in a gonge.
Whi is not þi table sett in þi cow stalle?   400
And whi etist þou not in þi shipun, as wele as in þin halle?
But al is good ynowȝ for þee where þat euere þou sittist,
Whi doiþ not þi cow make myry wedir in þi dish?
But, Iacke, in þis mater appose þou | þe monkes,   f. 8ᵛ
For þei kepen þis ser'i'monie more streiter þan freris.   405
　　More ouer þou meuest, Iak, anoþer mater,
If oure patrouns be perfit and oure reule also,
Whi renne we to Rome to be assoilid
Of þe oþ þat we han maad & be popis freris?
Iak, summe rennen to Rome but mo þer ben at hoom,   410
And dewli done her deuer aftir þat þei han chosen,

---

393 approued] appr¼roued.　　　　　　　　395 blundir ȝe] vndur ȝou.
405 serimonie: -i- (1) ?UR.

& þat þe lollardis forþinken ful soore.

ȝe wolden þat þere were as many freris as þer ben moones,

& þouȝ þere were oon lesse ȝe ȝaue neuere tale,

415 þat ȝe myȝten haue ȝour reyke & prechen what ȝou list,

& wiþ ȝour priuy pestilence enpoisoun þe peple.

Iak, þat Iudas was a shrewe, what was Crist þe worse?

& so þat summe ben exempt & rennen to ȝour ritis,

And summe bi apostasie ben Sathanas seruauntis,

420 Whi shulde oure patrouns be euer þe lasse perfit?

Ferþermore, whi make ȝe ȝou as men dede,

Siþ in begginge ȝe ben as quic as ben ony oþer,

And vnsemeli it is to see deed men begge?

Iak, me þinkiþ þou lernedist neuere of Poulis pistlis,

425 Whiche in a fewe shorte wordes answeriþ to þi sentence:

Quasi morientes et ecce viuimus. Glossa: quasi
morientes, id est, de vicio in vicium secundum
opinionem aliquorum; et ecce viuimus, in bonis
operibus in rei veritate.

430 So þouȝ we ben deed to þe world, aftir þin opynyon,

ȝit is oure soule in þe bodi, & grace in þe soule.

Whi, seist þou, suffre ȝe not ȝour children to come in to ȝour
conseil,

If it be good & able and aftir Goddis lawe?

A! Iak mafey, me merueiliþ moche of þin lewidheed;

435 Herdist þou neuere how Crist was transfigurid in þe hil,

And þer to his priuyte he chees but þree apostlis,

f. 9ʳ Forbedinge | hem to telle þat conceil ony ferþer,

And so were þere nyne fro þat conceil refusid.

Crist also took to him alle his twelue apostlis

440 And tretide of his passioun in riȝt priuy maner

And þe rude peple þat folowiden knewe no þing þerof.

Shal we, Iak, þerfore seie his conceil was not able,

Suspect & not good confourmed to Goddis lawe?

Anoþer cause resonable, me þinkiþ I can telle,

445 For counceil owith to be kept & not to be clatrid,

434 me: -e *from* y ?UR.

And children ben ay clatringe, as þou wel knowest.
Anoþer skil may be groundid of Salomons sawis:
To him, he seiþ, þat is wijs, it longiþ to kepe conceil,
And children ful seldun ben foundun wijs.
Iak, wolt þou telle þi knave as myche as þi wyf?   450
    Forþermore þou spekest of oure costly housis,
þou seist it were more almes to helpen þe nedy,
þan to make siche housynge to men þat ben deede,
To whiche longiþ but graues & mornynge housis.
Iak, is not a man beter þan a rude best?   455
3it makist þou to þi sheep a shepen, & to þi hors a stable,
And many a pore man þer is þat haþ noon hillyng,
But oonli heuen is his hous, þe best† stond keuered.
Whi houses þou not pore men as wele as þi beestis?
'Take hede' to sumwhat þat ⌜I⌝ seid biforen,   460
And þou answere to my question answer to þin owne.
    þou carpist also of oure ⌜couentis⌝ & sparist þe soþe:
þou seist we ben more ryal þan ony lordis.
Couentis haue we noon 'Iacke' but cloistrers we ben callid,
Foundid afor wiþ charite or þat he were flemyd;   465
'But' siþ entride envie and reuyd haþ oure houses,
þat vnneþes þe hillinge | hangith on þe sparres.   f. 9ᵛ
& 3it þou þinkist hem ouer good—yuel fare þou þerfore.
Iak, where saw þou euer frere houses þour3out þe rewme,
Lich in ony r'e'alte to þe toure of Londoun,   470
To Wyndesore, to Wodestoke, to Wallingforde, to Shene,
To Herforde, to Eltham, to Westmynster, to Douer?
How maist 'þou' for rebukyng lye so lowde,
To saye þat oure ⌜couentis passen⌝ þe lordes?
But so longe, by my leute, þou hast lerned to lyen,   475
þat þi tonge is lett'er'oun of lyes, þou lettist for no shame.
    We leten, þou seist, to lymytours, al þis rewme to ferme,
As þat we were welders & lordes of alle.

458 best] beste's': -es UR.   460 take hede: margin M.   I] is.   462 cou-
entis] coueitise.   464 jacke: margin corrector.   466 but: interlined and
margin for cancelled and M.   470 realte: -e- corrector.   473 þou: corrector.
474 couentis passen] coueitise passiþ.   476 letteroun: -er- corrector.

Vnsikir þing soþly it were to sette to ferme,
480 And fooles were þe fe'r'meres to taken it to tax.
I trowe þou menys þe pardonysters of Seint Thomas of Acres,
Of Antoun, or of Runcevale, þat rennen so fast aboute.
For of þe kynges rewme haue we no more astate
þan þou hast of paradis or of þe blisse of heuen,
485 For þe which, y trowe, þou maist of hasilwode singe.
  Why, seist þou, paye ȝe to no taliage to oure cristen kynge,
Siþ Crist paiede tribut to þe heþene emperour?
Iak, of no dewte ne of no dette paide Crist noo tribute,
But oonliche of mekenesse, performynge þe lawe,
490 & forto fleen occasioun of aftirward apechinge
Whan þat afor Pilat he shulde be forjugid.
But aftir þe scripture preesthode shulde not paien
To tax ne to taliage wiþ þe comun peple;
For whan þe folk of Israhel were putt vndir seruage,
495 Pharao suffride preestes in her former fredome
To be saued & susteyned of þe comoun store.
f. 10ʳ But now is þe compleynt | of Ieremye trewe,
þe prince of prouynces sugette 'is' vndir tribute.
Not for þanne þe comun lawe may wel suffren
500 þat preesthode ⌐mot⌐ paye ⌐but⌐ bi assent of prelatis,
Freli of her owne wille, no þing constreynede.
And þus prelatis & 'persouns'† aftir her state,
Ben stended to paien what þat nede askiþ,
But neiþir freres ne annuellers saue now late.
505 God woot it worchipeth not to beggen of beggers.
  Off lettris of broþirhood, also Iak þou spekist,
And wounders þat we wynnen noon of pore men & of preestis,
& ȝit ȝe desiren þat euery man shulde haue ȝour ⌐lettris⌐.
Of pore mennes preieris to be perseuers we wolden,
510 And of her lettris, & of her sele, if autentike þei weren.

---

491 whan: -n ?*corrector over erasure.*   495 fredome: *over erasure.*
498 prouynces: -s *corrector over erasure.*   is: *corrector.*   499 not for
þanne . . . 500 MS. may: *over erasure.*   500 mot] may. *after* paye: and
cancelled M.   but] *om.*   bi: -i *over erasure?*   502 persouns: *margin cor-*
rector.   aftir] *perilous aftir.*   508 lettris] *om.*

But of ȝour preestis pat*er* nost*er*s we desire*n* noo*n*,
For comu*n*liche h*er* blake bedes þei dele*n* to freris,
But þei shal cleue vnto þi chekes & Cristis curse also.

As wiʼsʼsely as we holde*n* ʻvsʼ noʻtʼ more p*er*fit þan ony oþer,
Ne no suffragies ⌐ʻsellenʼ¬ for a certey*n* bi ȝere,   515
Ne make*n* me*n* more p*er*fit þan h*er* blessid baptisme,
For praier may not satyllyn but oonliche on þe*m* alle.
And so þat gilde*n* ⌐trentel¬ þat þou spekist of,
þat now is purchasid of preestis out of freris hondis,
Delyueriþ *n*oo soule out of þe peyne of helle,   520
Ne purge*n* may of purgatory but as it is des*er*ued,
For charite is þe mesure þat demeþ þat meyne.

Also þou seist, Iak, þat we me*n* enforme*n*,
þat oure holy abite shulde helpe*n* me*n* fro helle,
And nameliche þo þat be*n* beried þeri*n*ne,   525
And Cristis cloþis dide not so, ne noo*n* of þe apostlis.
Iak, þat frere was ou*er* lewid þat lernede ⌐þee¬ þis lessou*n*,
Or on þi ficul fantasie þʻouʼ faynyst þis fable,
For Aus | tyns ne P*re*chours proponc*n* no siche pointis.   f. 10ᵛ
Wheþ*er* þe Carmes of her copes mowe mayntenen siche an
    erro*ur*,   530
Or wheþ*er* Seint Frau*n*ce hath gete*n* to his habite
þat v*er*tu be his g*r*ace, witt*er*ly ⌐I ne¬† wote,
But wel I wote þat Cristis cloith helide a wo*m*ma*n*
From þe longe fluxe of blood, as þe gospel telliþ.
But his p*re*destinacio*n* may onlich saue soulis,   535
And his p*r*iuy prescie*n*s may dampne who*m* hi*m* list.

Iak, ferþ*er*more of felony þou felly vs enpechest,
Of stelyng of childre*n* to drawe he*m* to oure sectis.
To tille folk to Godward I holde it no þeft,
But if þou calle Crist a þeef þat dide þe same,   540
Sayy*n*ge to þe riche ma*n*, go and selle þi goodis
And ȝif he*m* to þe pore, ȝif þou wole be p*er*fit,

514 wissely: -s- (1), wysly (*margin*) *corrector*.   vs: *corrector*.   not: -t *corrector*.
515 sellen] ʻselleʼ: *corrector*.   518 trentel] trentels.   527 þee] þe.
528 þou: -u *from cancelled* -at ?*corrector*.   529 proponen: -ro-, -en
corrector.   532 I ne] me ʻneʼ: ne *corrector*.   534 blood: b- *from* s.

And aftirward folowe me & be my disciple.
And in þe same gospel se what he seiþ also—
545 Who so forsaket not his fadir & his modir,
His sone and his douȝtir, his sistir and his broþir,
His lond and his tenementes, & him seluen also,
He nys not worþi to ben my folower.
And to his twelfe chosen, eftsoones he seide:
550 Behold fro þe world I haue chosen ȝou alle,
þat ȝe gon and beren fruyte & ȝour fruyte may dwellyn.
And þus to reuen þe world & spoilen him of his persouns,
It ne is no robery but Criste appreued þefte.
þou seist also ferþermore þat prestis shul not enprisoun,
555 For it nys not foundid in al Goddis lawe,
But ⌐vndirnym⌐ bi charite & so wynnen her broþir,
And ȝif he wil not be so wonnen haue him as heþene;
f. 11ʳ & þus bi þin opynyon | no man shulde be enprisound.
But, Iakke, in þi frensy þou fonnest more & more—
560 þou wenyst to make to me a diche, þou fallist þi silf þerinne.
For if þou pursue þi purpos þou assentist þi silf in tresoun,
Menusynge þe kyngis maieste, priuyng him of his power.
For if we taken þe gospel aftir þe menynge,
Neþir ⌐emperour⌐ ne kyng may honge ne drawe,
565 Heued ne enprisoun ⌐ne⌐ haunte no domes,
But al in fair manere shulen ben vndirnomen;
And who wil not amenden him ȝeue him þe brydil,
And ⌐boþe⌐ robbers & reuers, mansleeris & treytours,
And al maner mawfesours, shulden ben vnpounishid.
570 Iak, þe pope haþ a prisoun & ȝit he is a prest,
þe bishop of Cantirbury & of Londoun also,
And many oþer bishopis bi leeue of her kyng.
Art þou hardy to seien it is not Goddis lawe?
But y blame þee not gretli þouȝ þou bere hem heuy,
575 For goldsmythis of þi crafte ofte ⌐haue þei⌐ hem haunted

545 forsake] forsake'þ': -þ UR.   551 þat: *corrector over erasure.*
556 vndirnym] vndirmyn.   564 emperour] Empour.   565 ne] no.
568 boþe] be.   569 mawfesours: *from* mawfe⟨·⟩ons.   575 haue þei]
haueþ.   haunted: -d *corrector.*

And ȝit þei shulen ofter, bi þe helpe of heuen.

Also þou seist no sacrament we couetyn ne desiren,
But schrift & biryynge þat longeþ to þe peple.
Alas, Iak, for shame, whi art þou so fals,
Forto reuerse þi silf in þin owne sawes?   580
þou seidist in þi begynnynge, whan þou seidist of freres,
þei sellen seuen sacramentes with Symoundis eyris,
And now þat we coueite noon but þe sacrament of schrifte,
For beriynge is no sacrament but an almesdede.
þow jawdewyne, þou jangeler, how stande þis to gider?   585
By verre contradiccion þou concludist þi silf,
And bryngest þee to þe mete þere I wolde haue þee.
Who wolde take entent to suche wreches wordes,
þat neuere more ȝeueþ tale to be take with | a lesyng?   f. 11ᵛ

Whi, axist þou ferþermore, wil we no't' shryuen   590
Ne birien þe pore as wel as þe riche,
And do oþer dedes of almes done at her nede?
But if we schryue not þe pore whi ben perssons so wrothe,
And paroche preestes also, for schryuynge of her ⌐parishens⌐,
For euery lenten vs aȝen þei aleggen þe lawe   595
Off omnis vtriusque sexus, wiþ þe fauourable glooses.
But Iak do þi won & lette not to lyene,
I haue as leef þi leesing as þi soth saw,
For who is oonis suspect, he is half honged.

þou seist þat we prechen fallace & fables   600
& not Goddis gospel to good vndirstondinge,
& we ben more holdun þerto þan to alle oþer reulis,
For we wynnen more þerwith þan Crist & his apostlis.
What we ben holdun ⌐to⌐ I wil not forsake,
For moche of oure lyuynge is of þe gospel;   605
So dide Poul & oþer disciplis,
And lyuede of colectis made generali bi chirchis
For sustinance of prechours & also of þe pore.
And if þou leue not me, loke Poulis pistlis,
And þe glose þerwith & þere þou shalt fynde it.   610

590 not: -t ?UR.   594 parishens] paishens.   604 to] om.

Quis, inquit, militat suis stipendijs vnquam?
Et iterum, Dominus ordinauit hijs qui
euangelium annunciant, de euangelio viuere.
And so to his prechours Crist also þus seide:
615   *In quamcumque domum intraueritis, manete*
in eadem edentes et bibentes &c.
Dignus est enim operarius mercede sua.
Et ad Romanos: Probauerunt Macedones
et Achaya colleccionem facere in pauperes
620   *sanctorum qui sunt in Iherusalem.*
Aȝens 'þat' þat 'þou' saist, þat we prechen but fallace & fables
& leue þe gospel þat moste vs al saue,
Loke þat euery 'werke' is knowen pleinli bi his eende;
& so þe peple haþ þe pathes of feiþ & of bileue,
625   & God 'woote' frere's' prechinge hath wrouȝt to þis ende.
But ȝe han cast cursidly Cristendome to distroye
f. 12ʳ & of Cristis gospel make Macho | metis lawe,
Aȝens whom with opin mouth oþer while we romee,
And sumtyme brynge ȝou til a bay, if God wil it graunte.
630   For þis cause ȝe calle vs bastard branchis,
Pursuyng preestes to prisoun & to fire also.
But, Iak, þei ben bastard braunches þat launchen from oure
bileue,
& wriþyn wrongli away from Holy Chirche techinge.
Siche beren yuel fruyte & soure to atasten,
635   Worþi to noon oþer good but in þe fire to brenne.
And so forto pursue an heretike to fire or to prisoun,
I holde it more holsum þan to halewe a chirche,
In prisonynge of þe poysen þat morþerith many soulis,
Aftir Cristis doctrine in þe holy gospel:
640   *Omnis, inquit, arbor quae non fert fructum*
bonum excidetur et in ignem mittetur. Et iterum.

621 þat (1): *corrector.*   þou: *corrector.*   623 werke: *margin corrector.*
624 haþ: -a- *alteration,* -þ *corrector over erasure.*   625 *after* god: -dis
cancelled.   woote: *margin M.*   freres: -s *UR.*   626 distroye: u
cancelled after -o- *corrector.*   628 romee: -e *over partial erasure.*
633 wriþyn: -þ- *alteration.*   wrongli: -li *UR.*

Qui non manserit in me, mittetur foras sicut palmes,
et arescet: et colligent, et in ignem mittetur.

Disseuerynge ȝou from þe tree þat is Crist him silfe.

But how shulden freres pursue heresie,   645
And many of hem wite not what heresie meneþ?
Iak, I am not lettered but I am Frere Dawe,
& can telle wel a fyn what heresie amountith.
Heresie þat is Grw is diuisioun on Latyn,
þe whiche in oure langage meneþ sunderyng & partyng.   650
He þanne þat sundriþ him from Crist & his chirche
And frely forgiþ sentences contrarious to oure feiþ,
Siche manere of forgers heretikes we callen,
& also her felowis taken þe same name;
& her sory sentences ben clepid heresies,   655
But ⌐namely⌐ whan þei ben holdun of obstinat hertis,
& I shal þis mater more largely declare.

Sixe maner of heretikes ben foundun in þe lawe,
For he is callid an heretike þat rasiþ oure bileue.
& he is callid an heretike þat heresies sowith—   660
As Arrians, Wyclyfan`e´s, Sabellyanes, & oþer.
And þe corruptours of scripturis | heretikes ben holdun,   f. 12ᵛ
þat oþer wise vndirstondin þan þe Holigoost techiþ.
Also we clepen hem heretikes þat sacramentis sellyn,
Or ben from hem diuidid bi cursynge of þe chirche.   665
He is also an heretike þat doutiþ our bileue,
& wiþ a litil euydence goith out of þe waye.
And also an heretike him shulde we holde,
þat distrieþ priuyleges grauntid of þe pope.
þis sixe maners put ⌐Hostiensis⌐ in his Summe,   670
And if þis sentence be soth, y can noon oþer seien,
But þou & þi secte ben heretikes alle.

Iak, þou spekist forþermore of messis & of ⌐preieres⌐
And askist what we sellen ⌐whan⌐ `we´ seyen oure messe,

656 namely] nam⟨·⟩aly?: *after correction.*   whan: -n *over erasure.*   obstinat:
o- *alteration.*   659 rasiþ: -s- *corrector over two-letter erasure.*
661 wyclyfanes: -e- *corrector.*   670 Hostiensis] hostienser.   673
preieres] preires.   674 whan] wen: -n *M.*   we: *margin M.*

675 Wheþer þe sacrament, our preieres, or our traueile,
And if ony o`f' þis we done, þou arguest a greet errour.
Iak, vnto þis questioun onwyse may be ⌐answerid⌐,
Aftir þat Seint Austyn spekiþ of þe apostlis:
þe apostlis, a ⌐seiþ⌐, reseyued frely her breed,
680 Of hem þat freely token her techinge.
& so Iak, frely graunte we our masse to hem
þat freely ȝeuen vs her almesse,
& synnen no wyse bi noon oþer vice,
To selle no sacramentis ne spiritual preier.
685 And þus among freres gete þei no logginge
But bete hem to gretter men & geten her herbegag`e'
Of patronis of chirchis or priuyly with preestes,
⌐Which⌐ to fatte benefices wolde be promotid.
Iak,† suppose þat my labour y selle,
690 What wil þou seie þerto, do y ony symonye?
How þan shal þo persons seye þat setten her chirches to ferme—
þat ben more spiritual þan bodili traueile—
And þese paroche preestes þat ministren þe sacramentis
For a certen sawd bi ȝeer of ten mark or of twelfe,
f. 13ʳ And al þese annuellers þat syngen for a | tyme,
696 Takyng for her traueil as þei may acorde?
But þei can answere for hem silf & we shal for vs.
        Anoþer mater þer is meued, þat touchiþ begging þou seist,
þat we falsly Crist him silf disclaundren, to seie þat he beggid,
700 Siþ he was lord of al, & al in his demeyns.
But for þis mater Iacke, þou most vndirstonde
þat Crist in his godhede is lord of alle þingis,
As testimonie of scripture preueþ in many places.
As touching his manheed, he was nedi & pore,
705 For of his nede spake Dauid in his psalmes:
    Ego, inquit, mendicus sum et pauper;
    et Dominus sollicitus est mei.

676 of þis: *from* oþis *?UR.*   677 answerid] answeriþ.   679 seiþ]
seye.   686 herbegage: -e *margin corrector.*   688 Which] wich: -ch
corrector over erasure.   to: t- *corrector over erasure.*   689 suppose]
I suppose.

And aftir Austin & Ierom þis word of Crist was seid,
So þanne þese twey stonden wel to gidere:
þat Crist aftir oo kynde was lord of alle,　　　　　　　　710
And aftir þat oþer nedide to begge.
For if Crist seie soþ, him silf ne hadde noon harborow
To resten in his owne heed, & steken out þe stormes:
　　Vulpes, inquit, &c., vbi caput suum reclinet.
And if we shulen ȝeue credence to doctours wordes,　　715
Heere what seiþ Seint Ierom & Seint Bernard also:
　　Caue, inquit Ieronimus, ne mendicante Deo
　　tuo alienas diuicias augeas. Et Bernardus.
　　Vt te, Domine, per omnia nostre paupertati
　　conformares, quasi vnus in turba pauperum　　　720
　　stipem per hostia mendicabas.
Wherfore þou feynest fonnedli þat oure lord we sclaundre
Or ellis oure holy doctours diden not her deuer.
Iak, haue no merueyle þat y speke Latyn,
For oones I was a manciple at Mertoun Halle,　　　725
& þere y lernede Latyn bi roote of clerkes.
　　Of clamo'ur'us also begging þou chaterist & crijst,
And seist it is vttirli forbodun in Goddis lawe.
Iak, þe blynde begger sat bi þe weye
& lowde criede vpon Crist, as þe gospel telliþ, |　　730
But him was ȝouun iȝe siȝt, for al his grete noise.　　f. 13ᵛ
& also þe pore man at þe ⌈specious⌉ ȝate
Praiede to þe apostlis to parten of her almes,
& þer ⌈of beggerie⌉ vnreproued, of crokidnesse he was heelid.
I forȝete not þe laȝar þat beggide of þe riche,　　　735
And criede lowde at his ȝate to cachen his almes.
Where redist þou þat he was repreued of his begging?
I rede wel he was ful soone in Abrahams bosum.
　　þou makist also more ado for writing in oure tablis
Of sich mennes names þat ȝeuen vs her almes,　　　740
Wenynge þat God were a fool not knowinge mennes dedes

727 clamourus: -ur- *UR.*　　732 man: -a- *from* e.　　specious] specionus.
734 of beggerie] 'þe' begger: þe *UR for cancelled* of.

But if he were mengid bi weie of ȝour ⌐writyng⌐.
Iak, writyng was ordeyned for slipernes of mynde,
Not of God but of vs men, hirt in oure nature,
745 And bi bodili buystousnesse fallen to forȝetynge.
Now special preier, as clerkes seien, moste helpe'þ'† soulis,
& þat may not be done wiþouten special mynde.
þanne for oure forȝetfulnesse it nediþ vs to noten,
& þis is cause whi we writun in oure tablis.
750 And Esdras wroot a newe book to haue þe lawe in mynde;
To Seint Ioon in þe apocalips it was bodun also
þat priuy reuelacion to writun in his book,
For vnstabilnesse of mynde, seiþ þe comoun glose.
Whi also, þou axist, make ȝe so many maistris
755 Aȝens Cristis bidding in þe holi gospel?
Forsoþe, Iak, among oþer, þis is a lewid question,
Taking heed to þin astaate þou art but a knave,
& ȝit þou lokist þat þi knave shulde calle þee maistir.
Leue Iacke Iawdewyn, how kepist þou þe gospel?
f. 14ʳ Neuer þe les to | þi question answeriþ þe comoun glose:
761 þat neiþir þe acte of teching, neiþir þe acte of maistir
Ben forbodun of Crist, but oonli ambicion
And þe nyce appetite of worldly worship.
þou askist also ferþermore whos ben alle oure jewels,
765 & we seyen we han riȝt nouȝt in propre ne in comoun,
But gederen þe goodes of þe rewme to make þe pope riche.
Iak, þe ⌐two⌐ & twentiþe pope Ioon wroot aȝens þis mater,
& Frere Menours aȝens him, as her actis shewen;
Examyne her actis & loke who haþ þe beter.
770 I knowe noon oþer ordre þis perfitnesse approueþ.
þou grucchist also þat we gon two of vs to gider,
For of þe perfit apostlis wenten but oone aloone.
þou seist þat we pretenden þe perfeccioun of apostlis,
Parfay, Iak, in scripture þou failist here ful foule.

742 writyng] wrtyng.   743 slipernes: s- corrector.   744 nature: -e
corrector.   746 helpeþ] helpe'þ' þe: helpeþ, -þ UR.   751 was: twice,
second cancelled.   760 after answeriþ: word obliterated.   767 two] foure.

Herdes þou neuere þe processe of þe actis of þe apostlis,   775
In what maner þe Holigoost chees Bernabe & Poule
To gone boþe to gidere & Cristis seed to sowun.
And aftirward whan Bernabas from Poul was departid,
Anoþer felowe Tymothe toke Poul to his feere.
And ȝit þei weren perfit bi fastinge & bi preieris,   780
And resseyued hadde þe Holigoost bi þe apostlis hondis.
& þus we gon two to gider folwinge her stappis,
But more for þe myst'e'rie includid in þe noumbre,
Forto ⌐do⌐ workes of charite fulfilling þe lawe:
& two tablis of Moises þere þe lawe was writun,   785
And two cherubyns in þe temple, & two in þe tabernacle;
It was not good to Adam forto be aloone,
And Crist seiþ woo to sool in auenture þat he falle.

   Also for fraternite ful harde þou vs holdist,
To graunt part | of merit & also of messis   f. 14ᵛ
Bicause þat we witen not wheþer þat we ben in grace or in synne, 791
And happili for we praien for suche þat ben dampned in helle.
Iak, if þis cause were good, al preier were reproued,
And þanne were set at nouȝt boþe messe & matynes,
& holy bedis & orisons seid in Holi Chirche.   795
þanne shulde we leue Cristis bede, þe holy pater noster,
þanne was þe memento put ⌐falsly⌐ in þe masse,
And Hooli Chirche voidli or madli biddiþ preye,
And alle siche ȝonge impossibilitees folowen þerof.
For who is þat þat knowiþ him silf worþi forto preien,   800
But God bi reuelacion speciali wolde it shewe?
For noman, seiþ þe scripture, woot wheþer he is worþi loue,
Or ellis maugree but God it oonli knowiþ.
And who can telle, ferþermore, whiche shulde be dampned,
Siþ Goddis priuy domes man mai not comprehende?   805
And so shal noman preie for oþer, ne noman for him silf.
Iak, se now þin errour & sumtyme se'sse' for shame,

781 after resseyued: þe'i' from þe corrector, cancelled.   783 mysterie:
-y- (over two-letter erasure) -e- UR.   784 do] bi.   797 falsly] fassy.
807 sesse: -sse UR.

For þou jangelist as a jay & woost not what þou meenest.
More ouer þou mouest multipliyng of so many freris,
810 Whiche encresen combrouseli aȝens Goddis wille,
Siþ preestis wiþ oþer religious myȝte serue þe peple;
For twelue apostlis & fewe moo serueden al þe world,
And mo fyngris on myn hond þan foure & þe þombe
Amenusiþ my worching more þan it acresiþ.
815 And so þou seist þat freris letten Cristis growinge in to heuen.
Iacke, þou weenest þou wynne lond but þou concludist þi silf:
þou seist þat God alle þingis haþ maad in mesure, weiȝte, &
noumbre,
& þat euery frere is sum þing þou maist not denye; |
f. 15ʳ & þou seist freris ben maad aȝens Goddis wille,
820 þan haþ God maad sum þing þat he wolde not make,
And so his souereyne goodnesse is contrarious to him silfe.
Lo! Iakke Iospinel, what folowiþ of þi sawis.
Iakke, if ⌜þan⌝ a fewe moo myȝte seruen al þe world,
þanne myȝte a fewe preestes seruen a litil rewme—
825 Whi renne þanne þese ȝonge clerkes so faste to þe ordres
To encresen preestes aboue many hundridis,
And if freris ben combrouse, preestis ben wel more?
Or ellis telle a beter skil þanne þou hast begunne,
Whi þe toon is chargeaunt more þan þe toþer.
830 Also þe ensaumple of þin hond is no þing to purpos,
For kynde haþ determyned þe noumbre of þi fyngris,
& if it passe noumbre it is clepid monstruosite.
But God & Holi Chirche determyned noo noumbre
Of preestis ne of freris to helpen mannis soule,
835 For þe mo good þer ben þe better is Cristis spouse,
And þouȝ fewer myȝten done þat ⌜þat man⌝ nediþ,
Ȝit many hondis to gider maken liȝt werk.
Anoþer mater þou mouest, Iak, moost to be chargid,
Of þe solempne sacrament of Cristis owne bodye,
840 Conteyned in figure of brede, sacrifise for synne.

þou drawist a þorn out of þin hele & puttist it in oure,
þou berist vs on honde þat we seien þer is not Cristis bodye,
But roundnesse & whitenesse, and accident wiþouten suget.
Iak, we seie wiþ Holy Chirche þat þer is Cristis bodi
& not material breed with Wiclyf ȝour maistir,   845
þe whiche put þer but as a signe & not verre Cristis bodi,
Aftir a manere spekyng þat Holy Chirche vsiþ— |
As we clepen Crist a stoon, a lomb, & a lioun,   f. 15ᵛ
& noon of þese is Crist but oonli in figure.
þis heresie holde not we but ȝe his false folowers,   850
Priuyly as ȝe doren & opinli ȝe wolden
Ne were þe sharp ponishinge of ȝour former fadirs.
And now I wil þee telle þe freris confiteor
⌐Touching⌐ to þis sacrament how þat þei bileuen.
þei seie breed is turned in to fleish, & wyne in to blood,   855
þourȝ þe myȝt of oure God & vertue of his wordis:
þe fleish is mete, þe blood is drynke, & Crist dwelliþ,
No þing rasyd, no þing diuidid, but oonli broken in signe,
& as moche is in oo partie as is al þe hole.
þer leeueþ not of þe breed but oonli þe licnesse,   860
Which þat abidiþ þerinne noon substeyned substans;
It is deþ to yuel, lyf to good, encresing of oure grace.
It wole not be confect but oonli of a preest
þat lawfulli is ordeyned bi Holy Chirche keies.
And so carpenters ne sowters, card makers ne powchers,   865
Drapers ne cutellers, gi`r´delers, coferers, ne coruysers,
Ne no manere of artificeris þis sacrament mowe treten
But þe priuite of preesthode wer prickid in her soulis.
& ȝit ȝour sect susteynes wommen to seie massis,
Shewyng to trete a sacrament as preestes þat þei were,   870
Reuersynge holy doctours & decree of Holy Chirche.
    Allas! ȝour brymme blastis awake þe wilde ⌐wawis⌐,
& scailen sely Petership & putt it in hiȝe perile.

841 hele: -e- corrector.   842 not: -t from o corrector.   854 Touch-
ing] toucheng: -g UR. before toucheng: as cancelled.   858 rasyd: -sy-
?UR over three-letter erasure.   865 card makers: minim partially erased
after -d.   872 wawis] wawlis: -w- from l corrector?

Ne were God þe giour & kept þe stern,
875 Wiþ þe sterne stormes þat reufulli ȝe reisen,
Al shulde wende to wrak in to þe waast watris.
þe releef of Cristis feeste ȝe renden & ⌜rapyn⌝
f. 16ʳ þat his | almners þe postlis gaderid to gidere,
& ⌜dele⌝ it to dogges & ravenouse beestes,
880 & þe presciouse perlis ȝe strowun to hogges—
þe sutil metis of scripturis to cherlis stomakes
& maken hem als comoun as þe cart weye,
Aȝens Poulis sentence & Poulis owne doctrine:
Non, inquit Paulus, potui vobis scribere
885 *quasi spiritualibus, sed quasi carnalibus &c.*
Se also what Crist seiþ in þe holy gospel:
Multa habui vobis dicere: sed non &c.
Also 'in' many oþer place þus spekiþ he to his perfit disciplis:
Vobis datum est noscere misterium, regni Dei.
890 *Ceteris autem in parabolam &c.*
þan þe lewide & þe lered auȝt not yliche
þe ⌜scripture is⌝† scatrid in his priuy pointes.
Iak, þou seist at þe last þat charite is chacid
To vengyn oure defautis & mende vs of oure mysse,
895 Leuynge oure rotyn ritis, folowinge Goddis lawe.
Iak, oure ritis ben nouȝt rotyn, her rootis ben al freishe,
Plantid in þe gospel, as I seide biforen.
But good Iak, ȝour grace, where be ȝe foundid?
Not in Goddis gospel but in Sathanas pistile,
900 Wher of sorowe & of ⌜sorcerie⌝ noon is to seken,
But al maner of dolosite to ȝou is enditid,
As in þi lewid daliaunce apertli þou hast preued.
But moche mawgre mote þou haue þus to frayn a frere,
þat slily wolde haue slent aweye & noman haue greued.
905 But for þi grete labour þi gardoun þou shalt gete,

877 rapyn] ratyn. 878 almners: avmoners *margin corrector.* 879 dele]
delith. 880 ȝe: *corrector over three-letter erasure.* 888 in:
corrector. place þ-: *over erasure.* 892 scripture is] scripturis ben.
898 grace: *UR in lacuna.* 900 sorcerie] snowcrie. 904 slily: -i-
corrector over erasure.

þou shalt haue þe popis curse & al Holi Chirchis.
And if þou sett þis at nouȝt, God mowe sende þee more,
þe curse þat he haþ ȝouun to Caym, & Choreis sone also;
þou shalt also haue þe curse þat Crist ȝaf to Phariseis,
Figurid in þe ⌜figge⌝ tree þat neuere | bare fruyte aftir.   f. 16ᵛ
þou shalt haue þe weleaway of Gelboþ hilles,   911
þe sorowe of Sodome & al sinful citeis.
Take for þi faire speche þe preier of *deus laudem*,
þe greable gardoun for al opin sclaundris.
þou shalt haue þe malisoun of Moab & Ariel,   915
þe benysoun of Bethsaida shal make þy beddis heed.
&, Iakke, for þou apprisist not þe curse of Seint Franceis,
But scornyst þe malisoun of þe foure ordris,
Take þe malisoun þat God ȝaf to brekers of his lawe,
In þe book of Deutronomye, þe seuen & twenty chapitre.   920
But euere beware of Cristis curse & of cattis tailis,
þe which if þou haue grace to cacchen, neuere shal þou thryue.

   Now fare forþe to þi fourmures, & Iak, þou hem telle
þe mater of oure talkynge & loke how hem likiþ;
And if hem þinke not þi sawes sufficientli assoilid,   925
Lat hem senden aȝen, it shal be amendid:
And sai hem þat it nediþ not to sharpen oure clerkes,
For Frere Dawe is scharpe ynowȝ for al sich enditinge.
Fare wele Iak Iawdewyne, I þee God bitake,
& nomore of freris I þee rede to preche.   930
To lower state þan þei ben þou maist hem not dryue,
& if þei euere come to hiȝer, þe wers shal þou thryue.

   Explicit dictamen Fratris Daw Topias,
   quem in fine appellat Iohannem Walsingham,
   contra questiones Iohannis Vplond.

910 figge] figre.   917 apprisist: -ist *over erasure?*   926 senden:
-e- (1) *doubtful.*

UPLAND'S REJOINDER

An answere to þis tretis þat a frere haþ forgid—
He calliþ hy⟨m⟩self Daw Topias—aȝens me Iak Vplonde.
He groundiþ hym vpon seuen thynges, as his ordre askiþ:
Lesynges with losengery, cursynges & false glose,
5 Chidyng with blasfem`i´e, on chyteryng as chowȝes.
þow saist þi name is Dawe, it may riȝt wel be so,
For þou hast condiciones of a tame chowȝe:
He chiteriþ & he bribiþ alle þat he may gete,
þis he doþ in dede assay of hem þat know⟨iþ⟩.
10   Dawe, þou blabe`re´st blasfemies & reson hast þou non,
þou leggist oft Goddis lawe bot to a false entent—
Ȝee, falselier þan þe fende whan he saide to Crist
    Quia angelis suis mandauit de te.
    Daw, þou fablest of foxes & appliest hem to a puple
15 Of whom neþer þou knowyst kunnyng, ne her conuersacion,
Bot iche man þat witte haþ, & happe of discrecion,
May knowe þee & þin ordre, as Crist saiþ, bi þe werkes.
Take propirte of twey foxe⟨s⟩ & werkes of twye freres,
And þan þou fyndest hem in eche acorde, bot freres ben þe
    werse.
20 If þou saist þis is not so, bot groundid with out skil,
Loke how Sampson bonde þe foxes two & two to gedir,
Til þat þai destried þe corne alle about hem,
& þis was, as a doctour saiþ, þe figur of freres. |
Dawe, þou saist proudely I lie, for I telle þe trouþe;
25 For þat `⟨ȝe⟩´ ben not lege, men knowlechen wise,
For whan ȝe ben trespassoures, in theft or oþer vices,
Ȝour priour may at `his´ wille fette ȝou home to hym,
With out kynges commission, bot gret aȝen reson.
For oft ȝe leden a waye mennes wifes & ben sette in stokkes,

2 me: *very faint.*   10 blaberest: -ab- *over erasure.*   18 werkes:
over erasure.   22 destried: de- *clear photograph.*

Bot ʒour captaynes chalengen ʒow & asken not leue of kynges. 30
    Me merueliþ of þi lewdnes Dawe—or of wilful lesynges—
For Poule laborid wiþ his hondes, & oþer postilles also—
ʒee, oure gentil Iesu, as it is opunly knowe.
And þes were þe best prestes þat euer rose on grounde,
And þe best messes song, not lettyng hem her labour,   35
Bot suche bolde beggyng 'hatid þai' in worde & werke. |
    Dawe, þou spekist proudely apechyng our prestes,   f. 3ʳ
Bot of oon thyng am I certen, þai ben lasse euel þan ʒe.
For alle if þai synne oft, as it is wel knowen,
ʒit þe grounde þat þai haue is playnly Cristis religion,   40
And þowʒ þai straye oft þerfro ʒit mowe þai com to grace.
Bot ʒe han left þat grounde & ʒour patron boþe,
For as þe prophetes of Achab wer multiplied in many
And by oon holy prophet were þai alle destried,
So þe chirche is cropun now to multitude of cursid men,   45
Whiche of sadde bileue most nede be destried.
Bot I prayse noþer prest`es' ne þee for ʒour assent in symonye. |
    Daw, I haue askid questiones of þee '⟨&⟩' of þi freres,   f. 3ᵛ
Bot þat I lied oones on ʒ⟨ou⟩, knowe I me not gilty;
For Goddis lawe forbediþ þis in many place I wene,   50
And þowʒ I be Iak Vplonde ʒit drede 'I' Goddis lawe.
Bot I suppose þi secte tristiþ so meche in her habites,
þat þai kun lye of custom, as Peter propheciþ of hem:
    Fuerunt pseudoprophete in populo, magistri
    mendaces &c.   55
Bot to lie þus playnly & opunly on men,
ʒe count it no⟨t⟩ synne as ʒour wordes shewen.
ʒour freres ben taken alle day wiþ wymmen & wifes,
Bot of ʒour priuey sodomye ⌜speke⌝ I not '⟨here⟩';
Bot lat see Dawe if þou or any lyer of þin ordre   60
Can preue þis on oon of hem þat clepist my secte,
And sicurly shalt þou haue of me an hundriþ pounde.

---

36 *originally* in worde & werke þai hatid.   49 *after* þat: it *cancelled.*
50 lawe: -a- *partially obscured.*   *after* many: *inserted letter erased.*   place:
-ce *alteration.*   59 speke] spake.   here: *corrector?*

Daw, þou leggist Salomon for ȝour hie houses,
Bot 'olde' holy doctoures ben aȝen þee here,
65 And specialy Ierom, þat saiþ *in* þe lawe:
Who wil allege þe te*m*ple for glorie of our chirche,
Forsake he to be c*r*iste*n* & be he newe a Iewe.
  12ᵃ q̄ 2ᵃ Gloria episcopi.
For siþ þe pore Lorde, he saiþ, halowed his pore chirche,
70 Take 'we' C*r*istis crosse, he saiþ, & counte we delices claye.
 Daw, blaberere & blynde leder, þowȝ þou bigile symple hertes,
Wi*th* þi gildyn glose & wi*th* þi costly houses,
þou bigilest not Iak *with* ȝo*ur* theuishe logges.
  Vnde in euangelio, vos autem fecistis eam
75   *speluncam latronum.*|

_{f. 4ʳ} Topias, þou writist me to be a lewed man,
Bot lewed men p*r*echen not, as þou ca*n*st saye bot if þe list lye;
Bot I wot þou saist þ*us* by v*er*tuouse p*r*estes,
Bot þai ben ful bisie to edifie þe chirche
80 þat 'þe' m*u*ltitude of ȝou han allemost destried.
 For þe gospel saiþ,
  Surgent multi pseudoprophete.
Bot of he*m* ben fewe & gretly dispiside,
And of ȝou ful many, & eu*er* ⌈þe⌉ mo þe werse.
85 Me m*er*ueliþ, Daw, þou darst þ*us* lie on suche a gret clerke,
& *in* hys tyme knowen wel a v*er*tuouse man,
Of riche & pore þ*at* hy*m* þo knewe.
 Bot þou as blynde Bayarde berkest at þe mone,
As an olde mylne dog when he bygynniþ to dote;
90 Bot wel I wot þi baffyng, lye þou neu*er* so lowde,
May not menuse þis seint, þat lyued & tauȝt so truly.
  Quia dignus est operarius mercede sua. |

_{f. 4ᵛ} I drede me, Dawe, þe sentence of whiche þe p*r*ophet spekiþ,
Shal falle heuy on þin hede, & many of þi breþ*er*:
95 *Ve vobis qui dicitis bonum malum, et malum bonum.*

69 siþ: *over erasure.* *originally* saiþ he. halowed his pore: *over erasure.*
77 þe: -e *corrector?* *after* list: to *cancelled.* 78 Bot I wot þou:
over erasure. 84 þe] þo. 93 *after* whiche: *caret, no insertion.*
prophet: *over erasure.*

For alle trwe sentence þat we taken here,
þou turnest in to falsenes, þat woo shal þe bitide.
For to our secte þat is Cristis we drawen bot fewe puple,
For þou & oþer pseudo han marrid hem in þe way,
þat bot if God of his grace sende his honde of help,   100
þe chirche þat shuld folowe Crist is lykly to synke.
> Qui mihi ministrat, me sequatur. Attendite a
> fermento Phariseorum, quod est ypocrisis. |
> Homo apostata, vir inutilis, graditur ore peruerso.   f. 5ʳ
Dawe, þou hast liȝt conscience þus fynaly to deme,   105
For here þou damnest men to helle with out any condicion.
Whe haue leue of scripture to deme after mennes werkes,
Bot for to deme as þou dost, is to robbe God of his power;
For þe apostil saiþ,
> Noli ante tempus judicare, quoad usque veniat   110
> Dominus.
Litil wondir þowȝ lordis mysse tyme þat han suche confusoures.
> Quia si cecus cecum ducat, ambo in foueam cadunt.
þou saist þou kno⟨'w'i⟩st no lettre here, as if þou wer noo
   clerke;
To take a clerke as it shuld be, after his vndirstondyng,   115
þan sayst þou here more trwly þan in any oþer place.
Clerk is als meche 'to' mene as of þe sort of God,
And so þou preuist þi self non suche if þou loke riȝt,
Bot a liere apostata with alle his oþer ⟨poin⟩tes. |
   Daw dirt, þou claterist meche of ordires of aungeles in heuen, f. 5ᵛ
Bot lykkyn not þes to þin ordre, ne þin ordre to hem;   121
For þai ben ordenid of God þere with outen synne,
And þin is ordened of man, with many rotun rites.
And so as þe prestes of Bel stale vndir þe awter,
To bigile þe kyng to thefly cache here lyflode,   125
So ȝe forge ȝour falshed, vndir ydil ypocrisie,
To bigile þe puple, boþe pore & riche,
'&' as þe prestes fayned þat Bel ete þe kynges sacrifise,
So ȝour wikk⟨i⟩d wynnyng, ȝe saye, wirchipiþ God. |

123 þin: *twice, second cancelled.*   125 thefly: th- *over erasure.*

f. 6ʳ   ȝit Daw, in þis mater þou broylist vp many lesynges,
131   For grounde of þin ordre 'not' groundid in þe gospel;
        For see þes thre vertues, whiche þou here rehersist,
        Faylen in þin ordre welny in euery persone.
        For in obedience, & chastite, & pouerte also,
135   ȝe folowen more Anticrist þan Iesu Crist our lorde;
        ȝe ben more obedient to ȝour owne reules
        þan to þe reules of Crist groundid in lawe.
        And as to chastite of body, ȝe breken it ful oft;
        Bot chastite of soule, forsakyng Crist our spouse,
140   For ȝe ben apostatas gon bak fro Holichirche.
            Initium omnis peccati apostatare a Deo.
        As to verrei pouerte, who þat wil riȝt loke,
        ȝe ben þe most couetouse of alle men in erþe;
        For with symonye, & begrye, & sellyng of shrift,
145   ȝe pillen boþe gret & smal & priue hem of bileue.
            Auaricia, quod est ydolorum seruitus. |
f. 6ᵛ   Dawe, þou ratelist many thynges, bot grounde hast þou non,
        For where groundist þou in Goddis lawe to close men in stones
        Bot if it were wode men or giloures of þe puple,
150   Siþ alle þat is not groundid smacchiþ grete synne,
        Bot if ȝe taken, as ȝe vsen, arseworde þis gospel:
            Non potest ciuitas abscondi super montem posita.
        Or ellis,
            Neque accendunt lucernam et ponunt eam
155   *sub modio.*
        Or wher fyndist þou Dawkyn, þat men shulden kille her breþer,
        Siþ Crist our aller duke brouȝt vs verrei pees,
        Bot if þou be of 'þe' ranes þat ran fro Anticristis nose,
            Pacem relinquo vobis, pacem meam do vobis. |
f. 7ʳ   Touchyng þis pagyn Dawe, þi lesynges ben ful rif,
161   For her þou spekist of twey lyues & ȝe don noþer wel:
        For Martha groundid hir labour fully in Goddis lawe,
        So may not ȝe ȝour beggyng, ne ȝour castelles nouþer.
        Bot of contemplacion ȝe vsen not bot as foxes,

        131 not: *for cancelled* as.   138 *after* to: þe *cancelled*.

So in þis ȝe leuen Crist, Martha & Marie boþ.   165
    As touchyng ȝiftes to pore men, ȝe pike þat þai shulde haue,
Boþe of godes & faiþe of soule, I Iak can see non oþer.
    Panis egentium vita pauperis est; qui defraudat
    eum homo sanguinis est.
    We can not make mariage, Dawe, ne pursue no diuorse,   170
We wynne not meche money with þes, as þi secte doþ ful oft.
    Quod Deus coniunxit, homo non separet. |
    I praise not, Dawe, þe stremerse þat þou herof spekest,   f. 7ᵛ
Bot of suche wide cloþing, tateris & tagges,
It hirtiþ myn hert heuyly, I wil þat þou it wite.   175
Bot ȝour ypocrites habit, to whiche ȝe ben harde weddid,
Doþ more harme þan þes, bi þes two skilles:
Oon for þe coloure þat ⌈signifieþ⌉ sadnes,
Whan ȝe ben most vnstedfast of any folk in erþe;
An oþer for ȝour disformed shap þat signifieþ ȝour holine⟨s⟩,   180
So if it be soþ þat ȝe þerof saye,
It wold with litil help make an ape a seint.
þe tipet is a comyn reule if it be not superflue,
& so it doþ gode to bynde a manne⟨s⟩ hede;
Bot ȝour misse shapen shelde, bihynde at ȝour shulderes,   185
Blowiþ ȝour ypocrisie & blyndiþ many foles.
    Genimina viperarum, quis demonstrauit vobis
    fugere a ventura ira? |
    ⟨Ȝ⟩it, Dawe, me thynkiþ þou vsist þi customale condicion,   f. 8ʳ
þou hast so lerned to lye, þou ⟨c⟩anst not leue werk.   190
Bot ȝit I am gladde þou groundist þe on þe gospel.
    Diabolus est mendax, et pater eius.
þe secte þat þou seggist of, I wot is Iesu Cristis,
Tellen litil by cloþing, bot now oon now oþer.
þowȝ þou accuse þe menours haue I not 'to' do,   195
Bot wel I wot ȝe ben alle drawen in oo maner draggee.
    Lewde Dawe, whi laist þou forþe so many blunt resones,
For Salomon spekiþ not of silence propirde to an house,

---

178 signifieþ] siginfieþ.   191 gospel: -l *from* s?   198 ffor salomon
speki-: *over erasure.*

Bot of silence in iche place, in tyme & in reson.

200 Bot þe cursid ypocrisie of etyng of ȝour fleshe,

Shuld iche man despise for ȝour rotun rewle;

And so þes similitudes, with þes solu⟨c⟩iones,

Ben not worþe þe deuellis d⟨ir⟩t Dawe ⟨. . .⟩ |

f. 8ᵛ   Daw, þi wordes ben many & euer medled with venym,

205 For aȝenes gode men strecche I no malice,

Ne non of þilk Cristis secte þat myn callist,

Bot aȝenes heritikes, bosteres, & lieres,

Whiche han chosen hem a reule with blablereres of Baal.

And ȝit shal tyde þe tyme when Iosie shal regne,

210 & make an ende of suche fendes & 'Cristis' reule shal renue.

Ȝee, Iamnes & Mambres japid not so þe kyng,

As þou with þi cursid secte þe kyng & þe puple.

Attendite a falsis prophetis, qui veniunt ad vos
in vestimentis ouium.

215 I til þee Daw, with out dout þes wordes ben saide of ȝou,

With oþer pregnant prophecies of Peter & of Poule. |

f. 9ʳ   Daw, þou laborist fast to lede þi self to helle,

& blyndest many lewde foles with þi stynk⟨y⟩ng breþe;

For bi þis apis argument 'þat' þou here now ratelist,

220 He þat drynkiþ a quart wyne most nedis drynk a galon.

Bot aȝen house in mesure, Dawe, grucche I riȝt nouȝt,

And þowȝ þou saye ascorne a shepe house I haue,

þat haþ more grounde in Goddis lawe þan alle ȝour Caymes
castelles:

I thank God I beldid it with trwe bygeten gode,

225 Bot ȝe ȝoures with beggery, bargenyng, & robberye—

For grounde haue þai non bot if it be here.

Non habemus hic manentem ciuitatem. Et idem,
Ve qui edificatis ciuitatem in sanguinibus,
Et ve qui coniungitis domum ad domum. |

f. 9ᵛ   Ȝit, Dawe, þowȝ þou accuses't' pardoneres þat ben fals,

231 þou louest lesse a trwe prest þan þou dost hem alle,

211 japid not so þe kyng: *over erasure.*   212 þe kyng & þe: *over erasure*
230 pardoneres: -res *over erasure.*

For þai gon neere ʒou apostatas in gilyng of þe puple.
Bot þat 'ʒe' ferme to limitoures it may no⟨t⟩ be denyed,
Lye þou neuer so lowde & þerto sette a sele,
Bot þus with many fals meenes oppresse þe cuntrees.   235

    Bot as to paiyng of tribut as Crist hym self did,
þou lyknest ʒou to Pharoes, & so ʒe ben & werse,
Aʒenes Cristis paiyng & alle oþer mekenes:
þou autorisest ʒour pride aʒenes his holi werkes.
    Qui non est mecum, contra me est: et qui   240
    non colligit mecum, dispergit. |

    Dawe, I saide first to þee oon of þi groundes was cursyng,   f. 10ʳ
Whare autorisist þou þis lewde ⟨saw⟩, answere nowe;
þi resones ben a staf of rede þat liʒtly persen þe honde.
I meruel þat þou a clerk blaberst þus blyndely,   245
þou takest comynly no grounde of Crist ne of his lawe,
Bot eþer of þe pope as if he were þi God,
Or of oþer fantasies þat han no grounde hem self.
For whi shuld not alle prestes be meke after Crist
In payng of tribut & alle oþer werkes?   250
Daw, lat ⟨b⟩e þi false glose, it driuiþ þee to þe deuel.
    Benedicite, et nolite maledicere. |

    Lo Daw, with þi draffe þou liest on þe gospel,   f. 10ᵛ
For Crist said it hym self, þe vertu passid fro me;
And here þou maist see I knowe a b fro a bole fote,   255
For I cacche þee in lesynges þat þou laist on þe gospel.

    Bot þus to stele a childe is a gretter theft
þan to stele an oxe, for þe theft is more.
Dawe, for þou saist ʒe robbe hym fro þe worlde,
ʒe maken hym more worldly þan euer his fadir—   260
ʒee, þowʒ he were a plowman lyuyng trwe lyf,
ʒe robbe hym fro þe trwe reule & maken hym apostata,
A begger & 'a' sodomit, for suche þai ben many.

---

238 Aʒenes: *over erasure.*   242 þi: -i *alteration.*   245 clerk: -k *clear*
photograph.   246 all *but* lawe: *over erasure.*   247 eþer of: -er of
clear photograph.   249 whi: *clear photograph.*   251 ⟨b⟩e: -e *visible*
photograph.

Ve vobis qui facitis vnum proselitum. Suple,
265   *filium gehenne duplo quam vos.* |

f. 11ʳ   Daw, I do þee wel to wite, frentike am I not,
Bot it semiþ þi sotil witte ʽmarriþ' many man.
Bot how stondiþ þis to gedir: ȝe sle men *in* ȝo*ur* prison,
Ȝe haue ȝo*ur con*spiracies whe*n* ⌐ȝou⌐ gode likiþ,
270   Ȝe damne þe trwe, ȝe hyen þe false, deme Dawe wher þis be
gode.
And þe kyng by his juges trwe execute his lawe
As he did now late whan he hangid ȝou traytour*es*,
Wilt þou Dawe, all*e*gates, compere ȝou to ʽþe' kyng
Or to oþ*er* lordes þ*at* han her grounde i*n* God?
275   Lefe, fole, þi losengerie & studie Cristis lyf.
Que conuentio Christi ad Belial? Quid
communicabit cacabus ad ollam? |

f. 11ᵛ   Daw, how maist þou saye for shame þ*at* C*r*ist stale þ*us* childre,
And Poule beggid as ȝe don, ȝe lyuen bi þe gospel?
280   Ȝee Dawe, ȝe selle derrer*e* lesynges & poyson,
þan eu*er* did Poule alle his holy writyng.
Eu*er* þou likynest ȝou to Crist whan ȝe ben verrei Anticr*i*st,
And if bisshopes byside wel to knowe alle ȝo*ur* dedes
þai fonde ȝou werse þan harlotes or joguloures eþ*er*;
285   For ȝe begge or ȝe p*r*eche, many tymes & oft,
Somen men & threten he*m*, bot if þai ȝif ȝou gode,
Bot þe harlot wil drawe þe blode of his arse
Or he ask any gode or any rewarde.
And Daw, truly ȝo*ur* dedes co*n*trarie C*r*ist.
290   *Mordent dentibus et predicant pacem; et si quis*
non dederit in ore eorum quippiam,
sanctificant super eum proelium. |

f. 12ʳ   Daw, here þou blaberist ʽto' gedir falsenes & trouþe;
For a bastarde is he þat holdiþ aȝenes þe soþe,
295   God & trwe men discusse wher þat be ȝe or I.
For if ⌐þou callist holichirche⌐ þe techyng of Crist,

269 ȝou] ȝe.   274 -þer lordes: *over erasure.*   296 þou callist holi-
chirche] þou ?ʽseyst': þou *over erasure*, seyst *for cancelled* holichirche *T.*

þe reules of apostles, þe lyf of hem alle,
I summitte me to hem, & wil while I lyue.
If þou callist, Dawe, ʒour Dominikis reules,
With determinacion of many false prestes,   300
Holichirche—as I wene as oft þou hast done—
I forsake þe for euer, with þis cursid chirche.
   Odiui ecclesiam malignantium.
   If 'þou' purposist to pursuwe & drawe men to depe,
I meruel not meche for it is þin office;   305
þe fadires of freres, whiche were þe Pharisees,
Pursuwed Crist to þe paynful depe—
⌐ʒee¬, callid hym a blasfeme as 'ʒe' clepen 'hem' heritikes
þat holde aʒenes ʒour falsehede, 'alle' if þai men truþe.
   Et vos implete mensuram patrum vestrorum. | 310
   Daw, þou hast lerned so long to lye þou wenest þou saist soþ f. 12ᵛ
Whan þou liest most l⟨o⟩wde & sclaunderist þe truþe.
þou saidist þou were no lettred man, þou preuest þi self fals,
For þou spekist of jerarchies, of herisies also—
þou art gilty in alle þes poyntes, & þi breþer boþe,   315
þat I wolde preue apertly if þat þe tyme suffrid.
Lok ʒour lyuyng, ʒour prechyng, with oþer opun dedes,
& laye it by þe apostles lyf & se how þai acorde;
And, as I wene, þe Holigost appreueþ neþer nouþer.
Me thynkiþ ʒe ben tapsteres in alle þat 'ʒe' don: 320
ʒe tappe ʒour absoluciones þat ʒe bye at Rome—
ʒour prechyng, ʒour praying, & also ʒour berying.
Bot þou accusist oþer men þat han bot þe mote
In þe comparison of alle ʒour gret synnes.
   Ypocrita, eice primo trabem de oculo tuo.   325
   Dawe, ʒe folowen Crist as greyhounde doþ þe hare,
For as God ʒaf Kyng Saule in his wodenes,
So ʒe ben clekkid out to pursuwe Holichirche.
   Periculum in falsis fratribus. |
   ʒit, Dawe, þou drawist in many fals prompynges,   f. 13ʳ
For to hirt symple men, bot me neuer a del;   331

308 ʒee] ʒe.   312 lowde: -o- *blotted.*   317 opun dede-: *over erasure.*

For Crist in his membres beggid ful oft

For synne of þe puple when þai were at mischef,

Bot as suche bolde beggeres in bodily hele,

335 Begged neuer Crist ne non of his membres.

For 'Crist' þat is truþe, may in no wise

Contrarie him self, ne God þat is his fadir,

For in many places þai damnen suche sturdy beggyng.

And so, Dawe, þou dotest 'allegyng' þe water,

340 þe asse, or þe herberowe, for he was lorde of alle.

And so þou mysse takist Ierom, & lyest on Bernarde,

For Alrede his clerke wrote þis reson

þat þou mysse layst & dokkist it as þe ⌐likiþ⌐.

Herfor a clerke saiþ, þat euel mot he spede,

345 þat beggiþ of þe puple more þan is nede.

    Mendax mendicus non est veritatis amicus.

    Nutantes transferantur filij eius et mendicent.

God gif þe grace to knowe how þou art Iudas childe,

Whiche psalme þou leggist to me as to an euel entent.† |

f. 13ᵛ 3it, Dawe, þou hewist hye & puttist þi mouþe in heuen,

351 þ⟨y⟩ tong likkiþ þe chesefat & þe garner also,

And þe pore wedowes porse, þow3 she haue bot a peny,

And 3it, Dawe Dotypolle, þou iustifiest þis harlotrie.

    Why lykkennest þou writyng of names, whiche þou dost for money,

355 To þe holi scripture þat is our bileue,

For God ne any godeman appreued neuer þis symonye?

    †þou approuest 3our capped maisters with a glasen glose,

Whiche galpen after grace, bi symonye 3our sister,

And after sitten on hie dece & glosen lordes & ladies;

360 And þis is no liknes bitwix my knaue & hem,

For of þes & suche it ben þat Crist spekiþ in his gospel.

    Amant enim primos recubitus in cenis, et primas

    cathedras in synagogis, et vocari ab hominibus Rabbi. |

---

343 likiþ] likist: -t *visible photograph.*   349 *See* 349 n.   351 þy: -y *alteration.*   354 why: -y *alteration over three-letter erasure.*   357 þou] 'but' þou: but *T.*   358–9 symonye 3our sister And: *over erasure.*

Daw, þou herdist me not grucche þat ȝe went two to gedir, f. 14ʳ

For oþer 'while' ȝe gon three, a womman is þat oon; 365

Bot wheþer ȝe go two or oon, if ȝe wol do wele,

It were a gret ioye to me, God wot þe soþe.

Bot wel I wote þat charite may not duelle þere,

Where couetise crepiþ in '&' lecherie is loggid;

þerfor, Dawe, allegge 'þou' no figur for þin ordre 370

Bot if it be Zambr⟨e⟩ with Corby his lotby,

Or Iamnes & Mambres, Pharaouse freres.

Hij sunt qui penetrant domos, et ducunt

mulierculas oneratas peccatis.† |

Oft Dawe, in þi writtyng þou wryngist out contradiction, f. 15ʳ

Bot ȝit þou puttist defaut to prestes, as erst þou didist to 376
curates;

I wot þai ben defectif, bot ȝit stondiþ Cristis religion,

Of whose defaut I dout not, Dawe, ȝe ben 'þe' chef cause.

Bi þis it suwiþ not God bot Sathanas brouȝt ȝou in.

þou saist, Dawe, as þou felist, þat þere is Cristis body; 380

Bot I afferme faiþfully þat þat is Cristis body.

Daw, aske þi capped maisters as if þai were heritikes,

What is þe sacr⟨e⟩d host—& grounde hem in scripture—

To whiche we knele & doffe our hodes & don alle þis wirchip.

And I bileue þat† sacred whiche is boþe whit & rounde, 385

Is verrei Cristis body, as men shuld bileue,

& did to þe tyme þat Sathanas was vnbounde.

þe wittnesse of þis reson is Crist & his apostles,

With many holi doctoures of þe thousande ȝere;

Bot þis ȝe falsely forsake, with alle ȝour secte or many, 390

& blynden þe puple 'with' heresie, & leuen Goddis lawe,

For ȝe sayen þer is Cristis body & nouȝt þat sacred host.

Commutauerunt veritatem Dei in mendacium.†

369 couetise: -e *over erasure.* 371 lotby: *over erasure.* 374 *See*
374 n. 380 as þou: *twice, second cancelled.* 385 þat] þat 'oste':
oste *T.* 391 blynden: *over erasure.* 393 *See* 393 n.

COMMENTARY

JACK UPLAND

1. Iacke Vplond: Jack the Countryman. Cp. Foxe's headnote: 'a Dialogue or questions moued in the person of a certaine vplandish and simple ploughman of the countrey' (*Actes* (1570), i. 341).

2–3. Not an abstract but a concrete image. Cp. 'for þise habitis crien to þe folc holynesse & stablenesse, þat god wole haue hid to hym, & þus þei ben ofte false signes & garnementis of ypocritis, as crist clepiþ ofte pharisees' (*Tractatus*, Matthew, p. 302); 'þe fend vsiþ hise ypocrisie, & contrarieliche to crist moueþ men bi sensible signes . . . & þus ornamentis þat þise freris ordris vsen ben toolis to bigyle þe peple, & to feede heere bodiliche eye, & robbe þe eye of heere soule' (pp. 321, 323); 'And þese men seien þat siche holynesse stondiþ in her colours, and bodily abitis, wiþ oþer feyned signes' (*Vae*, Arnold, ii. 384).

2–3. 2 John 7: 'For many deceyuours wenten out in to the world, whiche knowlechen not Jhesu Crist for to haue come in flesch; this is deceyuour and antecrist'; Matt. xxiv. 24: 'Forsothe false Cristis and false prophetis schulen ryse, and thei schulen ȝyue grete tokenes and wondris; so that also the chosyne be ledd in to errour.'

4. Cp. 'Oure bileue techiþ us þat crist is boþe god & man, & so he is al myȝty, al witty, & al ful of good wille' (*Tractatus*, Matthew, p. 320); 'Crist Almyghty, al-witty, and alle wel willynge' (*Fifty Heresies*, Arnold, iii. 379).

4–7. Gen. i. 26: 'Make we man to the ymage and oure lickenesse'; 1 Thess. i. 3: '*we* myndeful of ȝoure werk of feith, and traueil, and charite, and susteynyng of the hope of oure Lord Jhesu Crist'.

7–59. The image of the *états du monde* is a commonplace in the literature of the later Middle Ages. On the fourteenth and fifteenth-century English forms, see R. Mohl, *The Three Estates in Medieval and Renaissance Literature* (New York, 1933), pp. 97–139.

11–14. 1 Tim. iv. 12–13: 'be thou ensaumple of feithful men in word, in lyuynge, in charite, in feith, in chastite. The while I come, taak tent to redinge.'

13. holi | alle H. Cp. C *in holy liuyng*, plainly a gloss.

16. office H / *offyces* C. *Office* = 'the special kind of activity proper to anything' (*OED*, *office* sb. 3 = *function* sb. 3) is meant rather than the restricted sense 'ecclesiastical services' suggested by C.

16–17. Cp. *PT* 33–34: 'For clerkes saye, we shullen be fayn / For hir lyvelod [to] swete and swinke.'

21–29. Licences for non-residence could be obtained without difficulty for purposes of study at a university, for service in an important household, or to serve the Crown. Cp. Wyclif's career: while at Oxford he drew the bulk of his income from two rural parishes which he held in succession, mainly as an absentee—Fillingham in Lincolnshire (1361–8) and Ludgershall in Buckinghamshire (1368–74); he also held the prebend of Aust in the collegiate church of Westbury-on-Trym, granted by Urban V in 1362. He entered the service of the Crown probably in 1372; from July to September 1374 he was employed on a diplomatic mission to Bruges. Such profitable abuse was the cause of much complaint on the part of the commons and the parish clergy. For 23–25, cp. *PT* 317–19:

> Hir tything, and hir offring both,
> They cleymeth it by possessioun;
> Therof nill they none forgo.

For simony, see 80–82 and *n.*

25. *almes and as for worldli bisines* H / *allmes* C. Taking the phrase with 25–27 is unsatisfactory, since 25–27 deal with spiritual rather than secular affairs. Taking it with 23–25 (which do deal with worldly business) gives better sense but difficult syntax. With some hesitation I exclude the phrase; it may be a descriptive shoulder note incorporated into the text.

31–33. Upland ascribes to errant seculars this tenderness to criticism. Cp. also *PT* 171–2: 'And though the soth thou of hem tell / In greet cursinge shalt thou fall.' But it was true of all religious; for such charges against the friars, cp. *PPC* 538–42, *Fifty Heresies*, Arnold, iii. 387.

40. *comoun peple* H / *comons* C. To this point H's usage is consistent: *lordis . . . preestis . . . comouns* (7–9); *Preestis office . . . Lordis office . . . Comouns office* (11, 14, 16); but *to preestis . . . To lordis . . . To þe comoun peple* (22, 34, 40). C may be original, but H is the harder reading.

40–42. Possibly a reference to the discontent that was the aftermath of the Black Death, when competition for labour from trades and industries encouraged many to abandon the land. Thus in Essex at the end of the fourteenth century, a ploughman named John Pretylwell was enticed away by a maltmaker who offered him 26*s.* 8*d.* a year, with food and clothing; two labourers in East Tilbury became shipmen *pro maiori lucro* and others on the Essex coast became *draggatores de oystres.* Such competition resulted in a law forbidding the setting of labourers' children to learn a trade if they were wanted on the land

(K. M. Kenyon, 'Labour Conditions in Essex in the Reign of Richard II', *Econ. Hist. Rev.* iv (1934), 429–51, quoted by M. McKisack, *The Fourteenth Century, 1307–1399* (Oxford, 1959), p. 340. Craftsmen get little shrift from either Upland or Daw: see *FDR* 575, 865–7.

46–53. Cp. 'And þus þe Chirche here is foule deformed from children of God to þe fendis lymes, and herto vertues ben transposid to vices; as mekenes is cowardise, and felnesse of pride is clepid riȝtwisnesse for to maynteyne Goddis riȝt, and wraþþe is clepid manhede, and myldenesse is shepenesse, and envye is condicioun of Goddis child to venge him, and slouþe is lordlynesse, as God restiþ evermore; coveitise is prudence to be riche and myȝti, as glotonie is largenesse, and leccherie is myry play; Goddis servaunt is an ypocrite, and an eretike is sad in feiþ. And þus alle vertues ben transposid to vicis, and so holy Chirche to synagoge of Saþanas' (*Vae*, Arnold, ii. 387). Cp. *PT* 501–24, Gower, *Vox Clamantis*, Bk. 7, Cap. iv (*Works*, ed. G. C. Macaulay, iv (Oxford, 1902), 278 f.). See Introduction, pp. 35–36.

48. *ffelnes and pride to wisdom and talnes* H / om. C. 'Shrewdness to wisdom and pride to courage'. For *felnes* = 'shrewdness' *OED* (*fellness* 2) cites two examples from *WV1* (*WV2* at Job v. 13 glosses in one MS. *wylynesse*, at Prov. i. 4 *warnesse* and *to eschewe yuelis*) both rendering Lat. *astutia*; *MED* (*felnesse* n. 2 (a)) adds a third from *Proc. Privy C.* (1439). *MED* glosses 'astuteness, sagacity, wisdom', but Upland's setting of *felnes* against *wisdom* and the glosses from *WV2* suggest a more dyslogistic sense. *OED* does not record *tallness* until 1535 and then only in the sense 'greatness of stature'; but adj. *tall* commonly means 'courageous', and here *talnes* is best taken as an unrecorded early form of the noun = 'courage, valour'.

53. synagoge of Satanas: Rev. ii. 9, iii. 9.

55. *of* H / *&* C. Taking *wagis* figuratively as 'reward, recompense' gives the better sense and allows the construction of H to be kept.

61. *cloistris & sellis* H / *in cloysters in cellys* C. Upland's favourite conjunction is *and*, and he makes excessive use of it. C often substitutes prepositions (as here, see also 240), conjunctions (127, 346, 350), quasi-conjunctions (239), relative pronouns (234); or he edits away (118–19 n., 312) or simply omits (368).

63. þre partis: the estates of 7–9.

65. *mamelynge / murþringe* H / *murmuryng & grudgyng* C. It is just possible to defend H in the light of mendicant sanctions against the eating of meat: cp. *UR* 200, *PPC* 779–82. But *mete* 'flesh of animals' is difficult; *OED* cites a single example from the fourteenth century, but the general sense 'food' would fit the context as well. The earliest certain use of *mete* = 'meat' is *c.* 1460.

C is clearly a gloss and suggests that *murþringe* is a corruption of *mamelynge* = 'mumbling, muttering' and 'musing, chewing'; cp. *PP*, A. viii. 130 (and Kane's note), B. v. 21, xi. 408. 'Musing' is perhaps best: 'the friars live a life of idleness, secure from poverty . . . thinking about food and extravagant clothes'.

66–67. *& þouȝ þei weren þe heire & þe hood / & þouȝ þei weren þe heire & þe hood ouer þe iȝen* H / *& þan þei vary in þer hartis when þer hode hangyth ouer þer eyn* C. C is corrupt here and so, I think, is H. The explanation lies in the proverb 'Cucullus non facit monachum', and more particularly in a variation of it 'Non tonsura facit monachum, non horrida vestis' found (at l. 9) in a poem beginning 'Quid deceat monachum, vel qualis debeat esse' (pr. T. Wright, *Anglo-Latin Satirical Poets* (Rolls Series, 1872), ii. 175 f.), ascribed by Wright to Neckam but more usually assigned to one Roger, a monk of Caen and contemporary of St. Anselm (among whose works the verse is also printed). I am indebted to Dr. R. W. Hunt for the ascription.

67. Cp. *PPC* 701–2: 'In fraitour & in fermori her fostringe is synne / It is her mete at iche a mel her most sustenaunce.'

69–70. *last brouȝte into þe chirche*: the mendicants were the latest of the great regular orders to be established: the Franciscans, the first, founded 1209. Cp. 'þes ben speciali men of þes newe ordris, and moost þese freris þat last comen ynne' (*Vae*, Arnold, ii. 379).

71. *settis of Antecristis sowinge of dyuers* H / *om.* C. C results from homoeoteleuton.

71. Friars were itinerant and missionary and must have been the most familiar kind of 'foreigners'—people from another region or district—in the largely rural England of the Middle Ages.

72. *not obediente to bisshopis*: mendicants lay outside episcopal jurisdiction (like the larger exempt abbeys, Carthusians, Cistercians, Premonstratensians); they were subject only to their own superior or general. Daw (51–52) hedges in his reply: *We obeien to bishopes as boxomnesse askiþ / Alþowȝ not so fer forþ as seculer preestes.* Cp. *180–1 n.*

73–74. Matt. vi. 26: 'thei sowen nat, ne repyn, neither gadren in to bernys'. An early constitution of the Franciscans closely regulated the admission into the order of those who were not clerks already competently instructed in grammar or logic, or clerics or laymen 'mightily edifying' to clergy and people. Thereafter the laymen accounted 'edifying' seem to have been chiefly those who were useful in performing menial tasks as servants for the brethren. But even the number of these was restricted, and most of the rough work came to be done by outside labour (R. B. Brooke, *Early Franciscan Government* (Cambridge, 1959), pp. 243–5).

74. *whete corn ne gras* / *wode corn ne gras* H / *corne wode nor grasse* C. In a context which has to do with crops 'wood' is suspicious. H had difficulty with the passage: *e* of *wode* possibly inserted later; *wode* and *cor* separated by hair-line; *n* added after *cor* with caret, no space before following *ne*.

The passage is quoted twice in *FDR*: *Wede corn ne gras wil ȝe not hewen* (34), *Wede corn ne gras haue we not to hewen* (55). On the basis of these *wede* readings supported by 1536 *weden* (H and C were unknown to him) Skeat argues that *wode* (1536 *woode*) 'is almost certainly an error for *weede*'. But his conjecture discounts the use of *FDR hew* in the unparalleled sense 'reap, cut (crops)'.

Upland's reading probably derives from Matt. vi. 26 and Matt. xiii. 24–30. The latter, the parable of the wheat and the tares, is a commonplace of medieval preaching and was proverbial at least by the mid fifteenth century. Cp. *ODEP*, p. 699, 'Therfor eny man may care, Lest the wede growe over the whete', cited from MS. Harley 5396 (*c.* 1450). In later versions *wheat* becomes *corn*. It may be that H should read *whetecorn*, for which see *OED, wheat-corn*.

ne good / *ne godd* H / *nor do oþer good* C. If H *godd* = *God* it gives awkward syntax and sense. Lines 69–75 deal with secular relationships and responsibilities, the world of business and man's place in it, with works and the friars' neglect of them; divine and spiritual authority and the friars' claim to it are the subject-matter of 75–78. God's intrusion into 69–75 would spoil the rhetorical antithesis. *do* is probably unoriginal: C often introduces words left to be understood in H, and the idea of 'doing' is supplied by *tilien, sowen, weden*, and *repen*.

75–76. Matt. xviii. 18: 'what euere thingis ȝee shulen bynde vpon erthe, tho shulen be bounden and in heuenes; and what euere thingis ȝee shulen vnbynde vpon erthe, tho shulen be vnbounden and in heuenes'.

76. *a mannes lijf to saue* H / *om.* C. In H this stands awkwardly after 75 *but oonli hem silf*. Transposition to follow *in heuen and in erþe* gives excellent sense. C's is part of a larger omission resulting from homoeoteleuton.

76–77. Cp. *PT* 167–8: 'To putte pennyes in hir purse / They woll sell both heven and hell.'

78. *hem silf* / *hem silf saued or dampned* H / *þemself* C. H completes the sense, but its explicitness argues against originality.

79. *confessouris & confundouris of lordis & ladies*: Richard II and in his last years Henry IV chose their confessors from among the Dominicans. Henry V chose his from the Carmelites; two of them, Thomas Netter of Walden and Stephen Patrington, were bitter

opponents of the Lollards; both were advanced in the Church. Netter became prior provincial of the Carmelites, Patrington Bishop of St. David's. Cp. *PPC* 708–9: 'And bigileþ þe grete wiþ glauerynge wordes / Wiþ glosinge of godspells þei gods worde turneþ.' See 379–82 and *n.*, *UR* 112, *UR* 359.

81–82. Simonundis eiris: Simon Magus offered money to the Apostles in exchange for the power of bestowing the Holy Ghost by the laying on of hands (Acts viii. 18–19). Hence the type of one who buys or sells ecclesiastical preferments etc. and trafficks in sacred things.

þe fyue ordris / *þe foure ordris* H / *v orders* C. Against C is the fact that the minor orders were moribund by 1300; in the late fourteenth century they would hardly be worth attacking. At *PP*, A. viii. 176 none of the seventeen extant MSS. covering a period of transmission of more than 130 years reads *five* in the line 'þei₃ þou be founde in þe fraternite among þe foure ordris'; but the late C text reads *fyue* at ix. 191, x. 343, and xvi. 81. *FDR* 84 reads *Iakke, of þi foli þou feynest fife ordres*, which supports C's harder reading.

fyue ordris: the fifth order is probably the Crutched Friars; at the beginning of the fifteenth century they seem to have had five priories in England. Of other minor orders, the Friars of the Sack were dissolved in England in 1317; three others listed by Knowles and Hadcock mustered only four houses between them, all almost certainly extinct by the end of the fourteenth century. See D. Knowles and R. N. Hadcock, *Medieval Religious Houses: England and Wales* (London, 1953), pp. 204–8.

falsli / *falsist* H / *last* C. C would give the attractive antithesis *last* / *first* and, in this 'verse' extract, reduce the weight of the first half-line with its hypermetrical three alliterating stresses. But 86 *Pharesies* etc. has the same variation, and it must be admitted here.

FDR 85–86 reads *And ₃it ben þer but foure foundid in þe lawe / Falsly as þou seist, & soone shal be distroied.* H *falsist* must be taken in the strained sense 'the falsest people' if it is to give adequate sense, and after the rising invective of 69–82 such an epithet is lame. *FDR falsly* = 'falsely established in our faith' is better: the beginning of Upland's catechism at 101 f. deals with the validity of the mendicants' foundation, and Daw's reading could be taken as looking forward to it.

86. Caymes castel-makers: *Caymes castels* a name for friars' convents, a commonplace of Lollard polemic. Caym or Caim was the usual fourteenth- and fifteenth-century spelling, and this was convenient for the detractors of the friars:

> Nou se the sothe whedre it be swa,
> That frer Carmes come of a k,
> The frer Austynes come of a,
> Frer Jacobynes of i,

> Of m comen the frer Menours;
> Thus grounded Caym thes four ordours,
> That fillen the world ful of errours,
> And of ypocrisy.

Wright, *Political Poems*, i. 266, quoted by Skeat, *PPC* 486 n. For Wyclif's own similar account, see *Trialogus*, Bk. iv, Cap. 33, ed. G. Lechler (Oxford, 1869), p. 362.

86–87. Matt. xxiii. 13–29, 2 Pet. ii. 1.

90–92. Matt. xxii. 37–40.

94–95. Probably Jas. i. 27: 'This is a clene religioun, and vnwemmyd anentis God and the fadir, for to visite pupilles, *that is, fadirles or modirles, or bothe,* and widewes in her tribulacioun.'

97. frere H / *fryer of what order art þou & who mad þi ordre what be þi rulys* C. C's insertion of this line (it appears at 103–4 in H) is puzzling. If merely a case of the scribe's eye dropping from 97 *fryer* to the same word in 103, it is not clear (1) why he did not omit all the intervening text (as, for example, at 227–8, 396–8) but after copying 103–4 returned to 97 and continued to copy exactly where he had originally left off, with no omission of text; (2) why, when C reaches 103, he omits the middle part of the quotation—*& who mad þi ordre*—instead of copying out the whole passage again.

98. ordre / *ordris* H / *ordre* C. There are six places where the context will allow either singular or plural of this word, and the MSS. differ in four ·

H	C
97–98. þin ordris and þi rulis	ordre & rulys
148. ordris & rulis	order & rule
322. summe of ȝoure ordre	summe of yower orders
330. summe of ȝoure ordris	some of yower orders
348. bynde hem to ȝoure ordris	bynd þem to yower orders
383. ȝoure ordris ben	yower order is

That Upland intends a singular at 98 is clear from the pronoun *þin*. At 148 singular *patrun* and the sense of the paragraph demand singular *ordre*. At 330 and 348 MS. evidence suggests the plural and the contexts also support a generalized plural sense. At 322 and 383 either singular or plural is admissible, and I let H stand in both cases.

98. Goddis lawe: the scriptures, a name much used by the Lollards. Cp. 115 *Cristis lawe* = 'the gospels'.

103. and who made þin ordre H / om. C. For C's omission, see 97 n.

103–6. Presumably an allusion to the late foundation of the mendicant orders. Cp. 69–70 and *n.*, 399–400.

107–8. Cp. 'First, freris seyn þat hor religioun, founden of synful men, is more perfite þen þat religion or ordir þo whiche Crist hymself made' (*Fifty Heresies*, Arnold, iii. 367).

109. *rulist þou þee | rulist þee* H | *dost þou not rewle þi self* C. Omission of the subject pronoun in the second person is unusual in ME. Cp. 276 reflexive *groundist þou þee* supported by C *dost þou grownd þe*.

111–13. Cp. 'Also freris chargen more brekyng of hor owne tradiciouns þen brekyng of þo comaundementis of God. Ffor a frere schal more be punysched for brekyng of one of hom, þen for brekyng of Gods heestis' (*Fifty Heresies*, Arnold, iii. 372); see e.g. *122–9 n.*, *161–3 n.*

111. *rulis* H | *rule* C. Upland is referring to rules in the sense of principles or regulations governing individual conduct rather than to the code of discipline of which these regulations are a part. This seems clear from the parallel *heestis* in the next line.

114–15. See *94–95 n.*

115. *Cristis lawe*: the gospels. Cp. *98 n.*

118–19. *to þore feble men and þore blynd and þore lame* H | *to poore febyll men blynd & lame* C. Emphatic parallelism is characteristic of *Upland*, and C usually edits. Cp. 208 n., 263 f., 266–7 n., 390–1; see also 287–8 and 292–4 where H is supported by C in both places.

118–19. In many places Christ bids men give to the poor (Matt. xix. 21, Luke xiv. 13, 21, etc.), but nowhere on pain of damnation. Cp. 'þo comaundement of Crist, of gyvynge of almes to pore feble men, to pore croked men, to pore blynde men'; 'þei ben wode þat mennes almes schulde be rightly departid amonge pore men, nedy, feble, crokid, and blinde—ffor þen þei seyn þei ben undone' (*Fifty Heresies*, Arnold, iii. 372, iii. 387).

122–9. A decree of Boniface VIII (c. 2, in VI°, De clerici, III, 24; Friedberg, *Corpus*, ii. 1065) made excommunication the penalty for abandoning the regular habit. Cp. 'Freris also ben stronglier weddid wiþ hor roten habite, ageyns þo fredome of þo gospel, þen þo housbande is wiþ his wif by ordynaunce of God. Ffor þo housbande may lawefully be absente fro his wif by a moneth, an half ȝeer, and sumtyme seven ȝeer . . . Bot if a frere be oute of his roten habite, ȝhe, an hour, he is apostata' (*Fifty Heresies*, Arnold, iii. 389).

125. *abite* H | *habytys* C. The noun occurs six times in the text (125, 128, 130, 133, 135, 205); H has the singular in every case, against plurals in C here and at 130; C omits the word at 133. For other examples of confusion between singular and plural nouns see 16 n., 111 n., 166–7, 210 n., etc.

134–6. Cp. 'Ffor if a frere leefe his bodily habite, to þo whiche he is not bounden by Gods lawe, he is holden apostata and scharply pursued, sumtyme to prisoun, and sumtyme to þo deth'; 'Also freris seyn, if a mon be oones professid to hor religioun, he may nevere leeve hit and be saved, þof he be nevere so unable þerto, for al tyme of his lif' (*Fifty Heresies*, Arnold, iii. 373, 369).

137. *seye* H / *Syr* C. There is contextual support in both MSS. for *seye*: 134 H (and C) & *ʒif ʒe seie*, 135 C *Tell me than fryer* (H simply *ffrere*). 137 H *seye*, 135 C *Tell me*, may both result from the pull of the verb at 134; but C *syr* is the easier reading. Without complete conviction I let H stand.

ʒou / *om.* H / *yow* C. Upland regularly uses the dative of interest in such constructions, as at 142, 149, 173, 292. Cp. 153 n.

137–9. Seynt Gregori: 'Nemo quippe vestimenta praecipua nisi ad inanem gloriam quaerit, videlicet, ut honorabilior caeteris esse videatur' (*Homiliarum in Evangelia II*, Homil. xl, Migne, *PL* lxxvi. 1305). Cp. *366–70 n*.

140–3. scapalarie: scapular, the special garment of the monastic orders; worn over the habit, it consists of a piece of cloth the width of the shoulders reaching front and back almost to the ground, it has an opening for the head in the middle, and hangs from the shoulders. The original scapular of the Dominicans was made so that it also acted as a covering for the head, and thus as a hood. *copis*: cope, a piece of cloth of semicircular shape, open in front and fastened at the breast with a band or clasp. Daw replies (368–79) that his hood signifies suffering in adversity or the business of his order, the scapular obedience to his superiors, the cope charity. For the knotted girdle, see *FDR 380 n*.

   Cp. 'ʒif þise cloþis ben gurde & more large in widnesse, þei beren on hem more synne, for more ypocrisie in hem. And knottis þat bitokenen penaunce hongynge bifore fro þe bodi ben signes of ypocrisie & noon oþer holynesse' (*Tractatus*, Matthew, p. 316); cp. also the complaint of the ploughman against the friars *PPC* 550: 'þei schapen her chapolories & streccheþ hem brode'. See 137–9, *PPC* 550–3.

142. *cloþis* H / *clothe* C. Either reading would suit the sense of the passage. In replying to this criticism Daw says *of oure presciouse cloþis fast þou carpist* (351), but at 356 he also refers to precious *cloþ*.

148. *ordre & rulis* / *ordris & rulis* H / *order & rule* C. For *ordre* see 98 n. If C's singular *rule* is admitted the phrase is tautological. Such doublets are characteristic of C but are seldom found in H. Cp. 17 H *prestis*, C *ministers or preastys*; 23 H *hire*, C *stipendys or wagys*; 29 H *wynnynge*, C *lucre & avawntage*, 36 H *vertues*, C *vertuusnes & good conuersacion*; 129 H *holden*, C *holden & taken*; 151 H *hard*, C *harde & strayt*, etc. *FDR* 406–7 reads *More ouer þou meuest, Iak, anoþer mater* / *If oure patrouns be perfit and oure reule also*; but *reule* here is equivalent to Upland's *order*. Cp. 111 n.

149. dispensacioun: the Register of the prior general of the Austin Friars lists the dispensations granted by the General Chapter of the order at Asti, 1419; those granted to English members are printed by F. Roth, *The English Austin Friars, 1249–1538* (New York, 1961), ii. 289–93. *court*: probably the General or Provincial Chapter. But it may refer to Rome itself; the Register (Roth, p. 292) mentions papal dispensation for accepting a benefice granted to one John Multon.

153. *take ʒou | make* H | *gett yow* C. The sense requires *take* as in 152; C seems here to preserve an original dative parallel to 153 HC *bynde ʒou.* Cp. 137 n.

155. *hise | his* HC. H omits final *e* in the plural only here and 169.

157–8. Presumably a reference to the claim of the Carmelites to be direct descendants of Elijah (taken up into heaven by the 'spirit of the Lord' in a whirlwind) and the 'sons of the prophets'. Cp. 2 Kings ii, *PPC* 382–3.

160. professid: a regular made his profession after a year in his order. Cp. Lydgate's account of his own profession (as a Benedictine):

> Entryng this tyme into relygioun,
>   Onto the plowe I put forth myne hond,
> A yere complete made my professioun.

(EETS, ES cvii (1911), 354.) One who abandoned his order after he had completed the year of his novitiate was legally an apostate:

> Out of the ordre thof I be gone,
>   Apostota ne am I none,
> Of twelve monethes me wanted one,
>   And odde days nyen or ten.

(Wright, *Political Poems*, i. 268.) Cp. 130–6.

161–3. do pursue men: for the power of the mendicants with the secular arm see the commission dated 15 November 1399 to all sheriffs, who, when required by Augustinian superiors, are to have it proclaimed 'that all vagabond members of the Order pretending to be exempted by the apostolic see from regular observances are to return to their priories and houses within two months, or face arrest' (Roth, *Austin Friars*, ii. 258). On the friars' persecution of heretics and apostates, see 214–19, 247–50, *PPC* 655–68.

162. *do pursue | to pursue* H | *do pursue* C. C seems here to preserve an original causal *do*; cp. 374–5 *do prisone hem* for the same construction.

165–7. The Franciscans especially were secretive about their corporate business. The sessions of their Chapters were held in private, and no unauthorized person, no secular, and no member of another order was permitted to attend. St. Bonaventure laid it down that if not a member of it, as penance for merely coming to the place where a General or Provincial Chapter was being held, Franciscans were to wear a probationer's hood for a week (Brooke, *Franciscan Government*, pp. 211, 277). Cp. 'Freris also of grete cautel bynden novycis to unknowen þing, for þei wil not suffre hom knowe hor privetees of hor reule and hor lif, til þat þei ben professid' (*Fifty Heresies*, Arnold, iii. 397).

168–76. The extravagance of friars' houses was much censured. For a Dominican house, cp. *PPC* 159 f.:

> Y ȝemede vpon þat house & ȝerne þeron loked,
> Whouȝ þe pileres weren y-peynt and pulched ful clene,
> And queynteli i-coruen wiþ curiouse knottes,
> Wiþ wyndowes well y-wrouȝt wide vp o-lofte.
>
> .   .   .
>
> Wiþ arches on eueriche half & belliche y-corven,
> Wiþ crochetes on corners wiþ knottes of golde,
> Wyde wyndowes y-wrouȝt y-written full þikke,
> Schynen wiþ schapen scheldes to schewen aboute.

Cp. 'And evere þei passen foule Crist and his apostils; ffor where Crist had not to reste inne his heved, freris, feyned beggers, have lordly plasis, þat almoste þorw Englond þei may iche nyght lye on hor owne' (*Fifty Heresies*, Arnold, iii. 368), and 368, *366–70 n.*

In fact, the charge fitted the monks better than the friars. Cp. the remarks of Professor David Knowles: 'the shift towards a more comfortable and elaborate career never greatly affected the architectural style or furnishings of the friaries. The letters and surveys and inventories of the commissioners at the Dissolution make it clear that the friars had few costly fittings, and that the buildings were on the whole modest in scale and style' ('The Monastic Buildings of England', *The Historian and Character* (Cambridge, 1963), p. 209). The persistent accusations of the Lollards may be the result of honest confusion, more likely of intentional misrepresentation.

168–9. Cp. Matt. viii. 20: 'Foxis han dichis, *or borowis*, and briddis of the eir *han* nestis, but mannes sone hath nat wher he reste his heued.'

168–72. Cp. 'And þerfore Crist and his apostlis maden no grete chirchis ne cloystris, bot wenten fro cuntrey to cuntrey, preching þo gospel, and teching men to do hor almes to pore men, and not to waste housis' (*Fifty Heresies*, Arnold, iii. 380). Cp. *PPC* 155–215.

169. hise | his HC. See 155 n.

170. Cp. *PT* 355: 'The pore to pill is all hir pray.'

172–3. housis of mornynge | grauis or housis of mornynge HC. *FDR* 453–4 reads *to men þat ben deede | . . . longiþ but graues & mornynge housis.* Doublets are characteristic of C but rarely occur in H (see

148 n.); *housis of mornynge* suits the contextual imagery and is the harder reading; *grauis* is probably a gloss.

177. *sette* H / *lett* C. Cp. *FDR* 477 *We leten, þou seist, to lymytours, al þis rewme to ferme,* 479 *Vnsikir þing soþly it were to sette to ferme.* Either reading is possible (see *OED*, *set* vb. iv. 27, *let* vb.[1] i. 8), but perhaps C is the easier, since it can be explained by the alliterative pull of following *londe, lymytouris,* and *lordis.*

ʒoure / *ʒour* H. This pronoun lacks *e* only here and at 193, 385. All are corrections. There are more than sixty examples of *ʒoure* in the text.

177. lymytouris: limiter, a friar licensed to beg as a procurator for his house in a certain carefully delimited district attached to each friary; such districts were thus 'farmed out'.

180–1. 1 Pet. ii. 13: 'Be ʒe suget to eche creature of man, for God; other to the kyng, as precellent.' Cp. 'þei ben not reulid by Gods lawe, ne lawes of þo Chirche, ne lawes of þo kyng. Ffor þei glosen Gods lawe as hom likes, and ben exempt fro bischopis and oþer ordinaries . . . And men seyn þei ben not lege men to þo kynge ne sugett to his lawes' (*Fifty Heresies*, Arnold, iii. 384). See *72 n.*

182–3. See 168–76 and *n.*

183. *cloþis* H / *coloris* C. *OED*, *cloth* sb. i. 5 records 'painted clothes' for tapestries only from 1542; but *MED* quotes an example of 1389.

184. *kyng* H / *cristen kyng* C. *FDR* 486 supports C, but the explicitness argues against originality.

185. *þore men* / *þore men þat ʒe þilen* H / *poore men* C. H goes against the normal direction of variation, and its explicitness argues against originality.

185–6. Matt. xxii. 21.

187–94. For a broad attack on the abuse of letters of fraternity, see *Fifty Heresies* xv. Arnold, iii. 377–8; *JU 335–41 n.*

191–2. Luke xviii. 9: 'Forsoth he seide also to sum men, that tristiden in hem silf, as riʒtful, and dispiseden othere', and cp. Isa. lxv. 5.

192. *þat ʒe most stonde* / *þat most stonde* H / *þat ye stond most* C. The sense requires the personal pronoun.

193. *ʒoure.* See 177 n.

199. trentale: trental, a set of thirty requiem masses said on the same day or on different days. This and other kinds of intercessory prayer were much demanded of the mendicants. Thus, John Woodhouse of Kimberley, Norfolk, a member of the royal household under Henry IV and Henry V, when providing for six days' exequies directed that on the first night the Carmelites of Norwich were to officiate, for the three following days the services were to be conducted by each of the other mendicant orders in the city; not till the fifth day were the secular clergy of the city to come in (E. F. Jacob, *The Fifteenth Century, 1399–1485* (Oxford, 1961), p. 297).

204–8. Burial in a friar's habit (usually extended to benefactors, see *335–41 n.*) was thought to excuse the soul the torments of purgatory and hell. Cp. 'freris . . . techen lordis, and namely ladies, þat if þei dyen in Frounceys habite þei schul nevere cum in helle for vertu þerof; and certis þis is an open heresie, dampnynge alle þat tristen þus into hor lyves ende' (*Fifty Heresies*, Arnold, iii. 382). The Franciscans especially encouraged the belief; Daw (529–32) disclaims the fable on behalf of Austins and Dominicans, suggesting that perhaps Carmelites or Franciscans might maintain such an error.

207. hiȝ H / *om.* C. Only once (at 225) does Upland fail to add an adjective to emphasize the extravagance of the friars' houses, and there he is not attacking the friaries as such but the practice of burying the rich within the precincts. At 168 they are *costli housis*, at 171 *gay housis*, and at 368 *curious & costlew housis*. Such attacks on the friaries are a commonplace of Lollard polemic. Cp. *168–76 n.*, PPC 207–8.

208. make cotis for many men to saue many soulis H / *make cootis for men þat þer sowllys may be savyd* C. For Upland's appetite for repetition and emphatic parallelism and C's habit of editing, see 118–19 n.

209–11. On the stealing of children by the mendicants cp. the vivid anecdote in Fitzralph's *Defensio Curatorum* (EETS, os 167 (1925), 56): 'And as þe comyn fame telliþ, after þat children ben bigiled into her ordre, þe children haueþ no fredome for to wende out, but beþ holden wiþ hem aȝenus her owne wille forto þei be professed in þe ordre. & ȝett more me seiþ, þat in þe mene tyme, þe children beþ nouȝt suffred to speke wiþ fader noþer wiþ modir, but vnder keping and drede of freres. In euydence herof, þis day as ich come out of myn Inne, come to me a good man of Englond þat is comen to þis court for socour and remedye; and he tolde me þat anoon after Ester þat last was at Oxenford, freres bynsame hym his sone þat was nouȝt xiii ȝere olde, & he came þider to speke wiþ his sone & moste nouȝt speke wiþ his sone, but vnder warde & keping of freres.' See *347–53 n.*

210. þefte / *þeste* H. 1536 *sith yat theft* (sig. Av^r).

heeste / *heestis* H / *commandment* C. H's plural may be the result of the strongly plural context; the sense strictly requires a singular.

211–13. Cp. 'And þof þis synguler ordir were more perfite þen Cristis, ȝitt he wot nevere wheþer hit be to dampnacioun of þo childe, for he wot not to what state God hafs ordeyned hym' (*Fifty Heresies*, Arnold, iii. 374); 'And where many children bi Cristis ordre shulden be saaf, þei shulen now be dampned bi taking of þes false ordris, for a frere can teche no more þat þis child shal be beter bi takinge of his ordre and kepinge of his reule, þan þis frere can telle þat God ȝaf him þis mannis oxe' (*Vae*, Arnold, ii. 380).

214–19. Matt. xviii. 17: 'Forsothe ȝif he shal not heere the chirche, be hee to thee as an hethen'; cp. Isa. lxv. 5: 'whiche seien *to an hethene man*, Go thou awei fro me, neiȝ thou not to me, for thou art vncleene'. For Augustine's teaching, see *Ep.* 211, the basis of the so-called Rule of St. Augustine. Upland probably alludes to the admonition he gives to those women who indulge in wanton looks: 'Convicta vero secundum praepositae vel presbyteri arbitrium debet emendatoriam sustinere vindictam: quam si ferre recusaverit, et si ipsa non abscesserit, de vestra societate projiciatur' (Migne, *PL* xxxiii. 962). Cp. 'Ffor þis þei suen scharplyer, and punyschen herfore; and þis privey horedame makes myche harme. As Crist biddes, undertake thryes oure broþer, and at þo fourt tyme forsake hom as hethen men' (*De Blasphemia*, Arnold, iii. 417); 'Freris also kepen not correpcioun of þo gospel ageyns hor breþer þat trespassen, bot cruely done hom to peyneful prisoun. Bot þis is not þo meke suynge of Jesus Crist, for he and his apostils prisoneden not synful men in þis lif, bot scharply reproved hor synne, and at þo laste, when þei wolden not amende hom, tauȝten gode men to comyne not wiþ hom' (*Fifty Heresies*, Arnold, iii. 383).

216. *wynne hem* H / *wyn hyn* C. Upland switches from plural subject in the first sentence of the paragraph to singular in the second, consequently the MSS. show some confusion of pronominal forms. The sense seems to require plural *hem* here but at 219 singular *hym* as in C.

217. *ne bi þe chirche* H / *om.* C. The security of the text is confirmed by Matt. xviii. 17.

218. *techiþ* / *techiþ vs* H / *teachith yow* C. The grammar of H's *techiþ vs to putte hym from þee* is capricious and suggests corruption. C's pronouns *yow . . . yower . . . yow* are suspiciously consistent and probably editorial. At 115 *techiþ* is followed by an object pronoun in both H and C. But at 215 H and C agree in omitting the pronoun in a construction otherwise identical with this. Omission gives good sense here and eliminates the pronominal confusion of H.

from þee as an heþen man H / *om.* C. Matt. xviii. 17 and *FDR* 557 *haue him as heþene* both support H.

220–5. Cp. 'Freris drawen to hom confessioun and birying of riche men by mony sotil meenes, and messe pens, and trentals, bot þei wil not cum to pore mennis dirige, ne resseyve hom to be biryed amonge hom' (*Fifty Heresies*, Arnold, iii. 374). Cp. *PPC* 468–71:

> Þei coueten confessions to kachen some hire,
> And sepultures also some wayten to cacchen;
> But oþer cures of Cristen þei coueten nouȝt to haue,
> But þere as wynnynge liþ he lokeþ none oþer.

Burial within the precincts of a mendicant house was much sought
after. For those buried in a Dominican house cp. *PPC* 181–8:

> Tombes opon tabernacles tyld opon lofte,
> Housed in hirnes harde set abouten,
> Of armede alabaustre clad for þe nones,
> Made vpon marbel in many maner wyse,
> Knyghtes in her conisantes clad for þe nones,
> All it semed seyntes y-sacred opon erþe;
> And louely ladies y-wrouȝt leyen by her sydes
> In many gay garmentes þat weren gold-beten.

Daw ignores Upland's question about burying the poor as well as the
rich; and well he might—see Stow's list of burials in the London
Blackfriars, *Survey*, ed. C. L. Kingsford (Oxford, 1908), i. 340–1.

226. *þe gospel / gospels* H / *yower gospell* C. The singular appears everywhere in H but here. Its meaning is variously (1) the holy scriptures
generally (as at 11) or (2) the record of Christ's life and teaching (as at
296). Here it probably refers to the gospel passage read at the com-
munion service. The plural with singular sense is found occasionally in
ME. used of a particular gospel (see *OED*, *gospel* sb. 2b) but not in any
of the meanings found in *Upland*. H may be the result of the plural
pressure of the passage.

227–8. *as ȝe doen at riche mennes housis and schoppis þat mai go to
chirche* H / *om.* C. C results from homoeoteleuton.

230. *diriges*: in the office for the dead according to the use of Sarum,
at the vigils (celebrated always on the day before the masses for the
dead) nine psalms were ordered to be sung, followed, when the body
was present, by nine different antiphons; but when the body was not
present, by one and the same antiphon—either the *Placebo* (Ps. cxiv. 9)
or *Dirige* (Ps. v. 9: 'Dirige in conspectu tuo viam meam'). These
vigils must have made the word *dirige*, loudly repeated after each of
the nine psalms at the beginning of the antiphon, very familiar; hence
it came to express funeral exequies generally. In 1417 one Richard
Bruton bequeathed 2*s.* 4*d.* to each priest of the Augustinian houses of
Bristol, London, and Winchester with the obligation to say thirty
masses within forty days after his death; 2o*d.* to each Austin who is not
a priest to say twenty times *Placebo* and *Dirige* (Roth, *Austin Friars*, ii.
286).

233–6. On the homilists' (and especially mendicant) appetite for *fals
fablis* and *feined myraclys*, see G. R. Owst, *Preaching in Medieval
England* (Cambridge, 1926), Ch. vi. John Myrc's *Festial* (EETS, ES
xcvi (1905)) is a collection of the sort Upland censures here. Of it Owst
says: 'With Myrc the text of canonical scriptures would seem almost
out of favour. He revels in the most fanciful and impossible anecdotes
about sacred characters; he is fascinated irresistibly by the lurid and

the painful; he seems to offer his listeners little short of a new super-stition and wizardry blessed by the Church, in place of the old for-bidden paganisms to which they still cling so lovingly' (p. 245). This echoes Richard de Bury's complaint (specifically against the friars) six hundred years earlier: 'they rely upon some treatises of small value, from which they derive strange heresies and apocryphal imbecilities, not for the refreshment of souls, but rather for tickling the ears of the listeners' ('quibusdam quaternis parvi valoris insistunt, de quibus Hiberas naenias et apocrypha deliramenta producunt, non ad refocil-lativum animarum edulium, sed ad pruritum potius aurium audi-torum'), *Philobiblon*, ed. E. C. Thomas (London, 1888), vi, par. 88. Cp. 'capped freris . . . senden oute ydiotis ful of covetise to preche, not þo gospel, bot cronyclis, fablis, and leesingis' (*Fifty Heresies*, Arnold, iii. 376); 'Sum prechen fablis, and sum veyn storys; sum docken holy writt, and summe feynen lesyngis; and so lore of Goddis lawe is al putt abac' (*Vae*, Arnold, ii. 379).

234. *&* H/*which* C. In *Upland* as in ME. generally *þat* is the dominant form of the relative pronoun; *which(e)* occurs only twice in H, once (382) governed by *of*, once (235) governed by *bi*; after 380 *synnes* it results from the scribe erroneously copying the same phrase twice. C is therefore an improbable nominative form.

234. Mark xvi. 15: 'And he seide to hem, ȝe goynge in to al the world, preche the gospel to ech creature.'

235. *to bodi & to soule* H/ *to bodie & sowle* C. Where a noun doublet is governed by the preposition *to* Upland usually prefixes it to both nouns as here; cp. 1, 248, 331, 401, 403. C keeps the second *to* at 1, 331, and 401; at 248 he omits both; at 403 he recasts so that *to . . . to* becomes *before . . . before*. The exceptions at 48, 50, and 52 in H are probably to be explained by Upland's reluctance to add to the plethora of prepositions in the passage and the fact that the whole passage may be taken over from an independent source (see Introduc-tion, pp. 35–36). Such duplication is also found with other prepositions, cp. *in* at 14, 76, 145, 147, *bi* at 18, 217, 278–9.

240–1. *ȝe winnen more wiþ*/*ȝe winnen more money wiþ* H/*ye wyn more with* C. FDR 600 f. *þou seist . . . we wynnen more þerwith*, 1536 (sig. A vi^r) *ye winne more by yeare wyth* support C. H has been exten-sively corrected and the explicitness probably results from doctoring.

241. *In principio*: the special reverence accorded to the opening words of St. John's Gospel was much used by the mendicants. Cp. Chaucer, *CT*, A. 254: 'And þus God wole þat þou leve to muse on doutis þat he wole hide, as of oure Ladi, and Seint Joon, and oþer seintis þat foolis glaveren, and bringiþ þis ynne as bileve, for þei hopen to wynne herbi' (*Vae*, Arnold, ii. 389).

246. ȝeer / ȝeris H / *yere* C. Plurals occur also at HC 20, 105, 400 all in this phrase, and all uninflected. H may result from contextual pressure of inflected plurals.

247. foolis: 'scoundrels' applied to the mendicants, see *241 n.* Cp. *PPC* 455–6: 'A! broþer,' quaþ he þo 'beware of þo foles! / For Crist seyde him-selfe of swiche y ȝou warne.'

247–50. Cp. 'if þer be any frere þat is a prest . . . able to travel to sowe Gods wordis amonge þo puple, if he do þis offis frely . . . þei wil poursue hym as apostata, and drawe hym to prisoun, and sey þat he is cursed for þis dede'; 'þei pursuen prestis, for þei reproven hor synnes as God biddes, bothe to brenne hom, and þo gospels of Crist written in Englische, to moost lernyng of oure nacioun' (*Fifty Heresies*, Arnold, iii. 368, 393).

248. to prisonynge & to fire H / *prisonyng & burnyng* C. *FDR* 631 reads *to prisoun & to fire,* 636 *to fire or to prisoun. FDR* may preserve the original reading, HC having introduced the gerund and participle on analogy of following *prechinge, sillinge.*

249–50. Matt. x. 8: 'frely ȝe han taken, frely ȝeue ȝe'.

253. wode H / *farr owt of þe way* C. C's exemplar must have read *wide* for original *wode,* and C's reading is an attempt to make sense out of it.

254–6. & þe more etc. The expanded passage here in C is a gloss to make sense of Upland's concinnity. Upland's sardonic remark that friars *woot not what an eresie is for to seye* is glossed accurately in *FDR* at 645–6: *But how shulden freres pursue heresie / And many of hem wite not what heresie meneþ?*

257–8. Probably Jas. v. 16: 'preye ȝe for eche other, that ȝe be saued. Forsothe the contynuel preyer of a iust man is miche worth.'

257–62. Cp. 'þise ordris witen not wheþer þat þei shal come to heuene, & so wheþer þat heere preyeris profiten to hem or any oþer man . . . & algatis siþ it is proprid to god to parte meritis as hym likiþ, & noon man may approue hise meritis but as god iugiþ þat it is worþi; & þus þis preyere of þise ordris is of a nest of blasfemye & chaffaryng of fendis preyere bi þe craft of symonye' (*Tractatus,* Matthew, p. 317).

260. sillen / sillist H / *so to sell* C. MS. *and sillist þou* is in the hand of the first corrector; strictly an infinitive parallel to *take* is required.

261–2. Balams boost: Num. xxii f. There Balaam is presented in a favourable light, but in NT he is cited as a type of avarice. So 2 Pet. ii. 15: 'the weie of Balaam of Bosor, the which louede hijre of wickidnesse.' *Gizies lepre*: 4 Kings (RV 2 Kings) v. Gehazi is here, as often, cited as the type of simonist. Cp. 'giezi, þat ran aftir naaman and toke ȝiftis of hym þorow occasion of þat grace so minystred, was a symonyent (Matthew, p. 378).

266–7. þou louest coueitousli more a penye þanne þin owen soule H / *þou lovist cuvitusnes more þan þi owne sowll* C. The sixfold repetition of *penye* is characteristic of Upland's style. Cp. 118–19 n.

267. quicke & dede H / *om.* C. 1536 (sig. A vi^v) reads *thou louest to lyttel mede for thy soule* and is certainly corrupt. By the fourteenth century the phrase is found outside traditional liturgical contexts. See *MED, ded* adj. 2c.

268–9. Matt. xxvi. 15.

272–81. For a full attack on the mendicant justification of begging see *De Blasphemia*, Arnold, iii. 410–19. For 272–6 cp. 'þen sith iche open beggynge is þus scharply dampned in holy writt, hit is a foule erroure to mayntene hit; bot hit is more erroure to sey þat Crist was suche a begger, for þen he moste have ben contrarie to his owne lawe' (*Fifty Heresies*, Arnold, iii. 372).

282. tablis: lists of benefactors for whom prayers were offered up.

285–90. That they pandered to the rich and ignored the poor was a constant complaint against the friars. Cp. *PPC* 368–9: 'Y pray þe, where ben þei pryue wiþ any pore wiʒtes / þat maie not amenden her hous ne amenden hemseluen?'; 'freris beggen wiþouten nede for hor owne riche secte, and not for pore bedraden men þat may not go' (*Fifty Heresies*, Arnold, iii. 383).

286. salarie H / *service* C. H *salarie* in the restricted sense 'stipend of a priest'—especially a chantry priest—current *c.* 1390 to *c.* 1520 (*OED, salary* sb. 1) is probably original.

289. þei / he H / *ye* C. Neither H nor C is satisfactory.

289. moornynge clopis: presumably a reference to the Dominicans. Cp. *PPC* 696–7: 'Blak, þat bytokneþ bale for oure synne / And mournynge for misdede of hem þat þis vseþ.'

292–3. Cp. Matt. xxv. 43: 'I was herberlesse, and ʒee gedriden nat me; nakid, and ʒee couereden nat me; seik, and in prisoun, and ʒee visitiden nat me.'

293–4. Cp. *PPC* 595–8:

> And broþer, when bernes ben full & holly tyme passed,
> Þanne comen cursed freres & croucheþ full lowe;
> A losel, a lymitour ouer all þe lond lepeþ,
> And loke, þat he leue non house þat somwhat he ne lacche.

and cp. 'men þat trauelen þus moten take sike men & helpe hem wiþ siche goodis' (*Tractatus*, Matthew, p. 300).

295-6. Matt. xxiii. 10: 'Nether be ȝe clepid maistirs, for oon is ȝour maistre, Crist.' *maistris*: masters of arts or divinity. The friars had a great appetite for learning; the Lollard objection is summed up in *PPC* 831 f.:

> Þise maystres of dyvinitie many, als y trowe,
> Folwen nouȝt fully þe feiþ as fele of þe lewede
>
> .   .   .   .
>
> It mot ben a man of also mek an herte,
> Þat myȝte wiþ his good lijf þat Holly Gost fongen;
> And þanne nedeþ him nouȝt neuer for to studyen.

The infiltration of the regular orders into the universities was much resented by the seculars: in February 1382 Nicholas Hereford preaching at Oxford argued that any clerk who was a member of a religious order committed apostasy by taking a degree. He was applauded by his audience (including the two proctors) and the chancellor of the university refused to interfere when applied to (McFarlane, *Wycliffe*, p. 106).

297. contrarien: a favourite Lollard word, especially in the phrase to 'contrary' Christ. It probably derives from the lawyers' use of *contrarietas*, the term invented by the twelfth-century commentators on the *Digest* and the *Code*: commenting on all this material they often had to deal with an apparent *contrarietas*, which they sought to resolve (M. Deanesly, *The Significance of the Lollard Bible* (London, 1951), p. 11). Cp. the similar use of the verb at 243.

298-306. St. Francis originally intended that his order should be devoted to absolute poverty, and wholly dependent upon alms for subsistence. This was the spirit of the earliest friars, but the ideal quickly became difficult to sustain; property was acquired in the shape of converted houses, and goods in the shape of furnishings and other necessary things.

By the middle of the thirteenth century the order was split: those who would revert to the Franciscan ideal of poverty (the so-called Spirituals) on the one hand, those who argued that it was impossible on the other. The split was papered over by a legal fiction (referred to in 299-301) which settled nothing: the bull *Exiit qui seminat* (1279) confirmed the Franciscans' complete renunciation of property *in communi*, and confirmed that all property given to the order was vested in the Holy See. The controversy flared up again early in the fourteenth century, and John XXII intervened on the side of the orthodox wing with two important bulls: *Ad conditorem* (1322) abolished the ruling of 1279 and *Cum inter nonnullos* (1323) declared it a heresy to assert that Christ and the Apostles had not owned any property (W. A. Pantin, *The English Church in the Fourteenth Century* (Cambridge, 1955), pp. 123-4). See *FDR* 764-9 and *n.*, and on the whole question D. L. Douie, *The Nature and the Effect of the Heresy of the Fraticelli* (Manchester, 1932), esp. pp. 153 f.

307. Luke xiv. 13, 21: 'But whanne thou makist a feeste, clepe pore men, feble men, crokid, and blynde, and thou schalt be blessid' and 'brynge in hidur pore men, and feble, and blynde, and crokid'.

309–11. But cp. Mark vi. 7: 'And he clepide twelue, and bigan for to sende hem bi tweyne.' Daw also quotes the journeying of Paul and Barnabas (776–7) and Paul and Timothy (779).

322. *ordre* H / *orders* C. See 98 n.

322–9. The friars' reluctance to touch money and their use of *bursarii* or small boys to collect the alms given to them was a part of the general controversy over the *usus pauper* (*298–306 n.*). For the extremes to which the mendicants went to avoid handling money, see G. G. Coulton, *Five Centuries of Religion*, iii (Cambridge, 1936), 404–5, where he quotes the *De Planctu Ecclesiae* of the Spanish Franciscan Alvarez Pelayo.

324. þe cros & þe kyngis heed: on the two sides of a coin. See the puns in *PP*, B. v. 244, C. xviii. 199 f.

326–9. Luke xvi. 14–15: 'Forsoth Farisees, that weren coueytouse, herden alle thes thingis, and thei scornyden him. And he seide to hem . . . sothli God knowith ȝoure hertis.'

330–4. Cp. 'And siþ he þat steelis an oxe or a kow is dampnable by Gods lawe, and monnis also, myche more he þat steelis a monnis childe' (*Fifty Heresies*, Arnold, iii. 374); 'þes wordis tellen opinly of making of freris, hou þei comen þeefly, boþe bi water and bi lond, to robben men of her children þat ben betere þan oxen' (*Vae*, Arnold, ii. 380); see *209–11 n.*, *347–53 n.*

335. *foole hardi* H / *foolische hardy* C. C is attested by *OED* only from the sixteenth century. But cp. also *FDR* 789 *ful harde*, 1536 (sig. Bii[r]) *so hardy*.

335–41. lettris of fraternyte: letters granted (by both monks and friars) under the conventual seal to lay benefactors of a house which admitted them to brotherhood (of the third order, in the practice of the Dominicans) and imparted to the persons admitted the benefit of all the masses, fasts, prayers, and other good works done or to be done throughout the order. Such lay brethren were usually buried in the precincts of the house and were usually dressed for burial in a friar's habit. Cp. 187–90, 204–8. See *Fifty Heresies*, Arnold, iii. 377–8, *De Blasphemia*, Arnold, iii. 420 f. For 335–7 cp. 'þei graunten letters of bretherhed under hor comyne seele, þat hor breþer schal have part of alle hor gode dedes' (*De Blasphemia*, Arnold, iii. 420).

345–6. Matt. x. 8. Cp. 'but ȝif þei sillen þus þis þing, þei ben þe fendis disciplis, siþ Crist biddiþ to ȝyve freely, as þei token freely of him' (*Vae*, Arnold, ii. 382).

347–53. bigile ynnocent children: cp. the case of William Heydok, a priest in the diocese of Norwich, who entered an Augustinian friary at the age of ten and made his profession when only eleven. A year and a half later he obtained leave from the superior of his house to go to a university. In ignorance of the law he left off his habit and had himself ordained priest. He had made his profession against the will of his relatives and friends and would never have made it had he reached the years of reason. His request to remain a priest was granted (*Cal. Pap. Reg.* iv. 352, dated 31 August 1402, cited Roth, ii. 266–7). On 30 September 1402 the Great Parliament of Westminster demanded that infants should not be received into any mendicant order without the consent of parents or relatives. The Commons demanded the twenty-first year as the minimum age for reception, but the king insisted on the fourteenth. The Decree was signed by the Provincials of all four orders (*Rot. Parl. III, Annales Henrici IV*, Rolls Series 28 (3), 349, cited Roth, p. 267).

Cp. 'And so þei steelen childir fro fadir and modir, sumtyme soche as ben unable to þo ordir, and sumtyme soche as schulden susteyne hor fadir and modir by comaundement of God' (*Fifty Heresies*, Arnold, iii. 373); see further *Fifty Heresies*, Cap. xliii (Arnold, iii. 397), *209–11 n.*

349. *wille* H / *willys* C. The singular used collectively gives the best sense. For examples of this characteristic variation see 98 n.

349–51. Mark vii. 10–13: 'For Moyses seide, Worschipe thi fadir and thi modir; and he that cursith fadir or modir, die he by deeth. But ȝe seien, If a man seie to fadir or modir, Corban, that is, What euer ȝifte is of me, it schal profite to thee; and ouer ȝe suffren not hym do ony thing to fadir or modir, and ȝe breken the word of God bi ȝoure tradicioun, that ȝe han ȝouun; and ȝe don many suche thingis.'

354–7. Cp. 'freris ben moste perilouse enemyes to holy Chirche and al oure lond, for þei letten curatis of hor offis . . . Ffor if curatis diden hor offis in gode lyve and trewe prechinge, as þei ben holden upon peyne of dampnynge in helle, þer were clerkis ynowhe, of bischops, parsouns, and oþer prestis, and, in caas, over mony to þo puple' (*Fifty Heresies*, Arnold, iii. 400); 'Ffor chaunouns, munkes, and freris schulden noȝt þen have stonden in sted bot few pore prestis schulde have sufficid to þo Chirche by pure Cristis lawe' (*De Blasphemia*, Arnold, iii. 418).

In May 1418 a man was examined at Salisbury on suspicion of heresy; he possessed English books, one of which declared that a reasonable number of priests was sufficient to do the sacraments and to preach, for bastard branches and idle drones waste goods and prevent profitable preaching (J. A. F. Thomson, *The Later Lollards, 1414–1520* (Oxford, 1965), p. 27).

357–9. Wisd. xi. 21: 'But and thou hast disposid alle thingis in mesure, and in noumbre, and in weiȝte.' Cp. 'Bot feyth and kynde techis us,

þat ordir of Crist is better, and þat he ordeyned his Chirche as beste
wolde be, nouþer to myche ne to litel, bot in gode mesure. Bot þo
bastarde braunchis of þo newe ordiris spronge in wiþoute auctorite of
God' (*De Blasphemia*, Arnold, iii. 417); 'it is good & resonable men to
haue chirchis in mesure, & in numbre, & in weyhte, aftir þe hooly
trinitee' (*Tractatus*, Matthew, p. 321).

357. It is perhaps a little earnest to take Upland's complaint about
the increase in the numbers of friars too literally, but the facts do not
support him. Knowles and Hadcock in estimating the number of friars
in England between 1216 and 1540 (Appendix, p. 363) show that they
were at their highest just before the Black Death of 1350 (5,016 in all);
the Black Death reduced them by more than half (to 2,075); by 1422
they had made a modest recovery (to 2,564), and by 1500 they stood at
3,050. The Black Death reduced the number of houses from 200 to
185; in 1500 there were still 185.

359–60. Mark iii. 14. There is no scriptural authority for Upland's
fewe oþere prestis. Possibly ironical, or implying 'with a few other
priests rather than many friars'.

362. Singular *helpiþ* may be scribal, corrupted by adjacent *man*; but
more probably the subject *foure fingris & a þombe* is a collective
singular.

oon hond / a hand C. Upland seems to mean 'one hand and not the
other', and the numeral seems appropriate rather than the generalized
form of C.

363–4. *treble . . . ordris* H / *trubyll . . . lordys* C. C's confusion arises
from his attempt to accommodate the two erroneous readings.

366–7. Cp. Matt. x. 9.

366–70. Cp. 'If freris, in more spense of housyng and mete, in
clothyng, in juwels, chargen more þo puple þen Crist wiþ his apostils,
how suen þei Crist in þis maner of lyvynge?' (*De Blasphemia*, Arnold,
iii. 416); 'þei . . . haven over myche richesse, bothe in grete waste
housis, in preciouse clothis, in grete feestis, and mony jewels and
tresoure' (*Fifty Heresies*, Arnold, iii. 372). Cp. 137–9 and *n.*, 168–76
and *n.*

367. *þe apostlis* H / *crist* C. If Upland is referring to Christ's injunction
in Matt. x. 8 f. then *apostlis* is the more exact reference and therefore
preferable. C is probably the result of scribal substitution for the sake
of emphasis.

373–6. The friars laid much emphasis on scholarship and teaching,
yet they did not produce their own books, since it would have involved
them in manual rather than intellectual work. Hence they bought books

and would be in competition with the poorer seculars as Upland complains. See C. H. Talbot, 'The Universities and the Mediaeval Library', *The English Library before 1700*, ed. F. Wormald and C. E. Wright (London, 1958), pp. 74–78. Cp. 'þei robben curatis of hor offis and gostly worschip, and letten hom to knowe Gods lawe, by holdynge bokis fro hom, and wiþdrawinge of hor vauntages, by whoche þei schulden have bokes and lerne' (*Fifty Heresies*, Arnold, iii. 396–7).

377–8. Mark iv. 14.

379–82. Cp. 'Also freris schewen not to þo puple hor grete synnes stably as God biddes, and namely to myghty men of þo worlde, bot flatren hom and glosen and norischen hom in synne . . . by flatryng and fals byheestis, þei leten men lyve in hor lustis and counforten hom þerinne' (*Fifty Heresies*, Arnold, iii. 376–7); 'þei leeden prelatis, lordis and ladies, justisis and oþer men by confessioun, and tellen hom not spedily hor synnes' (*Fifty Heresies*, Arnold, iii. 385); 'þus þei . . . deceyven riche men . . . and mayntenen or counforten hom to lyve in falsenesse, ageyns Jesus Crist' (*Fifty Heresies*, Arnold, iii. 372). Cp. 79–80 and *79 n.*

383. *ordris ben* H / *order is* C. See 98 n.

383–8. Cp. *Fifty Heresies*, Cap. xix. (Arnold, iii. 381–2).

384. pouert, chastite, & obediens: cp. *FDR 262 n.*

385. *ʒoure / ʒour* H. See 177 n.

388–9. Matt. xxiii. 2–3: 'Vpon the chaier of Moyses, scribis and Pharisees seeten. Therfore kepe ʒee, and do ʒee alle thingis, what euere thingis thei shulen seie to ʒou. But nyl ʒee do after her werkis; sothely thei seien, and don nat.' Cp. 'þus freris speken bi goddis lawe, but þei don euen þe reuers, as crist seiþ of pharisees, þat þei seyen but þei don not' (*Tractatus*, Matthew, p. 306).

390 f. For the sacramental confusion that these texts afford see also *FDR 838–71* (and *838 f. n.*), *UR* 380–93 (and *380 f. n.*).

390–3. Cp. 'Also freris perverten þo right feithe of þo sacrament of þo auter, and bringen in a newe heresie . . . when holi writt seis openly þat þis sacrament is bred þat we breken, and Gods body, þei seyn þat hit is nouþer bred ne Gods body, bot accident wiþouten sugett' (*Fifty Heresies*, Arnold, iii. 378).

394–400. Matt. xxvi. 26. For Paul's words, 1 Cor. x. 16: 'and the breed which we breken, where it is not the delynge, *or part takynge*, of the body of the Lord?' For St. Augustine's teaching see Sermon ccxxxiv (Migne, *PL* xxxviii. 1116): 'Non enim omnis panis, sed accipiens benedictionem Christi, fit corpus Christi.'

Cp. 'Ffor Crist seis þat, þis bred is my body; and Seynt Poule seis, Þo bred þat we breken is þo comunycacioun of þo Lordis body;

and Seynt Austyn seis, þat þat þing þat we seen is bred . . . Lord, what schulde move Crist Almyghty, al-witty, and alle wel willynge, to hide þis byleve of freris by a thousande ȝeer, and nevere to teche his apostils and so many seyntis þo right byleve, but to teche first þese ypocrites, þat comen nevere into þo Chirche til þo foule fende Sathanas was unbounden?' (*Fifty Heresies*, Arnold, iii. 379).

395–8. & seint poul seiþ þe breed þat we breken is goddis bodi and seynt austin seiþ þat not eche breed is goddis bodi but þat breed þat reseyueþ blissynge is goddis bodi & to þis acordiþ H / *& saynt paule saith euery brede is not godes body & to þis acordith* C. C results from double homoeoteleuton caused by 396, 397 *seiþ*, 397 *goddis bodi* and 398 *goddis bodi*. I let HC *acordiþ* stand despite the plural subject because of the extensive variation found in such constructions in ME., for which see Mustanoja, pp. 62–65.

399–400. Cp. John x. 1 : 'he that cometh not in by the dore in to the fold of the scheep, but stiȝeth vp by another weye, is nyȝt thef and day thef'.

402. *chasiþ* H / *compellith* C. Although *chase* = 'to oblige, urge' is not recorded in *OED* it is attested by *MED* (*chacen* v. 5(b)) in the early fifteenth century. It is demanded by the alliteration in this 'verse' extract, as is H *chalenge* (C *declare*).

403. *þis mys* / *þat þou may* C. In association with (*a*)*mend* (as here) *mys* is part of a common ME. alliterative tag (*OED*, *miss* sb.[1] ii. 3b). FDR 894 reads *mende vs of oure mysse*.

403–4. Cp. Ps. l (RV li). 5 : 'For my wickidnesse I knowe; and my synne aȝen me is euermor.'

406. *ritis* / *rutis* H / *roottys* C. Cp. FDR 896 *Iak, oure ritis ben nouȝt rotyn, her rootis ben al freishe.*

411. H continues with a passage clearly the work of an interpolator.

jacke in þi ianglinge charite þe wa⟨nti⟩s for þou pinchist at oure pouce as a parid schrewe þis is þe leþerist lessoun þat euer ȝit j herde of lerid or of lewid ⟨da⟩ies of my lijf Seynt ffraunc⟨e⟩s ⟨curs⟩ & al foure ordris come vpon þat fals þeef þat þus þee haþ ⟨en⟩formed for þe pointis of oure priuytees he haþ prickid to þ⟨. . . . .⟩ or þou 'art'[1] apostata & proued al þis þi silf

[1] art: ?C[1].

FRIAR DAW'S REPLY

1–2. Jer. ix. 1 : 'Who shal ȝyue to myn hed watir, and to myn eȝen a welle of teres? And I shal wepe dai and nyȝt the slayne men of the doȝter of my puple.' Cp. Lydgate's poem *Quis dabit meo capiti fontem lacrimarum?* on the same text:

Who shal yeve vn-to myn hed a welle
Of bitter terys my sorwys to compleyne,
Or a gret condewit of troubly watrys ffelle
Down to dystylle fro myn Eyen tweyne.

(EETS, ES cvii (1911), 324.) It is cited by J. Sparrow, *RES*, N.S. xiv
(1963), 61, n. 1), who owes the reference (as I do) to Professor Norman
Davis. See also the opening lines of the poem on the execution of
Richard Scrope, Archbishop of York, 8 June 1405, pr. Wright,
Political Poems ii. 114–18.

5–6. Seint Ioon: St. John the Divine, from the earliest times identified
with the Apostle: see 751. *prophecie*: Rev. vi. 12–13: see *7–9 n.*
Iohel in his soth sawis: quoted by Peter, Acts ii. 20: 'The sunne schal
be turned into derknessis, and the mone into blood.' The phenomena
are an apocalyptic commonplace.

7–9. Rev. vi. 12–13: 'and the sunne is maad blak, as a sack of heyre,
and al the moone is maad as blood. And sterres of heuen fellen doun
vpon the erthe.' Cp. Rev. viii. 10: 'and a greet sterre brennynge as a
litil brond, felle fro heuene'; ix. 1: 'a sterre hadde falle doun fro
heuene in to erthe'.

9. from heuen / on erþe MS. Repetition *on erþe / to þe erþe* and the absence
of any reference to 'heaven' so prominent in the source and associated
passages (see *7–9 n.*) are suspicious. These passages argue strongly in
favour of a reading *from heuen*.

11. For the sun's twelve points see Rev. xii. 1: 'And a greet token
apperide in heuene; a womman couerid, *or clothid*, with the sunne,
and the moone vndir hir feet, and in the heed of hir a coroun of twelue
sterris.'

15. grounding of þis / ground in goddis MS. For *grounding* = 'foundation'
('chiefly in immaterial sense') see *OED*, *grounding* 1 and cp. qn. 1395:
'Cristine men ben not holden for to bileve, withouten open groundinge
of holi scripture.' False joins are a regular source of corruption in this
text; see 104, 162, 257, 460, 532, 575, 879, 892.

16. Matt. xxii. 37–39.

17. sundring / hindring MS. Brotherhood is enjoined in 16; 'sundering'
gives the sharper contrast and restores the alliteration. Cp. 138 n.

18. and: quasi-adv. (as Lat. *et*) 'besides': 'But not on account of that
[sc. the commandment] is estrangement of classes now taught besides
the pursuit of poverty that Christ has approved.'

18. Luke vi. 20.

20. 'The wheat withers together with the nourishment it affords, and
we have no food.'

20. Cp. 'þe cockil cometh fourth ere þe corne ripe . . . Thenne fadeth þe flour of þe fals cockil'. *Mum and the Sothsegger,* ed. M. Day and R. Steele, EETS, os 199 (1936), M 62, 69.

21. For Samson's revenge on the Philistines see Judges xv. 4–5.

22. John xv. 1: 'I am a verri vyne, and my fadir is an erthe tilier.'

23. Achan | achor MS. Achan stole loot from Jericho (Joshua vi), was detected at Ai, and stoned at Achor (Joshua vii); substitution of man for place is demanded by the sense.

25–26. For Dathan, Abiram, and Korah, their pretensions to the priesthood, and their destruction see Num. xvi; for *senceres,* Num. xvi–xvii f. For Korah's son see 908 where he is linked with Cain; the York *Harrowing of Hell* (ed. K. Sisam, *Fourteenth Century Verse and Prose* (Oxford, 1921), xvi) at 305 f. lists Datan and Abiron with Cain, Judas, and 'Archedefell'.

27. For Elijah's contest with the priests of Baal at the sacrifice see 3 Kings (RV 1 Kings) xviii. 20 f.

28. Cp. 2 Tim. ii. 17: 'the word of hem crepith as a canker'.

30. formyng: 'persuading, instigating' unrecorded in *OED,* but the sense is attested in other parts of the verb (*OED, form* v.[1] 2c) and in the noun *former* (*OED, former* sb.[1] 2, only the two examples from this text—30, 36—cited). *MED* does not admit the sense.

31–32. Matt. xiii. 25, 38–39.

34. Here and at 55 Daw quotes from a passage in *Upland* apparently corrupt at an early stage of transmission: see *JU* 74 n. Both *hewen* and *wede* were probably present in Daw's copy of *Upland. Hewen* makes sense only in conjunction with HC 1536 *wo(o)de.* It does not follow that *hewen* is evidence for an original *wode* and that *wede* has been introduced in the course of transmission of *FDR.* The case for it depends upon one of three assumptions: (1) scribal misreading of *wode* as *wede* in both 34 and 55; (2) scribal misreading of *wode* as *wede* at either 34 or 55 and later alteration of the other *wode* to harmonize with it; (3) conscious scribal substitution of *wede* for *wode* in both 34 and 55. Of these (1) is possible but unlikely; (2) is improbable: a 'harmonizer' would surely realize that *hewen* lends its authority to *wode* rather than *wede*; (3) involves intentional alteration of two perfectly good readings to two manifestly less good. It seems likely that *FDR* 34 and 55 are substantially accurate paraphrases of the text that Daw had in front of him as he wrote.

36. yfourmed: unusual pp. form in this text, but repeated 256

41. *leyen hem a water*: 'overcome them', 'make of no effect or value' (*OED, water* sb. i, 11c). For the same idiom cp. *PPC* 782 'leyd hire in water'.

42. *summe* (1) / *summen* MS. The antecedent of threefold *summe* is 40 *questions*. MS. *summen* may = *sum men*, scribal corruption resulting from memory of the refrain (see *42 n.*). *Supposid* probably = 'alleged' (*OED, suppose* v. 11). The syntactical type occurs again in 200.

42. A formula with a very wide currency in the fifteenth century. Cp. 'some be lewde, some all be schreude / Go schrewes wher thei goo', the refrain to a poem *Women, women, loue of women, make bare purs with some men* (pr. from MS. Lambeth 306 (*c.* 1462), EETS, os 12 (1865), 25–26, earlier by T. Wright and J. O. Halliwell, *Reliquiae Antiquae*, i. (1841), 248–9); in another version from Balliol College MS. 354 (sixteenth century) pr. R. L. Greene, *The Early English Carols* (Oxford, 1935), no. 401A (also by Wright, *Songs and Carols of the Fifteenth Century*, Percy Society, xxiii (1847), 89–91, 'from a manuscript at present in the possession of the Editor'—now Bodleian MS. Eng. poet. e. 1) the refrain is 'For sum be lewed, And sum be shrewed; Go, shrew, whersoeuer ye go'. Cp. also 'Item, but if ye make such purvyauns that my prestes be paiid, and pore men, beside other charges, and purvey mony for me beside, outher ye gader shrewdly or ellis ye spend lewdly' (John Paston I to Margaret Paston *et al.*, dated 15 January 1465, *Paston Letters*, ed. Norman Davis (Oxford, 1958), p. 40).

Greene (who also prints the Lambeth version—401B) comments: 'The two widely differing versions of this carol probably represent the activities of at least two different authors, writing to the same air and according to an easy and suggestive formula' (p. 431). It may be that its popularity (perhaps a result of the currency of the songs) made it available for a polemical Daw as for an epistolary Paston: Daw makes much use of proverbs and proverbial tags—see, e.g., 45, 94, 232, 233, 280, 336, 485, 599, 837, etc.

46 f. A dislocated passage. According to emended line numbering, MS. reads: 49, 50, 47, 48, 51, 52, etc. But 47–48 go naturally with 40–46 and 49–50 with 51–52 (in reply to *JU* 72–73). Other possible reconstructions are: 46, 48, 47, 49, 50, etc., or 47, 46, 48, 49, 50, etc.; either would provide a more orthodox syntax, but both would posit a more complicated dislocation.

51–52. Daw sophisticates: friars were exempt from episcopal jurisdiction. See *JU 72 n.*

52. Full stop after this line should perhaps be delayed until after 54. But 49–52 stand alone satisfactorily and 53–54 go more naturally with 55 f.

57. Paul praises labour in a number of places, but especially in 1 and 2 Thess. See, e.g., 1 Thess. iv. 10–11: 'Forsothe, britheren, we preyen

ʒou, that . . . ʒe worche with ʒoure hondis, as we han comaundid to ʒou.' Cp. 2 Thess. iii. 8, 10, 12; 1 Thess. ii. 9, etc.

61–62. Cp. *JU* 16–17 and *n.*

64. vexest / vexes MS. For 2 sg. pres. ind. without *-t* cp. 459 *houses þou,* 481 *menys þe,* 507 *wounders þat,* 690 *wil þou,* 775 *herdes þou,* 922, 932 *shal þou.* Only here are the conditions for loss (*-t* before *þ-*) wanting.

73. sorowe & shendship: collective singular.

74. growe: strong pp. without *-n* unusual in this text, but cp. 589 *take.*

75. þe seuen sacramentes: traditionally Baptism, Confirmation, the Eucharist, Penance, Extreme Unction, Order, and Matrimony; they were enumerated by Peter Lombard, *Sentences,* Bk. 4, dist. i, num. 2.

76. wil / willen MS. No other example in the text of this auxiliary with *-n.* It is possible that one should read *wel* after *JU* 82 *paien wele.*

84–85. See *JU 83 n.*

88. Fiton: 'a familiar or possessing spirit; also, one possessed by such a spirit and acting as its mouthpiece' (*OED, python²*). Cp. Deut. xviii. 11: 'nether a man take counsel at hem that han a feend spekynge in the wombe' (Vulg. 'nec qui pythones consulat'); and Isa. xix. 3: 'and thei schulen axe her symylacris, and her false diuinouris, and her men that han vncleene spiritis spekinge in the wombe' (Vulg. 'pythones et ariolos').

89. þi god is a slepe: Elijah mocked his opponents thus in the contest referred to in 27. See 3 Kings (RV 1 Kings) xviii. 27.

92. Balames asse: Num. xxii. 28–30, cp. *JU 261–2 n.*

93. marren / marrer MS. Daw may have imported the proper noun from *JU* 85.

101–4. The pedagogic metaphors are clear in general outline but obscure in detail: *forme* = 'course of exercises leading to a degree' (*OED, form* sb. i, 11 c), *chaier* an allusion to the lecturer's seat in the schools. The references to a *lowe* chair and *rounde rollis* probably imply that the women's instruction was not religious but amorous. Daw's capacity for imaginative coarseness is clear from 126.

103. perfit / perfit in ʒour lawe MS. Hypermetrical; *in ʒour lawe* probably interpolated because the first half-line imputes a moral perfection that in the eyes of the orthodox no Lollard could lay claim to.

104. call on men for þer / callen hem forþ her MS. Sense and syntax are awkward; the emendations improve both. For *sister,* an exclamation used to attract attention, or for emphasis = 'seest thou! look!' (chiefly

Northern), see *English Dialect Dictionary, seesta*. There is another possible example of gen. *þer(e)* in 130.

105. þe castels of Caym: see *JU 86 n*.

109–11. For Solomon's temple see 3 Kings (RV 1 Kings) vi–viii. Daw's defence of the friars' sumptuous churches is based on Solomon's example and such texts as Exod. xxv. 8, 1 Chron. xxii. 11.

114–15. Perhaps a conflation of Matt. v. 16: 'So shyyne 3oure li3t before men, that thei see 3oure good werkis', and Matt. vii. 20: 'Therfore of her fruytis 3ee shulen knowe hem.' Cp. 623, *UR* 17, 107.

121. Matt. xxiii. 23.

122. Cp. Matt. vi. 16: 'But when 3ee fasten, nyl 3e be maad as ypocritis sorweful, for thei putten her facis out of *kyndly* termys, that thei seme fastynge to men.'

123. Matt. xxiii. 27: 'Woo to 3ou, scribis and Pharisees, ipocritis, that ben lic to sepulcris maad whijt, the whiche with outen forth semen faire to men; sothely with ynne thei ben ful of boonys of dead men, and al filthe.'

124. Cp. Eph. iv. 14: 'we ben not now litile children, mouynge as wawis, and be borun aboute with al wynd of techinge', and also Matt. xi. 7, Jas. i. 6, Jude vv. 12–13.

125–6. Perhaps the conscious adaptation of an image with which Daw—if, as seems likely, he was a Dominican—would be very familiar: the coat of arms of the Dominican order is a dog with a flaming torch in its mouth, and the image commemorates the prophetic dream of Dominic's mother before his birth. See, e.g., the seal of the Dominican Provincial of Scotland dated 1519: a full-length figure of Dominic with crucifix, behind him a dog running with a firebrand (W. de G. Birch, *Catalogue of Seals in the Department of Manuscripts in the British Museum*, iv (London, 1895), no. 15461). See also E. Mâle, *The Gothic Image* (London, repr. 1961), pp. 293–4.

126. *3our*(1) / *3ou* MS. For *3ou* as possessive see *OED you* iii. 8; three examples only are cited, two from a single book dated 1642, one from Elworthy's *West Somerset Word-Book* (1888). Cp. also *yow beche* = 'your bitch' in the Cely letters (A. Hanham, *MÆ*, xxvi (1957), 188). The same error is corrected in 103.

128. *crepith / crepit* MS. The first of four 3 sg. pres. inds. in -*t*; three (*crepit*, 135 *myng^t*, 137 *induct*) in the space of ten lines, *ow^t* at 445. 135 *myng^t*, 445 *ow^t* suspended on pattern of *with*; *crepit, induct* not suspended, probably represent uncertainty of scribal usage, *inducit* reinforced by Lat. *inducit*.

129. From here to 209 is a summary of Rev. viii–xi, interspersed with Daw's glosses.

134–5. *noieþ ... myngid / he noieþ ... he myngith* MS. The threefold *he* is syntactically clumsy and the clumsiness owes nothing to the source, Rev. viii. 7. I omit 134 *he* on the analogy of the same construction in 142 and 159; *myngid* is supported by the source (Vulg. *mixta, WV* 1 *mengid*).

136. *by þe tokenyng*: probably a version of 'by the same token' in the sense 'for the same reason', 'in the same way' (*OED, token* sb. 15).

138. *sunderers / hinderers* MS. 139–41 gloss 138, but not clearly. At 649 f. a parallel passage begins *Heresie þat is Grw is diuisioun on Latyn / Þe whiche in oure langage meneþ sunderyng, & partyng*, and *sunderyng* restores sense to 138–41. *OED* has *sunderer* only from nineteenth century, but *sunder* from OE., *sunderance, sundering* from ME. Cp. 17 n.

140. loue daies: in popular and literary writing any meeting of contending parties for the purpose of settling their dispute might be called a 'loveday'. It was used for private settlements out of court (but so called only in the records of the humblest); less frequently for regular cases of arbitration in which the court took an active interest; and for the settlement of all kinds of private and public quarrels, from the vicar's pacification of scolding women to treaty-making on the borders. The making of lovedays was not a monopoly of churchmen: private friends or public officials might undertake the office of peacemaker (J. W. Bennett, 'The Mediaeval Loveday', *Speculum*, xxxiii (1958), 351–70).

141. *we / ȝe* MS. Since Daw argues at length that Lollards are destroyers of social harmony, it is unlikely that he would allow them credit for trying to repair the damage once done.

151. *wiþ men / wiþinne?* MS. Abbreviation mark misplaced, but the scribe probably intended *wiþinne*. It makes odd sense in the context; before a plural object *wiþ* can mean 'among' (*OED, with* ii. 11 = *among* A. 6) which is preferable to 'within' in any of its senses.

157. Maximine: Maximinus, Arian Bishop of Hippo Regius, debated with Augustine on the subject of the Trinity, A.D. 427–8. Augustine wrote against him *Collatio cum Maximino* and *Contra Maximinum* (Migne, *PL* xlii. 709–42, 743–814). *Maniche*: it is doubtful whether Daw has Mani or his doctrines in mind here; he uses the name (as so often in the Middle Ages) as a catchword to express disapprobation. At 334–5, however (see *n.*), a more exact reference is probable.

162. *scricheth / westheth* MS. The corruption results from misjoining of original *ve scricheth*. 'Screech' (*OED, scritch* v.) is used from early ME. of the crying of birds.

170. *fift / first* MS. See Rev. ix. 1.

174. *lioun / a lioun* MS. For omission of indefinite article in similes where the second element is sg. cp. 173 *þei stongen as scorpioun*, 187 *ȝe ben toþed as lioun*. The usage owes nothing to the source (Rev. ix. 3–10), which is overwhelmingly plural. Cp. 222 n.

188. *þe / ȝour* MS. The clumsy construction may result from scribal introduction of possessive *ȝour*, encouraged by the sequence 183 *ȝe ben lyke scorpions*, 185 *ȝe ben also lich horses*, 187 *ȝe ben toþed as lioun*, in place of *þe* found in parallel constructions 176 *þe smorþering smoke is*, 179 *þe breses ben*.

190. *but*: probably = 'yet, however' and explained by the author's awareness of the uneasy consonance between the two parts of his allegory of the *haburions*. In 188–9 they are made from crafty devices and cunning tricks designed to trap innocent souls: yet (190) they are also made from iron, signifying obstinacy.

192. *at þe sixt / In þe siȝt of* MS. See Rev. ix. 13–14.

194. *þridde / ferþe* MS. See Rev. ix. 15, 18, and 198 below.

197–204. A confused, and I suspect corrupt, passage:

(1) at 195 the four angels signify *foure general synnes*. At 197 these are identified as *cediciouns supersticions þe glotouns & þe proude*. Substitution of personal *þe glotouns & þe proude* for the abstract sins implied by 195 *general*, and in contrast with preceding *cediciouns supersticions* and 199 *envie, pride*, and *leschry*, is awkward. It may be that in 197 original *glotony* and *pride* have been corrupted by the idea of personal agency contained in 196. But 202 *þe perfit, þe yuel* show that the idea of such agency was in Daw's mind, and it seems unlikely that corruption is here the result of anticipation.

(2) in the MS. 201 stands after 197 in the form *poerte preamblis to presse aforne anticristis comyng*; *presse* results from alteration of original *preise(n)*. The sense of the line is difficult to reconcile with its context, but if original *preisen* (='appraise, assess') is allowed to stand, and the line inserted after 200, it restores significance to the line itself and improves the sense of two otherwise uneasy passages. Translate 'four general sins established . . . to kill the third part of men with three deadly darts . . . since some are perfect, others wicked and others fickle, poverty comes in advance of Antichrist to appraise: the perfect won't be harmed, the wicked already are, etc.'

(3) MS. *þ'* in 198 I take as *þre* rather than *þer*; the possessive is possible, but *her* is the dominant form in the text, *þer(e)* occurring only at 130 (a doubtful case) and 104 (emendation). 'Three' refers to the envy, pride, and lechery of 199 which represent the three plagues of Rev. ix. 18—the *fiyr smoke and brymstone* of 194.

205. *voises in heuen seide | noise in heuen was made* MS. Cp. Rev. xi. 15 'And the seventh angel sounded; and there followed great voices in heaven, and they said, The kingdom of the world, etc.' The generalized reading of the MS. is slightly uncomfortable with the following 'that' clause.

207–9. An unusual concessive construction: dependent precedes non-dependent clause, *rengne* required in both clauses appears only in the second. Its omission in the first clause may be scribal.

210. *dubby*: unrecorded *OED*; *MED*, *dubben* 3 (d) (only this example cited) suggests 'to deal falsely with (Scripture), misinterpret'; but the sense required is 'dabble, meddle, tamper'.

210–15. For the convention of simulated ignorance cp. *PPC* 845–7:

> But, for y am a lewed man paraunter y miȝte
> Passen par auenture & in som poynt erren,
> Y will nouȝt þis matere maistrely auowen.

212–13. A curious figure, the evidence for which is scanty. *OED*, *windmill* 2 gives the first element attributive meaning 'a sign or character resembling [a windmill], as a cross or asterisk', providing only two other passages (dated 1581, 1898) in support. *ODEP* (p. 346) cites the passage as a proverb meaning 'entirely illiterate', but recording no other occurrence of the A/windmill comparison, and the B/bull's foot comparison not again until 1721. While the general sense is not in doubt, the precise significance of the comparisons remains obscure.

215. *priuy processe*: presumably the Revelation narrative paraphrased and glossed 129–209.

222. *wallis | þe wallis* MS. The uncorrected reading makes good sense and in its omission of the definite article is parallel to 227 *cam in to crede*. Cp. 174 n.

227–8. *iudicare*: see F. L. Utley, 'How Judicare Came in the Creed', *Mediaeval Studies*, viii (1946), 303–9, for a list of occurrences of the phrase and a full (though not wholly conclusive) discussion of its meaning. Utley misinterprets 225–6: 'the threat of Friar Daw Topias that the impatient Lollard Jack Upland will too soon find what Judgement can mean, while Topias himself is sitting comfortably at Christ's own side and laughing at Jack's plight' (p. 309); in 225–6 Daw is not speaking *in propria persona* but quoting *JU* 99–100.

229. Patience is masculine here, as is Charity in 465. Cp. also *PP*, B. xiii. 46–47.

229–30. Isa. xiv. 12.

231. *suposis* / *suposer* MS. For *-er* suspension instead of *-is* cp. 255, 670; for *-s* in 3 sg. cp. 201 *preamblis*, 869 *susteynes*.

232-3. For these two proverbs cp. (1) Chaucer, *Troilus*, i. 809 'Unknowe, unkist, and lost, that is unsought', Gower, *CA*, ii. 467 'And for men sein unknowe unkest', (2) *Troilus*, ii. 859-61 'swich manere folk, I gesse . . . Thei speken, but thei benten nevere his bowe'.

239-43. Daw alludes to the doctrine of the double procession of the Holy Ghost, according to which the Holy Ghost proceeds from the Father and the Son together. See *ODCC*, art. 'Double Procession of the Holy Ghost.'

243. *proceding*: many sixteenth-century examples in *OED*, only one (Paston) from the fifteenth, and in the special sense 'the taking of a university degree'. *OED* records sense 'coming, issuing forth' only from 1587 (*OED, proceeding* 5—also of the Holy Ghost). See *239-43 n.*

247-9. The 'organic' theory of society is a commonplace of medieval political thought. Its most famous development is probably that in Bk. 5, Ch. 2 of John of Salisbury's *Polycraticus*, where he states that the priesthood is the soul of the body (ed. C. C. J. Webb (Oxford, 1909), i. 282-3). Aquinas expresses Daw's point succinctly: 'potestas saecularis subditur spirituali, sicut corpus animae' (*Summa*, ii. 2, q. 60, art. 6, ad. 3). *decre*: that of Innocent III, c. 6, X, De maioritate, I, 33 (Friedberg, *Corpus*, ii. 196-8). *comoun lawe*: the general law of the Church as distinct from local laws made for a particular restricted purpose. For a full summary of the 'organic' theory and its several varieties see O. Gierke, *Political Theories of the Middle Age*, tr. F. W. Maitland (Cambridge, 1900), pp. 22 f.

248. With this line the scribe abandons verse lineation and until 257 writes continuously as prose with a double virgule to show line-division; from 258 to 346 he uses verse lineation again (except for 267 and 277); from 347 to the end as prose.

250-3. For a comprehensive defence of the religious see Aquinas, *Contra Impugnantes Dei Cultum et Religionem* (Opusculum xix). He mentions canons, monks, and Knights Templar (but not friars) together in Part One, Chapter II (see *Opuscula Theologica* ii, ed. R. M. Spiazzi, (Rome, 1954), par. 33). Chapter I of the same work is entitled 'Quid sit religio, et in quo perfectio religionis consistat'; such 'perfection' is the subject of Upland's first question (101-2) and the present passage is part of Daw's reply to it, which begins at 236.

255. *manniskynde* / *manere kyndes* MS. That Daw should count all types of communities or orders is not impossible (*telle* here = 'say'); that he should count all mankind is.

257. *bi tweyne & two | betwene two & two* MS. That Daw refers to the intrinsic harmony (*ordre* = 'harmonious arrangement') of a group of two rather than to that between two and two seems clear from Upland's questioning at 309–11 of the friars' habit of begging in pairs. The syntactical type 'by two and two' = 'in twos, in pairs' is a common one. But I offer the emendation with reservations: the MS. reading may refer to the four orders of 85.

261. *ensaumple*: quasi-adverbial with ellipsis of the verb—'see for example'.

262. *obedience, chastite, & pouerte*: the traditional three counsels of perfection. They are not *combined* anywhere in Christ's teaching. There seems to be no direct teaching of Jesus on obedience; on chastity in the sense of celibacy there is possible support in Matt. xix. 12: 'sunt eunuchi, qui se ipsos castrauerunt propter regnum caelorum'; and cp. 1 Cor. vii. 32. On poverty there is much more—see especially Mark x. 23–30.

263. *hope*: 'think, suppose' (*OED, hope* v. 4).

265–6. *þe postle*: John, 1 John ii. 16: 'Forwhi al thing that is in the world, is coueytise of flesch, and coueytise of iȝen, and pride of lijf.'

271. *Iacke boy*: *OED (Jack-boy)* 'a boy employed in menial work'. But Daw is simply addressing Upland by his Christian name as in 270 and employing *boy* in the contemptuous or abusive sense common in ME. E. J. Dobson, 'The Etymology and Meaning of *Boy*', *MÆ*, ix (1940), 121–54 (also *MÆ*, xii (1943), 71–76), does not list this example.

271–2. Probably a reference to Jas. i. 27, which Daw paraphrases at 314 f.

273. *yee | þee* MS. Cp. *JU* 114–16: *Approueþ Crist ony mo religiouns þan oon þat Synt Iame techiþ vs? If þou seist ȝhe, tel þou now in Cristis lawe where it is.*

275. *rewlis*: *JU* 117 (*Cristis*) *rule* = 'code of discipline' but here = 'principle regulating conduct'. Elsewhere Daw is careful to keep the distinction of meaning: 114 *rewle* = 'principle', 348, 407, 602 *reule* = 'code of regulations'. See also *JU* 111 n., *118–19 n.*

275–6. Possibly Luke xvi. 19–31, the parable of Dives and Lazarus, in which it is implied that damnation is the penalty of riches in this world.

280. *þee | þe* MS. The personal pronoun makes better sense than the instrumental of comparison. Only here and 527 has 2 sg. acc. or dat. single *e*.

280–1. Cp. 'What should we (quoth I) grease the fat sow in thars', *ODEP* (p. 263) from 1550 (Heywood). But see the Wakefield *Abel* (ed. A. C. Cawley, *The Wakefield Pageants in the Towneley Cycle* (Manchester, 1958), ll. 64–65): 'Go grese thi shepe vnder the toute / For that is the moste lefe.' I owe this reference to Professor Norman Davis.

282. *pistle | pistles* MS. James wrote only one epistle. Daw's plural may include the speech of St. James in Acts xv with its close parallels, but more probably it is a copyist's slip.

282 f. Jas. i. 27. See also 271–2, 314 f. Martha and Mary, Peter and John, Rachel and Leah are traditional pairs and types of the active and contemplative life. The classical exposition of the Two Lives is in Gregory, *Homil. in Ezechielem* II. ii. 8–11 (Migne, *PL* lxxvi. 953–5); cp. also *Moral.* vi. 56–61 (*PL* lxxv. 760–5), *Hom. in Ezech.* I. iii. 9–12 (*PL* lxxvi. 809–11).

Cp. Richard de Bury (*Philobiblon* v, par. 75) where, mentioning Martha and Mary, Rachel and Leah, he describes the labour of copying books as a union of the active and contemplative lives. Thomas there questions the usual assumption that the distinction between the Two Lives is based on Jas. i. 27; he suggests that it is more likely to have been derived from Aristotle, and cites Aquinas, *Summa* ii. 2, q. 179 f.

287–9. 'These lives are founded on love by diverse classes of people, by men who, establishing separate orders as a consequence of their vows, and affording us a manifest example, may teach us the Christian life.'

300–1. Ps. cxxxii (RV cxxxiii). 1: 'Lo! hou good and hou myrie *it is*; that britheren dwelle togidere.'

301. *se | siþ* MS. Ps. cxxxii. 1 has *ecce*.

303. For the community between the Apostles and all believers in their witness see Acts iv. 32: 'Forsoth of the multitude of men bileuynge ther was oon herte and oon soule', and also Acts ii. 42, iv. 35–37, v. 12.

312–13. Gen. xxviii. 12. The angels in Jacob's vision, alternating between heaven and earth, participate both in the active and the contemplative life. For the contemplative life enhanced by participation in the active see Gregory, *Hom. in Ezech.* II. ii. 15 (Migne, *PL* lxxvi. 957–8), *Regula Pastoralis* ii. 5 (*PL* lxxvii. 32–34), *Epp.* I. xxv (*PL* lxxvii. 468–79); for the union of the two especially appropriate in preachers see Gregory, *Moral.* vi. 56 (*PL* lxxv. 760–1), xxviii. 33 (*PL* lxxvi. 467).

314–21. An extended paraphrase of Jas. i. 27. See also 271–2, 282 f.

323. *not*: *JU* 120–1 reads *& ȝeue hem no þing aȝen.* *OED* (*not* ii, sb. 12) records the substantive use of *not* 'nought, nothing' between Wyclif and the early sixteenth century. So again 860.

328–9. Possibly corrupt. *Sweten* best taken as infinitive of 'sweat' = 'to suffer severely' (*OED, sweat* v. ii. 8): 'it is unnecessary to tell you what we give to the poor, for an act of charity ought to be secret and since it [sc. the act of charity = what we give] will suffer severely at your hands [i.e. come into your possession]'.

328–9. Matt. vi. 3–4: 'But whanne thou doist almes, knowe not thi left hond what thi riʒt hond doith, that thin almes be in hidils.'

332. *hem* / *him* MS. Paraphrasing *JU* 125 f. Daw keeps 2 pl. *ʒe* (330) used by Upland. For Upland's sgs. 125 *abite*, 126 *man, wijf, man,* Daw substitutes pls. 330 *abitis,* 331 *men, wyues,* 332 *þei*; but sg. *him* suggests that Daw's readings are editorial and not original in the text of *Upland* he is paraphrasing. See also Introduction, p. 33 and n.

334–5. Maniches errours: the ethic of the various Christian Dualist sects comprehensively known in the Middle Ages as Manichees, held that marriage and generation were crimes; but it disapproved of marriage more than of casual sexual intercourse, since the latter constitutes merely one isolated sin, the former a state of sin. Such a doctrine can obviously degenerate into a licence for casual promiscuity and unnatural vice, and those believers who did not proceed to full initiation in the Dualist faith made good use of it. In the West especially, far from the Eastern centres of the heresy, such garbled ideas were popular. As early as 1157 Archbishop Samson of Reims complained that Manichaeanism was being disseminated throughout his diocese by itinerant weavers who condemned marriage and encouraged sexual promiscuity. Their presence was discovered by the refusal of a girl to submit to the attentions of a young cleric. Such chastity was considered ominous, and the girl, when questioned, admitted that she believed virginity to be obligatory. Three years later they appeared in England, denying Baptism, Marriage, the Eucharist, and Catholic unity. Hence, throughout the Middle Ages, Manichees in Western Europe were associated with orgiastic obscenity (S. Runciman, *The Medieval Manichee* (Cambridge, 1947), pp. 121–2). See also *157 n.*

336. Probably adapted from Prov. vii. 19: 'For *myn* hosebonde is not in his hows; he is goon a ful long weie.' The Proverbs context suits the sense. Cp. also the poem against the friars (Wright, *Political Poems,* i. 264):

> For when the gode man is fro hame,
> And the frere comes to oure dame,
> He spares nauther for synne ne shame,
> That he ne dos his wille.

343. *mowe* / *mowe we* MS. UR's correction is unnecessary: a subject pronoun need not be expressed in ME. where it has been expressed in

a previous oblique case; or *mowe* may be a reduced form of *mow we*. 'And so we are able to commit apostasy in our souls, our religious habits notwithstanding.'

345. forme/former MS. 495, 852 *former* support the correction; but *forme* 'first, primeval' had a limited and declining currency in the fifteenth century.

345. 2 Cor. xi. 14: 'sothli he Sathanas transfygurith him into an aungel of ly3t'.

360. tipet: apparently the remnant of a scarf (*chaperon*) used to fasten a padded cap (*bourrelet*) to the shoulder of gowns and robes. See W. N. Hargreaves-Mawdsley, *A History of Academical Dress in Europe Until the End of the Eighteenth Century* (Oxford, 1963), p. 195 and fig. 11 (p. 192). Mr. Hargreaves-Mawdsley declares other uses of the term to be incorrect. But *UR* 183–4 suggests that it was also used to bind the head in some way; see also *CT*, A.3953.

362. MS. adds: *þe pokes of purchace hangen to þe erþe*, 'the extravagant long sleeves, the fruit of begging, hang to the ground'. But (1) richness of dress was not a Lollard vice, 360, 364–5 notwithstanding; (2) the accusation of begging is odd; Lollardy drew its support not from the abjectly poor but from the moderately prosperous class of artisans. See Daw's catalogue 865–7 and McFarlane, *Wycliffe*, p. 180. The imputation of 328–9 (if I understand them correctly— see 328–9 n.) cannot discount the weight of historical evidence; (3) the line spoils the balance of 362–3 and is difficult to reconcile with their sense. On the other hand such sartorial extravagance was much practised by the regular religious and was the object of attack throughout the fourteenth and fifteenth centuries. It may be that this is a piece of Lollard marginalia induced by indignation at 360–6 (perhaps with original *þi* for *þe*), subsequently incorporated into the text.

369. fremde/frende MS. A common ME. collocation; see *MED*, *fremed* (b). For the same error cp. *PT* 626—there in rhyme.

370. faire cloiþ of Salomons table: I know of no scriptural support.

371. Matt. xxii. 11–12.

374. Matt. v. 10–11: 'Blessid *be* thei that suffren persecucioun for ri3twisnesse, for the kyngdam of heuenes is herun. 3ee shulen be blessid, when men shulen curse 3ou, and shulen pursue 3ou, and shulen say al yuel a3eins 3ou lee3ing, for me'; cp. Heb. xi. 26, 1 Pet. iv. 14.

380. þe knottide girdil: after his conversion St. Francis girded himself with a rough cord in memory of the cords with which Christ had been bound during his Passion, and a white girdle with three knots came subsequently to form part of the Franciscan habit.

383. greye clopis: the traditional colour for the clothing of the lower classes (and that considered socially appropriate) in the Middle Ages was grey or black (see G. F. Jones, 'Sartorial Symbols in Mediaeval Literature', *MÆ*, xxv (1956), 66). Walsingham describes the itinerant preachers as *vestibus de russeto* (*Historia Anglicana*, ed. H. T. Riley, i (Rolls Series, 1863), 324). Cp. *PP*, B. xv. 162–3: '[Charite] . . . is as gladde of a goune of a graye russet / As of a tunicle of Tarse or of trye scarlet'.

385. Matt. vii. 15.

389–92. (1) *Esttacens sciens* etc.: Ecclus. xx. 6–7. (2) *Tempus tacendi* etc.: Eccles. iii. 7. (3) *Sicut urbs* etc.: Prov. xxv. 28. See also *UR* 198–9.

395. blundir ȝe / vndur ȝou MS. The emendation restores sense and alliteration if *blundir* is taken figuratively to mean 'misinterpret' (cp. l. 5 of the first interpolation *UR* 349 n.): 'and if, despite God's grace, you both misinterpret, you will go very badly astray'.

404–5. As early as the Council of Aix (817) it was decreed that monks should not eat outside the refectory. Thus, in the English *Regularis Concordia* of the tenth century it is stated that of those who dwell in a monastery, 'neither the abbot himself nor any of the brethren shall eat or drink outside the refectory except in the case of sickness' ('extra refectorium nec ipse abbas nec fratrum quispiam nisi causa infirmitatis manducet uel bibat'), *Regularis Concordia*, ed. T. Symons (London, 1953), p. 62.

406. meuest: the lack of distinction between *u* and *n* in this text is especially troublesome in the verbal homographs *meue / mene, moue / mone*. 809, 838 *moue / mone* probably = 'move' rather than 'moan' (despite apparent support from *JU* 1–2): *OED* (*moan* v.) doubts whether 'moan' as a verb is found before the sixteenth century.

Meue / mene are possible alternatives at eleven places. At 81, 358, 360, 381, 481, 646, 650, 808, *mene* 'to signify' is certainly intended, probably also at 250. At 406, 698 'signify' is impossible and 'move' rather than 'complain' (see *OED, mean* v.²) is probably intended since (1) the constructions in 406, 698, and those in 809, 838 where *moue* has been admitted are very similar, (2) 'move a matter' is a common idiom (see *OED, move* v. i. 14, 15b).

408–9. Lines separated by virgule after *op*, probably by a corrector. The emended division improves the metre.

426–9. 2 Cor. vi. 9: *Quasi morientes et ecce viuimus*. The rest of the quotation is from the interlinear gloss traditionally ascribed to Anselm of Laon.

435–7. Matt. xvii. 1–9.

439–40. Matt. xx. 17–19.

447–8. Cp. Prov. x. 19: 'In myche speche shal not lacke synne; who forsothe temperth his lippis, is most prudent.' A common Wisdom idea: see, e.g., Prov. xiii. 3, xxi. 23, xii. 13, xviii. 21, xxx. 32.

456. *shepen*: for the erroneous association with 'sheep' see *OED*, *shippon*. Again 401 *shipun*.

458. *best* / *bestes* MS. *-s* represented by flourish used by UR for *-s* in *FDR* 625 *freres*, and *-ur-* in 727 *clamourus*. The correction is unnecessary: *Þe bestes stond keuered* echoes 456, and 457–8 anticipate 459. MS. *best* taken absolutley 'people of highest rank' *MED, best* adj. as n. 1 (a)), hence 'the rich', gives satisfactory sense: it provides a sharp antithesis to 457 and allows 459 its full rhetorical value.

460. *I* / *is* MS. The passive is clumsy. Daw probably refers to 367 which 461 echoes. The sense of 461 is 'if you answer my question you answer your own'.

462. *couentis* / *coueitise* MS. Cp. 464 *couentis*. For the same error see 474.

465. Cp. 3.

470–2. The Tower of London, the palaces of Windsor and Westminster, the castle of Wallingford, and the manors of Woodstock, Sheen, Hertford, and Eltham were all royal residences at the end of the fourteenth and in the early fifteenth centuries.

474. *couentis passen* / *couetise passiþ* MS. Upland's charge is *ȝe maken ȝou courtis passinge lordis* (173–4).

477–80. See *JU 177 n.*

481–2. Daw here refers to the Hospitals of St. Thomas of Acre (or Acon) in Cheapside, St. Anthony in Threadneedle Street, and St. Mary Rouncivall at Charing Cross. Both St. Mary Rouncivall and St. Thomas of Acre seemed to have derived a large part of their income from the collection of alms; the latter shared with the Knights Templar the right to collect alms in churches once a year, and this must have been especially profitable after the suppression of the Templars in 1312. In 1397 the Pope issued a mandate to the bishops of England and Ireland ordering them to recommend to the people of their dioceses those seeking alms for the Hospital of St. Anthony, and not to extort anything from them or to hinder them in any way. As late as 1537 an agent of St. Anthony's was raising money by collecting offerings and selling hallowed bells for cattle (*VCH, London,* i. 491–5, 581–5).

Such indulgences must have been especially resented by the friars, and that Daw's indignation was justified is clear from regulations passed by Convocation in St. Paul's in 1424: pardoners were henceforth forbidden to proclaim indulgences except on behalf of the House of St. John's, St. Anthony's, or the Hospital of St. Thomas the Martyr at Rome (Wilkins, *Concilia*, iii. 429).

485. Proverbial? Cp. *Troilus*, v. 502–5:

> Quod Troilus, 'Now Lord me grace sende,
> That I may fynden, at myn hom-comynge
> Criseyde comen!' and therwith gan he synge.
> 'Ye, haselwode!' thoughte this Pandare.

and *Troilus*, iii. 890, v. 1174.

486. The apparently uneasy construction *paye ȝe to no taliage* is confirmed by 480 *to taken it to tax*, 492–3 *preesthode shulde not paien / to tax ne to taliage*. See *493 n.*

486–7. Matt. xxii. 21.

488–91. John xviii. 33 f.

493. to tax ne to taliage: this alliterative formula is an example of one of a number of stylistic devices widely used in English wills, charters, writs, and other legal instruments from very early times. For a discussion of the Anglo-Saxon appetite for such jingles see F. E. Harmer, *Anglo-Saxon Writs* (Manchester, 1952), pp. 85–92.

494–6. There is no scriptural authority for Daw's claim that Pharaoh gave the priests concessions during the bondage in Egypt: Artaxerxes did this in the time of Ezra. See 1 Esdras (RV Ezra) vii. 24: 'Also we make knowun to ȝou of alle the preestis . . . that ȝe han not power to put on hem tol, and tribute, and costis for keperis of the lond.'

497–8. Lam. i. 1: 'prince of prouynces mad is vnder tribute'. *Ieremye*: Jeremiah.

499. þe comun lawe: probably the bull *Clericis laicos* of Boniface VIII, 1296 (c. 3, in VI°, De immunitate, III, 23; Friedberg, *Corpus*, ii. 1062–3) asserting the complete immunity of the clergy from taxation by the state unless levied with papal permission, on threat of excommunication.

500. mot paye but bi / may paye bi MS. The sense is that the clergy are taxed not because the law allows that they must pay but because their superiors have agreed to it. See *499 n.*

502. Marginal *persouns* is probably a correction for *perilous* (a caret stands before *perilous* but no cancellation), marginal *pur-* in the same hand a miswriting.

502–4. Convocation of Canterbury, 3 October 1419, levied a noble from chaplains of parochial chantries (*annuellers*) of seven marks annual value and upwards. See Introduction, pp. 10 f.

505. 'There is no honour in begging from beggars.' Intransitive use of 'worship' unrecorded *OED*.

508. *ʒour lettris* / *ʒour* MS. Gap after *ʒour*, no erasure; ?ditto mark centrally placed. Cp. 169, 898 for other scribal lacunae. It may be that the scribe's copy was defective in all three places. From *JU* 187–90 (paraphrased here) *lettris* can be supplied with some confidence.

510. See *UR 234 n.*

512. *blake bedes*: probably 'wicked prayers'. *OED* allows *black* a figurative sense only from 1581, but *MED* the sense 'wicked' from the late fourteenth century. But Daw may refer to the beads of the rosary on which the *pater noster* was usually represented by every eleventh bead, of a different size and material from the rest. Cp. Gower, *CA*, viii. 2904–5.

527. *þee* / *þe* MS. See 280 n.

532. *I ne* / *me ne* MS. The impersonal construction with *wote* resulting from the correction is difficult. *Wote* is regularly constructed with the nominative (as in 533), and it seems better to assume corruption of an original *I ne*.

533–4. Matt. ix. 20 f.

541–3. Matt. xix. 16–22, esp. v. 21.

544–8. *þe same gospel*: probably Matthew, the one the medieval Church knew best. See Matt. x. 37 f. Only Matthew's account contains *worþi*; *his lond and his tenementes* does not occur in any of the sayings that resemble this.

545. *forsake* / *forsakeþ* MS. The sense requires the subjunctive rather than the indicative resulting from UR's correction.

550–1. John xv. 16: 'Ʒe han not chosun me, but I chees ʒou; and I haue put ʒou, that ʒe go, and brynge fruit, and ʒoure fruit dwelle.'

554–7. Matt. xviii. 15–17.

556. MS. *vndirmyn*: a miswriting occasionally found in fifteenth-century texts (see *OED*, *undermine* v.).

560. Ps. vii. 16: 'A lake he openede, and dalf it out; and fel in to the dich that he made.' A commonplace: see, e.g., Ps. ix. 15, lvii. 6; Prov. xxvi. 27, xxviii. 10; Eccles. x. 8, etc.

568. *boþe* / *be* MS. The MS. may represent the earlier form *beie* / *bo*, but elsewhere *boþe* is invariable. The construction with more than two nouns is attested from Chaucer.

575. *haue þei | haueþ* MS. *goldsmythis* can hardly be a collective singular, nor (in this text) *haueþ* a Southern plural. Cp. 879 n.

575. One Goldsmith (and presumably of that craft) was amongst eight accused of heresy at Leicester during the visitation by the metropolitan Courtenay of the diocese of Lincoln in 1389 (McFarlane, *Wycliffe*, p. 139). Peter Payne, Principal of St. Edmund Hall, a zealous upholder of Wyclifian principles, was forced to flee England for Bohemia, probably in 1413, to avoid a martyr's death. At the Council of Basle in 1433 one Partridge, himself a lapsed Lollard, taxed him with this and he admitted that he had fled with the retort 'Well, you may so if you like; but you were yourself once upon a time a smith of our craft' ('Bene, inquit, vultis sic, vos fuistis antiquus faber nostrae artis'). Peter of Zatéc, *Mon. Conc. Gen. Saec. XV*, i. 335, quoted by A. B. Emden, *An Oxford Hall in Medieval Times* (Oxford, 1927), p. 149. On Payne, see also McFarlane, *Wycliffe*, pp. 156–8.

Not only the religious disliked craftsmen, cp. *JU* 40–42; cp. also the lines (at p. 245) in the poem against the Lollards (Wright, *Political Poems* ii, 243–7):

> I trowe ther be no kniȝt alyve
> That wold have don so open a shame,
> For that crafte to studi or strive,
> Hit is no gentel mannes game.

578. *schrift & biryynge*: collective singular.

588. 'Who would take notice of the words of such a wretch?'

592. oþer dedes of almes: presumably Upland's 'saying of the gospel' at the bedside of the sick, and attendance at poor men's funerals (*JU* 226–32). Daw does not reply to these questions in detail.

596. omnis vtriusque sexus: a decretal (c. 12, X, De poenitentiis, V, 38) which compelled parishioners to be shriven by their parish priest once a year (Friedberg, *Corpus*, ii. 887–8). Cp. Fitzralph, *Defensio*, p. 48, ll. 25–28: 'þe secunde article is þis, þat stondyng þe statute þat was made in þe general consail, *Omnis vtriusque Sexus*, þe pope may nouȝt make þat parischons beþ nouȝt y-holde to schryue hem of alle her synnes ones a ȝere to her owne preste'; also *Defensio*, p. 51, ll. 11–14: 'euerech parischon þat leueþ al þe ȝere his ordynarie, þat is his parisch curatour, & schryueþ hym to a frere, trespaseþ aȝenes þe heeste of holy chirche, in þat decretal *Omnis vtriusque Sexus*'.

The friars' hatred of the decree is illustrated by the extraordinary interpretation of it advanced by a Dominican, Richard Helmslay, preaching in Newcastle in 1379–80 against the rights of the secular clergy: he argued that strictly the decree applied only to those who were literally *utriusque sexus*, i.e. hermaphrodites. The indignant clergy of Durham cited him to Rome and he was known throughout the Curia as *Frater Ricardus utriusque sexus*. He was ordered to make public recantation of his teaching at Durham and Newcastle (cited Pantin, *English Church*, p. 165 from MS. Bodley 158 f. 142ᵛ and Durham Cathedral Muniments, Registrum ii, f. 205).

598. For idiomatic *have* + adj. and the indicative, rather than *had* with subjunctive see *OED*, *have* v. B. i. 22b.

604. *to / om.* MS. The emendation allows the *holdun* clause to be taken in its most natural sense, parallel to the same construction in 602.

605–8. For 'living of the gospel' see 1 Cor. ix. 14 quoted by Daw at 612–13. Paul in the next verse denies that he ever did this. He never asked for money, though other churches sent voluntarily to help him. See Phil. iv. 16, 2 Cor. xi. 8, 9.

611–13. 1 Cor. ix. 7, 14. Nicholas of Lyra's gloss to v. 7 is: 'imo milites stipendia sumunt a populo terrae quam defendunt. Idem ostendit in agricolis & gregum pastoribus. Apostoli vero fuerunt milites contra haereticos insurgentes, & in vinea domini cultores, & gregis dominici pastores: propter quod a populo sumptus eis debebantur.' At v. 14 both Lyra and the interlinear gloss quote Luke x. 7: 'Dignus est enim operarius cibo suo [mercede sua].'

615–20. (1) *In quamcumque* etc.: Luke x. 5, 7. (2) *Probauerunt* etc.: Rom. xv. 26.

623. Matt. vii. 20: 'Therfore of her fruytis ȝee shulen knowe hem.' Cp. 115 and *n*.

624. *peple*: collective singular.

640–3. (1) *Omnis arbor* etc.: Matt. iii. 10. (2) *Qui non manserit* etc.: John xv. 6.

670. *hostiensis / hostienser* MS. See *670 n.*

670. *Hostiensis*: Henry of Segusia (Segusio, Susa), commonly called Hostiensis, an Italian canonist of great reputation; taught canon law at Paris, spent some time in England, died 1271. His *Summa Aurea* or *Summa Hostiensis* was an early authority on Gratian's *Decretum*.

677. *onwyse*: 'unwise'. For ME. *on-* = *un-* see *OED*, *un-* prefix¹ 4c.

678–80. *Seint Austyn spekiþ*: see *De vita et moribus clericorum suorum* (Sermons 355, 356, Migne, *PL* xxxix. 1568–81) for Augustine's teaching on poverty and the so-called 'Apostolic Rule'. But I cannot identify the text exactly.

679. *a seiþ / a seye* MS. The unstressed parenthesis accounts for 2 sg. masc. pron. *a*, provides conditions for corruption of the verb, and follows naturally from 678 *Seint Austyn spekiþ*.

684. One or more lines may have been omitted at this point: there is no satisfactory antecedent for 685 *þei*, and 685–8 are difficult to reconcile with 681–4.

689. suppose / I suppose MS. The MS. is difficult, the use of imperative *suppose* to introduce a hypothetical statement common.

702–3. Col. i. 16–18; cp. Col. ii. 9–10, Eph. i. 22–23, 1 Cor. xv. 27, Rom. ix. 5.

706–7. Ps. xxxix (RV xl). 18.

708. Jerome's gloss: 'Egenus et pauper Christus' (Migne, *PL* xxvi. 946); for Augustine's to the same effect see *PL* xxxvi. 450.

712–14. Matt. viii. 20.

716–21. I cannot identify the quotation from Jerome nor that from Bernard. But that ascribed to Bernard may be the work of Ailred: see *UR* 341–2 and *n.*

725–6. See Introduction, p. 7.

726. Cp. *PPC* 376–7: 'Loke a ribaut of hem þat can nouȝt wel reden / His rewle ne his respondes but be pure rote.'

727. The syntax of *also* is curious, but it does not affect the sense of the line.

729–31. Matt. xx. 29–34.

732–4. Acts iii. 2–10.

734. of beggerie / þe begger MS. UR's correction makes 734 *he* superfluous and the syntax uncomfortable: the emendation gives better sense and makes the construction parallel to 737 *he was repreued of his begging*.

735–8. Luke xvi. 20–22.

746. helpeþ soulis / helpeþ þe soulis MS. The indicative resulting from the correction is an improvement, but the syntax remains uneasy; there are eight other examples of plural 'souls' in the text, nowhere else in conjunction with the article.

750. Esdras wroot a newe book: 2 Esdras (RV Nehemiah) viii. Ezra, though a scribe, did not write the book of the law; he carried it to Israel.

751–3. Rev. i. 10–11: 'I herde aftir me a greet voys, as of a trumpe, seiynge, That thing that thou seest, wrijte in a book.' *þe comoun glose*: I cannot identify.

754–5. Probably Matt. xxiii. 10: 'Nether be ȝe clepid maistirs, for oon is ȝour maistre, Crist.'

760–3. þe comoun glose: Lyra on Matt. xxiii. 7 (*et vocari ab hominibus rabbi*): 'Desiderare enim scientiam et actum docendi non est malum, sed meritorium: sed desiderare nomen tantum, hoc est malum et superbiae peccatum.'

764–9. For John XXIV erroneously written for John XXII see 767 n. For the issues between the so-called 'spiritual' Franciscans and their order, *JU 298–306 n.* For John XXII's ruling, c. 5, Extrav. Joann. XXII, De verborum significatione, XIV (Friedberg, *Corpus*, ii. 1230–6).

Cp. Fitzralph, *Defensio*, p. 93: 'þe two & twentiþe pope Joon in his constitucioun þat bygynneþ, *Quia quorundam*, seiþ openlich þat þe þridde pope Nichol wiþcleped þe bulle of þe ferþe pope Alisaundre touchyng alle þe articles þat his declaracioun conteyneþ. Þe þridde pope Nichol declared how streyt schuld be þe pouert of frere menours. Also pope Nichol made declaracioun of þe trauail of freres & of her prechyng in a bischops diocesy þere freres beþ wiþseide.' For extensive references to the Franciscans' 'acts' in the controversy see Douie, *Heresy of the Fraticelli*, pp. 153–201.

767. two / foure MS. Figures are the cause of much scribal confusion in this text: see 170 n., 192 n., 194 n. The corruption probably arises from a double error: substitution of the familiar John XXIII (antipope to Popes Benedict XIII and Gregory XII from 1410 to 1415) for John XXII, with subsequent misreading of XXIII as XXIV.

774–81. Daw is here rather confused. On the choice of Barnabas and Paul by the Holy Ghost see Acts xiii. 2. For the contention between them which led to their separation, Barnabas taking Mark and Paul Timothy, see Acts xv. 39–40, xvi. 1–3. It is said of Paul and Barnabas only that they fasted and prayed: see Acts xiii. 3, where it is also said they they received the laying on of their fellow Apostles' hands. But at this laying on of hands they did not 'receive' the Holy Ghost: this occurs in a different connexion in Acts viii. 17, xix. 6.

Daw probably thought it discreet not to quote in his own support the story of St. Dominic's vision in St. Peter's, in which St. Peter and St. Paul gave him staff and book, with orders to preach the gospel. He then 'saw his sons spread throughout the world, two and two, preaching to the people the word of God' (*Legenda Aurea*, ed. F. S. Ellis (London, 1900), iv. 178).

785–8. For the two tables of Moses see Exod. xxxi. 18, for the two cherubim in the temple, 3 Kings (RV 1 Kings) vi. 23, and for two in the tabernacle, Exod. xxv. 18. For the dangers of Adam's solitariness, see Gen. ii. 18. In 788 Daw is mistaken in his attribution to Christ; the text is from Eccles. iv. 10: 'wo to hym þat is aloone, for whanne he fallith, he hath noon reisynge him'.

787. For the construction *it was not good to Adam* cp. Wyclif 'þis meke sittynge and deuout herynge of Cristis wordis was best to Magdeleyne'

('Of Feigned Contemplative Life' in Sisam, *Fourteenth Century Verse and Prose*, xi, B. 58–59).

789. ful harde: it may be that *JU* 335 *foole hardi* (C *foolische hardy*) is original; but 1536 *so hardy* supports *FDR*.

796–7. Cristis bede: Matt. vi. 9–13. *memento*: probably the commemoration of the faithful departed in the mass: 'Memento, Domine, famulorum, famularumque tuarum etc.' See *Missale Romanum* (ed. 1880), *Ritus Celebrandi Missam*, ix. 2 (p. xlix), and *PP*, C. xii. 51 n. where Skeat quotes Ps. cxxxi. 1: 'Memento, Domine, David etc.'

797. falsly | fassy MS. Wright *fally*, *OED* (*voidly* qn. 1402) emends to *falsly*.

802–3. Cp. 1 Cor. viii. 2–3: 'But if ony man gessith, that he kan ony thing, he hath not 3it knowe hou it bihoueth hym to kunne. And if ony man loueth God, this is knowun of hym.'

803. Perhaps 'or else he only knows in spite of God himself'.

805. Rom. xi. 33: 'A! the hi3nesse, *or depnesse*, of the richesse of wysdom and kunnynge of God; hou incomprehensyble ben his domes, and his weyis vnserchable.'

807. *sumtyme*: probably 'for a while', or perhaps 'for once in a while'.

815. JU 364–5 reads *lettip Cristis chirche*. Daw's *letten Cristis* is not necessarily corrupt; *Crist* can stand as ellipsis for 'Christ's church' as in 1 Cor. xii. 12.

823. *pan | pou3* MS. Correlation of *pan* and 824 *panne* ('if therefore . . . it follows that') gives better sense than either the MS. or the corrected reading.

835. Cp. Eph. v. 23: 'for the man is heed of the womman, as Crist is heed of the chirche'; cp. Rev. xxi. 9, *UR* 139.

836. *pat man nedip | nedip* MS. Metre and sense are defective. It is clear from 833–4 that what is 'necessary' is *to helpen mannis soule*.

838 f. Wyclif maintained that in the Eucharist the substance of the bread and wine remained after consecration, while Christ was in the sacrament 'not by way of multiplication, but virtually only, as a king is in every part of his kingdom' (not 'substantialiter et corporaliter', but 'vere et realiter, virtualiter et sacramentaliter') (*ODCC*, art. *Wycliffe*). The orthodox belief was that the whole substance of the bread and wine was converted into the whole substance of the Body and Blood of Christ, only the accidents (i.e. the appearances of the bread and wine) remaining.

848. For Christ as a stone see Eph. ii. 20; as a lamb, John i. 29; as a lion, Rev. v. 5.

853. confiteor: a general confession of sins, used in the Roman Rite at the beginning of mass; here used figuratively.

853–62. Daw takes over the dogma of transubstantiation verbatim from Aquinas's hymn *Lauda, Sion, salvatorem* (pr. F. J. E. Raby, *Oxford Book of Medieval Latin Verse* (Oxford, 1959), no. 262), composed for the feast of Corpus Christi at the request of Urban IV, institutor of the feast. Daw's account is a cento of lines from the second half of the hymn, stanza 6 to the end. Detailed parallels: *FDR* 855 'Dogma datur Christianis / quod in carnem transit panis / et vinum in sanguinem' (*Lauda* 31–33); *FDR* 857–9 'caro cibus, sanguis potus / manet tamen Christus totus' (*Lauda* 40–41), 'A sumente non concisus / non confractus, non divisus' (*Lauda* 43–44), 'nulla rei fit scissura / signi tantum fit fractura' (*Lauda* 59–60), 'tantum esse sub fragmento / quantum toto tegitur' (*Lauda* 57–58); *FDR* 862 'mors est malis, vita bonis' (*Lauda* 52).

857. dwelliþ: 'remains'. *Lauda* 41 (see *853–62 n.*) reads 'manet tamen Christus totus'. Cp. 551 *þat ʒe gon and beren fruyte & ʒour fruyte may dwellyn* quoting John xv. 16 'that ʒe go, and brynge fruit, and ʒoure fruit dwelle' (*WV*1; *maneat* Vulg., *abide* RV).

860. leeueþ not: leeueþ intransitive 'remain' (*OED, leave* v.[1] iii. 12, cp. qn. 1357 'There levyth in the auter no materyal bred'), *not* substantive 'nothing' (see 323 n.).

861. 'Whatever remains in it is quintessential matter which is, etc.'

862. Cp. 1 Cor. xi. 29: 'Forsoth he that etith and drynkith vnworthily, etith and drynkith dom, *or dampnacioun.*'

865–7. The Lollards drew most of their support from prosperous tradesmen and artisans. Those hanged on 13 January 1414 after the failure of Oldcastle's rising included a brewer, a carpenter, a dyer, a glover, 'and other craftsmen of smaller repute' (J. H. Wylie, *The Reign of Henry the Fifth*, i (Cambridge, 1914), 270). For other craftsmen in Oldcastle's rebellion see Wylie, i. 275–6. On middle-class support of the Lollards see McFarlane, *Wycliffe*, p. 180. Cp. also Daw on Upland's objection to prisons at 574–6; but this may be metaphorical —see *575 n.*

868. 'Unless the sacred mystery of priesthood should be planted in their souls'? *OED* records *prick* = 'plant' (*prick* v. iv. 22) only from 1627.

869. In the early Church women sometimes usurped clerical functions; cp. *PP*, B. v. 166–8:

> Seynt Gregorie was a gode pope and had a gode forwit,
> That no priouresse were prest for that he ordeigned.
> Thei had thanne ben *infamis* the firste day thei can so yuel hele conseille.

Skeat's note to this passage cites from Tyrwhitt the decretal of Gregory IX (I. v, tit. 38, c. x) which forbade such practices in the strongest terms. I know of no evidence to support Daw's accusation that the Lollards allowed women to celebrate mass. The interpolator of *UR* expressly rejects the charge (*UR* 393 n., ll. 21–24). But that there may have been some encroachment is suggested by the fact that in December 1448 John Yonge, a chaplain of the Holy Cross of the Temple, Bristol, admitted that he had claimed the right of free preaching *except for women* (Thomson, *Later Lollards*, p. 37).

877. *rapyn | ratyn* MS. For the alliterative phrase *rape and rend*, see *OED, rape* v.² 1b.

878. *almners*: 'almoners' may be read *alumers* (Wright *alumners*, so also *MED* under *aumener* n. (1) (a)), but the marginal correction *avmoners* confirms the form in the text. For *alumer* 'illuminator', 'one who enlightens', see *OED* and *MED, alumere*; the word is a *hapax* quoted from l. 8 of *Iesu Dulcis Memoria* (Harley 2253 version pr. T. Wright, *Specimens of Lyric Poetry*, Percy Society, iv (1842), no. xxv) 'Then thou so suete alumere'. But the context supports 'almoner' rather than 'illuminator', and the word is probably a ghost resulting from confusion of minims and consequent mistranscription. See *EPS*, x (1967), 57–59.

879. *dele it | delith it* MS. A Southern plural is unlikely, but corruptions resulting from false joins are common. Cp. 15 n., 575 n.

884–5. 1 Cor. iii. 1.

887. John xvi. 12.

889–90. Luke viii. 10.

892. *scripture is | scripturis ben* MS. If *scripturis* is a collective singular (cp. Mustanoja, p. 63, quoting *CT*, I. 1039) *ben* is difficult. Daw's argument is based on the secrecy he imputes to Christ in 435–41 and to the Bible in 210–15: 'the secrets of the Bible have been dissipated and betrayed'.

898. *(зour) grace*: a complimentary periphrasis here used ironically in conjunction with *good Iak* (*OED, grace* sb. ii. 16a).

899. Sathanas pistile: Epistola Luciferi, an anti-clerical satire in the form of an open letter to popes and bishops sardonically commending their life and pleading only for a little more loyalty to Beelzebub. Very popular in the Middle Ages, it was current in a number of versions: see G. Zippel, 'La lettera del Diavolo al clero, dal secolo XII alla Riforma', *Bullettino dell'Istituto Storico Italiano per il Medio Evo*, lxx (Rome, 1958), 125–79. A Latin version in the Register of John Trefnant, Bishop of Hereford (1389–1404), pr. Canterbury and York

Society, xx (1916), 401–5 is translated in Foxe's *Actes and Monumentes* (1570), i. 599–600. Its close association with Lollardy is suggested by the appearance of an English version immediately following, and in the same hand as, the copy of *Upland* in C.U.L. MS. Ff. vi. 2. I owe the reference to Zippel to Professor J. A. W. Bennett.

900. *sorcerie / snowcrie* MS. *OED* records *snowcrie* as *hapax* with 'meaning uncertain'. See Introduction, pp. 12–17, *EPS*, x (1967), 59–61.

908–10. For the curse of Cain see Gen. iv. 11 f.; for that on Korah's family and followers, Num. xvi. 25 f. (and *25–26 n.*); for Christ's cursing of the fig tree, Matt. xxi. 19.

911–12. For the defeat of the Israelites by the Philistines on Mount Gilboa see 1 Kings (RV 1 Samuel) xxxi. 1 f. On Sodom see Gen. xix.

913. *deus laudem*: Ps. cviii (RV cix). I owe this reference to Professor J. A. W. Bennett.

915–16. Moab was much cursed: see Amos ii, Isa. xv, etc. Ariel (the symbolic name for Jerusalem) is cursed in Isa. xxix. For Christ's woe against Bethsaida see Matt. xi. 21.

917. St. Francis cursed a Friar Minor, Brother John of Sciaca, who founded a place of study in Bologna without St. Francis's leave, because Francis had always intended his friars to pray rather than read. Brother John fell into a sickness and St. Francis refused to revoke his malediction. His end was spectacular: one day a ball of fire and sulphur came and smote through his body and the bed on which he was lying. With a foul stench the wretched man died and the devil received his soul (*Actus B. Francisci*, ed. P. Sabatier (Paris, 1902), pp. 183–4). Cp. the interpolation in *Upland* (*JU* 411 n.): 'Seynt ffraunces curs & al foure ordris come vpon þat fals þeef þat þus þee haþ enformed.'

919–20. For God's *malisoun* see Deut. xxvii. 15–26.

925. *þinke*: 'think' rather than 'seem'. Mustanoja, p. 436 lists a few impersonal uses of normally personal verbs from the fourteenth and fifteenth centuries.

933. *dictamen*: this technical term and much other evidence (such as the catalogue of heresies taken from the *Summa Aurea* of Henry of Segusia, 658–70) suggests that Daw was not innocent of formal scholastic training. For a discussion of the authorship see Introduction, pp. 7–9.

UPLAND'S REJOINDER

5. chyteryng as chowȝes: cp. Deut. xviii. 10: 'noon be foundun in thee . . . that axith questiouns of dyuynouris that dyuynen aboute the auteris, and that taketh hede to dremes and chiteryng of bryddis'. For 'ravenes gredynge, pies chiterynge' in divination see Owst, *'Sortilegium'*, *Studies Presented to Sir Hilary Jenkinson*, ed. J. Conway Davies (London, 1957), p. 302. Cp. 'So chiding and chatering [as choghe] was he euer', *Sothsegger*, EETS, os 199 (1936), M. 345.

9. knowiþ: I assume non-expression of subject pronoun *it*. Cp. 61 n., 194 n., 206.

13. Matt. iv. 6 cited from Ps. xc (RV xci). 11.

14. Judges xv. 4–5. See *FDR 21 n.*

16–17. See *FDR 114–15 n.* and cp. *FDR 623, UR 107.*

23. a doctour: Nicholas of Lyra in his moralization on the Judges text (xv. 4–5) quoted by Daw: 'Et sicut Samson per combinationem vulpium incendit segetes Philistinorum: sic Christus per praedicatores charitate combinatos succendit fidei charitate formata Gentilium corda.'

25. 'For wise men recognize that you are not loyal.'

27. See *JU 161–3 n.*

29. Cp. *58–59 n.*

32–33. 1 Cor. iv. 12: 'we trauelen worchinge with oure hondis' and Mark vi. 3: 'Whether this is not a carpenter?'

36. in worde & werke: apparently one of the inclusive formulas so common in ME.—'in every way, in all things'. Cp.

> Whom alle þe vij. sciences seruyd at wille,
> Bothe in werke and in worde weren at his heste,
> And more bunne at his bede þan boy til his maister.

Sothsegger, EETS, os 199 (1936), M. 356–8.

43–44. 3 Kings (RV 1 Kings) xviii. 20–40. Cp. *FDR 27 n.*

47. The pronominal variation is explicable if ȝour is taken to refer both to priests who practise simony and to Daw who implicitly approves of it.

52. habites: 'settled practice or usage' (*OED* only from 1581) rather than 'clothes'. There is support in 189–90, a passage very similar to 52–53. 'I imagine the members of your sect are so secure in their long established practices that they are able to lie without thinking about it.'

53. propheciþ: there is no other example in the text of reduced form of 3 sg. pres. ind.; but reduction of a stem ending in *i* is very probable.

54–55. 2 Pet. ii. 1.

58–59. A common charge against the friars. Cp. *PPC* 765–9:

> And comeren her stomakes wiþ curious drynkes,
> Þat makeþ swiche harlottes hordome vsen,
> And wiþ her wicked worde wymmen bitraieþ!
> God wold her wonynge were in wildernesse,
> And fals freres forboden þe fayre ladis chaumbres!

And also in a poem against the friars (Wright, *Political Poems*, ii. 249–50):

> Lat a freer of sum ordur
> *tecum pernoctare,*
> Odur thi wyff or thi doughtour
> *hic vult violare;*
> Or thi sun he weyl prefur,
> *sicut furtam fortis;*
> God gyffe syche a freer peyne
> *in inferni portis!*

See also 29, 364–5, *262–3 n.*

59. speke / spake MS. The sense seems to require a present tense.

59. Dom David Knowles points interestingly to Wyclif's own habit of making accusations of immorality by way of apophasis ('I will not mention', 'I leave to speak of', etc.) as here. He quotes 'taceo autem de corporali incontinencia' (*The Religious Orders in England*, ii (Cambridge, 1955), 103, n. 2). See *262–3 n.*

61. Omission of the subject pronoun in the second person is unusual in ME., but cp. 206 *þilk Cristis secte þat myn callist.*

63. 3 Kings (RV 1 Kings) vi–viii.

64–70. 'Because the poor Lord, he says, sanctified his poor church, we accept the cross of Christ and regard worldly goods as worthless' (69–70). *UR* quotes Gratian's *Decretum* c. 71, C. XII, q. 2, (Friedberg, *Corpus*, i. 710–11) referring to Jerome, *Ep.* 52, no. 6 (Migne, *PL* xxii. 532–3). *UR* 69 is a loose, 70 a close, translation of the decree: 'Nunc uero, cum paupertatem domus suae pauper Dominus dedicauit, portemus crucem, et delicias lutum putemus.'

71. Matt. xxiii. 16: 'Woo to зou, blynde lederis.'

72–73. It is unnecessary to assume pronominal confusion in these lines. In 105–11 Daw defends the friars' luxurious houses by referring to Solomon's temple as a precedent. Here UR is simply attacking Daw's tendentious use of his text, and the sense of 71–73 can best be brought out by a loose translation: 'though you may fool simple people with your (i.e. Daw's) persuasive gloss and your talk of rich buildings, you don't fool me into accepting your (i.e. friars') ill-founded convents.'

74–75. Mark xi. 17.

82. Matt. xxiv. 11.

84. þe / þo MS. Anticipation of following *mo* and 87 *þo* 'then' makes the miswriting an easy one.

85–87. The *gret clerke* of 85 and the *seint* of 91 is Wyclif, referred to by Daw in 150 f. The Lollards were generous in dispensing blessedness: Richard Fitzralph is more than once referred to as 'Saint Richard'. See, e.g., *De Blasphemia*, Arnold, iii. 412, 416.

88–90. Bayarde: a common name for a horse and 'as bold as blind Bayard' a proverbial comparison: cp. *CT*, G. 1413–14 'Ye been as bolde as is Bayard the blinde / That blundreth forth, and peril casteth noon' and *Troilus*, i. 218. The present passage suggests that Bayard was a name also given to dogs: *berkest* and *baffyng* imply it, as does the syntactically parallel simile of the *olde mylne dog*.

92. Luke x. 7. A favourite text for those who attacked the friars. Fitzralph uses it three times in the *Defensio*, pp. 62, ll. 24–26, 86, ll. 28–30, 90, l. 31.

95. Isa. v. 20.

102–4. (1) *Qui mihi ministrat* etc.: John xii. 26. (2) *Attendite* etc.: Luke xii. 1. (3) *Homo apostata* etc.: Prov. vi. 12.

107. See *FDR 114–15 n.* and cp. *FDR* 623, *UR* 17.

110–11. 1 Cor. iv. 5.

113. Matt. xv. 14.

119. *pointes*: Wright *partes*; but cp. the almost identical phrase 315 *in alle þes poyntes* in a very similar context (311–16).

124–5. For Daniel and the priests of Bel see Dan. xiv. 13–14 (RV Bel and Dragon, vv. 14–15).

139. Crist our spouse: Rev. xxi. 9: 'Come thou, I shal shewe to thee the spouse, wijf of the lomb' and cp. Eph. v. 23, *FDR* 835.

141. Initium etc.: a conflation of Ecclus. x. 14, 15: 'Initium superbiae hominis *apostatare a Deo* . . . *initium omnis peccati* est superbia.'

146. An adaptation of Col. iii. 5.

149. For other instances of formal *it* in contexts where it is virtually equivalent to 'they' see Mustanoja, pp. 132–3.

152–5. Matt. v. 14–15.

158. ranes: probably an adaptation of Lat. *rana* 'frog'. Cp. Rev. xvi. 13: 'Et uidi . . . de ore pseudoprophetae spiritus tres immundos in modum ranarum'; see Augustine, *Expositio in Apocalypsim,* Hom. xiii (*PL* xxxv. 2446–7). The sense is perhaps 'mucus'.

159. John xiv. 27.

160. pagyn: 'a part acted to deceive or impose upon any one; a trick' (*OED, pageant* sb. 1c); here probably 'specious argument'. Cp. 130.

160 f. See *FDR* 282 *f. n.*

165. UR does not associate Christ and Martha with Mary here as examples of the contemplative life, but more generally as examples of the Christian life.

168–9. Ecclus. xxxiv. 25.

172. Matt. xix. 6.

178. Presumably black, the colour of the Dominican habit. That UR guessed (I think rightly) that he was confuting a Dominican is clear from 299.

187–8. A conflation of Luke iii. 7: '*Genimina uiperarum,* quis ostendit uobis fugere a uentura ira?' and Matt. iii. 7: 'Progenies uiperarum, quis demonstrauit uobis fugere a futura ira?'

192. John viii. 44? Cp. l. 22 of the third interpolation (393 n.): 'al wey þou vsest þe craft of þyn old fader'.

194. tellen: 3 pl. pres. ind. referring to collective singular *secte,* with non-expression of subject pronoun. For 'set store by' see *OED, tell* v. iii. 25; *bot now oon now oþer* perhaps 'except for the occasional one', referring ironically to *FDR* 356–7.

198–9. See *FDR* 389–92 *n.*

200–1. Cp. *PPC* 779–82:

> We haue sene our-self in a schort tyme,
> Whou freres wolden no flech among þe folke vsen;
> But now þe harlottes han hid thilke rewle,
> And, for þe loue of oure lorde haue leyd hire in water.

203. A horizontal stroke, probably an abbreviation mark, stands after *dawe;* the letter over which it was presumably placed lost in cropping.

203. þe deuellis dirt: perhaps antedates the imprecatory use of the phrase recorded by *MED* (*drit* n. 3(d)) first from the Towneley plays a1460. A literal sense 'dung' suits the context, as also in 120.

209–10. For Josiah's reformation see 4 Kings (RV 2 Kings) xxii, xxiii, esp. xxiii. 4 f.

211. Iamnes & Mambres: referred to by Paul (2 Tim. iii. 8) as Moses' opponents; it is generally assumed that the Egyptian sorcerers of Exod. vii. 11, 22 are meant. The names are traditional from the earliest Christian times. Cp. *371–2 n.*

213–14. Matt. vii. 15.

223. Caymes castelles: see *JU 86 n.*

227. Heb. xiii. 14.

228. Hab. ii. 12.

229. Isa. v. 8.

230–2. UR's syntax is somewhat confused here: strictly 232 should precede 231, but the sense is clear.

233. See *JU 177 n.*

234. It is hardly necessary to document UR's irony, but it may be pointed out that in the Middle Ages no class of seal was free from suspicion of forgery. Thus, when in 1380 two men set out to forge a will they were able to buy at Paul's Gate a seal ready-made and with the device (a letter H) they required (I. S. Leadam and J. F. Baldwin, *Select Cases before the King's Council, 1243–1482*, Selden Society, xxxv (1918), 73); in a case before the Queen's Bench in Michaelmas Term 2 Henry IV, an Approver claimed to have found in a 'forcere' in a house he had burgled a counterfeit seal of lead, resembling the Great Seal of Henry IV, with which sixty letters and charters had been sealed (*Queen's Bench, Ancient Indictments*, 185. m. 53). I quote both examples from *A Guide to Seals in the Public Record Office* (London, 1954), p. 7, n. 4, p. 30, n. 2 (iii) respectively. Cp. also Daw's remark at 509–10: *Of pore mennes preieris to be perseuers we wolden | And of her lettris, & of her sele, if autentike þei weren.*

236. Matt. xvii. 24–27, xxii. 15–22.

240–1. A conflation of Matt. xii. 30: '*Qui non est mecum, contra me est*; et qui non congregat mecum, spargit' and Luke xi. 23: '*Qui non est mecum, aduersum me est: et qui non colligit mecum, dispergit.*'

242. See 3–4.

243. ⟨?s . ?w⟩: illegible MS., possible in photograph. *Saw* = 'decree' fits the context: it is the *cursyng* of 242, which in turn refers to *Cristis curse* of *FDR 513.*

244. Isa. xxxvi. 6: 'Lo! thou tristist on this brokun staf of rehed, on Egipt, on which if a man restith, it schal entre in to his hoond, and schal perse it.'

244. persen: it is unnecessary to emend to *persiþ*. The grammatical looseness results from UR's adaptation of Isa. xxxvi. 6; relative *þat* refers to *resones* rather than *rede* of the borrowed metaphor.

249–50. See *236 n.*

252. Rom. xii. 14.

254. Luke viii. 46.

255. The comparison is Daw's: see *FDR 212–13 n.*

257–8. Cp. *JU 330–4 n.*

262–3. Thomas Walsingham, the St. Alban's Chronicler, records an incident (in 1387) in which a crowd of 'Lollards' rioted in London, crying out, 'Let us rout these murderers, burn these sodomites, hang these traitors' (McFarlane, *Wycliffe*, p. 139).

Cp. 'Also freris ben foule envenymed wiþ gostly synne of Sodome, and so ben more cursid þen þo bodily Sodomytis, þat weren sodeynli deede by harde vengeaunce of God. For þei done gostily lecchorie by Gods worde, when þei prechen more hor owne fyndyngis, for worldly mucke, þen Cristis gospel for savynge of mennis soulis' (*Fifty Heresies,* Arnold, iii. 399). Such 'spiritual sodomy' seems appropriate here; but at 59 the context demands a literal sense. See *58–59 n.*

264–5. Matt. xxiii. 15. The *suple* word is odd. I can find nothing in the dictionaries to explain the use here, but Professor Norman Davis draws my attention to the following passage from the Paston Letters: 'Primo suggessit Sanctissimo Papae mentiendo quod coactus et constrictus [fuisset] metu parentum ordinem intrare. . . . Et primo, contra primum articulum, viz., quod metu parentum etc. quia, ut asserunt fide media quam plures fide digni quorum nomina perlongum esset enarrare, quod alter parentum, *suple* pater, neci submersionis suffocatus fuerat in Themisia diu antequam ordinem ingressus est praenotatus Johannes . . .', *Paston Letters,* ed. J. Gairdner (London and Exeter, 1904), no. 46 (1900 ed. no. 35) (B.M. Addit. MS. 27443, f. 93). The sense seems to be 'namely' or 'presumably', probably the former, and this would fit the present passage. The same document contains a second example of the word.

269. ʒou / ʒe MS. UR's uncertainty in historically impersonal constructions is illustrated by his divided usage in the 'marvel' verb; impersonal *me merueliþ* at 31, 85, personal *I meruel* at 245, 305. Here either pronoun or verb could result from contextual pressure, but the unstressed pronoun would be especially susceptible to the pull of fourfold *ʒe.* Cp. 343 n.

271–3. and: concessive 'even if, allowing that' with subjunctive; 273 *allegates* 'yet, nevertheless'. UR is replying to *FDR* 561–2; the sense is: 'admitting that the king does have supreme authority, exercised through his judges administering the law . . . would you nevertheless compare yourself to him?'

271–2. Skeat (p. xxxvii) suggests that this refers to the hanging of eight Franciscans at Tyburn in June 1402, for being implicated in a plot against the life of Henry IV. For the arguments which lead me to reject this, see Introduction, pp. 9–19.

276–7. (1) *Que conuentio* etc.: 2 Cor. vi. 15. (2) *Quid communicabit* etc.: Ecclus. xiii. 3.

290–2. Mic. iii. 5.

296. þou callist holichirche / þou seyst MS. The interpolator's emendation is not very satisfactory. The sense requires something to balance the antithesis of 299–302 and the obvious reading is *callist holichirche* of 299–301. 'If you call holychurch Christ's teaching etc. then I submit myself to it; but if you call holychurch Dominic's rules etc. then I forsake you and your accursed church for ever.'

303. Ps. xxv (RV xxvi). 5.

308. ʒee / ʒe (1) MS. The sense requires affirmative 'yea' which elsewhere has doubled *e*.

308. See Mark xiv. 64, Matt. ix. 3, John x. 36.

310. Matt. xxiii. 32.

325. Matt. vii. 5.

327. For Saul's persecution of David see 1 Kings (RV 1 Sam.) xviii. 10 f.

329. 2 Cor. xi. 26.

332–3. 'For Christ's disciples often begged when they were in distress as a result of the people's sinful neglect.' The *synne* is that described in *JU* 279–81.

338. þai: refers to the scriptures, generalized from *FDR* 703.

339–40. The allusions are not obvious and the exact sense is not clear, but the general drift of UR's argument is to assert Christ's divine lordship against Daw's attempt to emphasize his humanity in support of the friars' begging. It is best to take *allegyng* in the sense 'setting aside, annulling' (see *OED*, *allay* v.[1] for the formal and semantic confusions that in ME. make such a meaning possible) and *water*, *asse*, and *herberowe* as referring to three episodes in the life of Christ which support UR's claim of his lordship: (1) Matt. xiv. 25–29: Christ's walking on the waters (or possibly Matt. viii. 24–26, his

rebuking of the winds and the sea); (2) Matt. xxi. 1–4: Christ's send-
ing of the two disciples to find the ass on which he is to make
his triumphal entry into Jerusalem; (3) Matt. xxvi. 17–19: Christ's
requisitioning of the house in which he and his disciples are to eat the
Last Supper. (1) Illustrates his divine authority, (2) and (3) his divine
prescience. The sense is that Daw is foolish because he wilfully
ignores such occasions as these when Christ demonstrated the fullness
of his divine power.

341–2. Ierom, Bernarde, Alrede: see *FDR* 716–21 and *n.* Ailred,
Abbot of Rievaulx, was a disciple of St. Bernard, often referred to
as 'the Bernard of the North'. UR's ascription to Ailred of Daw's
citation from Bernard may be correct, but I am unable to identify it.

343. *likiþ | likist* MS. The four 2 sg. pres. inds. of 341, 343 probably
account for *likist, þe* probably preserves the construction intended by
the author. Cp. 269 n.

344–5. I cannot identify UR's *clerke*.

346. Perhaps an adaptation of Prov. xxvi. 28: 'Lingua fallax non
amat veritatem.' The whole passage in Prov., vv. 24 f, fits UR's
attack on Daw's misrepresentations here.

347. Ps. cviii (RV cix). 10.

348. Iudas childe: the phrase 'Judas's children' was often used to
describe the wicked. As a monster of iniquity Judas is equated with
Cain and the devil himself. Cp. l. 11 of the second interpolation
(374 n.): '& so þe deuyl & caym with judas ben ʒoure fadirs'.

349. *whiche*: 'whichever' referring to Daw's tendentious quotation
from Ps. xxxix (RV xl). 18 in 706–7. After this line the first interpolation (transcribed below, discussed Introduction, pp. 40–41) begins.
Lines 1–2 run on from UR's text, upper margin f. 13ʳ; 3–8 upper
margin f. 13ᵛ—for which see frontispiece.

> for ʒit þou schuldest be damned more softly in helle
>   *nutantes transferentur filij &c.*
> þou sp'i'llest much breþe daw with legyng of þy tyxtes
> for summe þou legest kenely to a fals entente
> but of oþer þou blundyrst as a blynde buserde   5
> for þes pore of whom þou spekyst myʒt not helpe hem selfe
> but ʒoure prowde loseng⟨erse⟩ þat ⟨ru⟩nne abowt as snekdrawers
> ben neyþer pore ne febil & so juge þou how þes to acorde

350. This proverb in the form 'He that heweth to hye, with chippes
he may lese his sight' is already in Usk (*Testament of Love*, ed. Skeat,
Chaucerian and Other Pieces, p. 38) 'an olde proverbe'. *ODEP*
(p. 293) first records it from *c.* 1330 (Manning).

351. Hardly a proverb, but cp. 'Other . . . merchants . . . sore abhor-
ryng the Italian nacion for lickyng the fat from their beards, and
taking from them their accustomed livyng' (*ODEP*, p. 363, only from
1548). Cp. also Langland's description of Covetousness, *PP*, B. v.
194: 'And as a bondman of his bacoun his berde was bidraueled.'

362–3. Matt. xxiii. 6–7: cp. *PPC* 557–8: 'He mot bygynne þat borde
a beggere, (wiþ sorwe!) / And first sitten in se in her synagoges', and
PPC 761.

364–5. See *58–59 n.*

371–2. *Zambre, Corby*: Num. xxv. 6–8, 14–15. *Iamnes, Mambres:
211 n.*

373–4. 2 Tim. iii. 6.

374. After this line the second interpolation begins. All lower margin
of f. 14ᵛ.

> þou argust topias wonderly as if þou were an asse
> for þou legest ȝoure selde bedys to þe pater noster þat crist him selue
>   made
> but wel j wote þat alle ȝe gate neuer apeny
> with þe pater noster but with ȝoure famulorum
> þat ȝe sey is beter ȝe gete many poundes   5
> for crist made þat one for better may none be
> but ȝe with ȝoure ypocrisy han autorised þat oþer
> to blynde with þe pupyl for ȝoure cursed grounde
> & þou god god made al þinge in mesure & in wyȝte as þe scripture seyþe
> it folowþ not he made ȝou for ȝe ben oute of mesure   10
> & so þe deuyl & caym with 'judas' ben ȝoure fadirs

380 f. See *FDR 838 f.n.* The technical terms of the Eucharistic
controversy may have achieved popular currency, with consequent
debasement and loss of exactness. Such vulgarization may perhaps be
seen in Uthred of Boldon's advice to the monks of Durham proceeding
to the university: 'it is no good losing the substance for the sake of the
accidents' (quoted Pantin, *English Church*, p. 174). But this could rather
be the putting of learning to the service of wit.

In any case it is difficult not to side with Daw against his inter-
locutors. Upland (390–3) ascribes to the friars the Wyclifian heresy
that after consecration the bread remains both in accidents and
substance. As Daw complains (841) *þou drawist a þorn out of þin hele
& puttist it in oure*; he goes on to restate the orthodox doctrine (844–
62). Of UR's reply I can make nothing; but I feel safe in assuming
confusion of thought rather than corruption of the text.

387. Rev. xx. 7: 'And whan a thousynd ȝeeres shulen be endid,
Sathanas shal be vnbounde of his prisoun', and Rev. xx. 2–3.

389. of þe thousande ȝere: see *387 n.*

393. Rom. i. 25.

393. After this line the third and final interpolation begins. Lines 1–13 (*sikir*) lower margin f. 15ᵛ, 13 (*of*)—25 (*þe*) lower margin f. 16ʳ, 25 (*at*)—28 upper margin f. 16ʳ.

To make with þe a dialogge j holde it bot wast¹
for þou marys⟨t⟩ þy lesynges lowde with þy false heresyes
men may se by þy writin⟨g⟩ here þou jangelyng jay
how þou by leuest not in þe sacrid oste
for we sey alle þe sacrid oste þat is sene with eye   5
is verey cristes body but þy sette seyþ not soo
but 3e sey þer is cristes body but 3e tel not where
but crist seyþ þis is my body & not þer is my body
whi 3e templers messe sellers grante 3e not cristes wordes
syþ 3e chafyr þus þerwith by gylyng þe pupil   10
lete 3ou⟨re⟩ sette write 3oure byleue of þis sacrid osste
& preche it as 3e wr⟨i⟩te it & sette þerto 3oure sele
& j am sikir of my feyþ 3e schul be stonde to deþe
& þan schal 3oure castils cache hem new maysters
for 3e² wil not grante ne but³ few of 3oure ordirs   15
þe ost sac⟨rid⟩e⁴ white & rounde is verey cristes body
j pray oure lord jesu þat sone be it sene
who is in þe trew wey wheþer 3e oþer we
but towching men of crafte whom þou dipisyst
al þey schulde medle hem to know her byleue   20
but as wele of her sacryng as wymmen syngyge messe
al wey þou vsest þe craft of þyn old fader
why darst not þow oþer summe of 3ou false heretykis
fynde owte such on & preue 3oure lesynges soþe
& þerfor daw j sey ⟨no⟩more to þe⁵ at þis tyme   25
but þou ert on of þe falsest þat euer j saw write
for makomete & serginus in al her grete lawe⁶
'wrot'⁷ not so many lesynges as ben here in þy writynges

¹ 3it spekiþ jak vplonde: *margin.*
² *after* 3e: we *cancelled.*
³ but: *possibly* bot.
⁴ sacride: -ride *alteration.*
⁵ *possibly word after* þe; to þe *repeated upper margin, partially erased.*
⁶ lawe: -e *over erasure.*
⁷ wrot: wr- *over erasure.*

APPENDIX

TABLE OF PARALLEL PASSAGES

Exact line references are given wherever possible, but where the argument is diffuse only an approximate reference is supplied

JU	FDR	JU	FDR	FDR	UR	FDR	UR
69–78	31–66	182–6	486–505	21 f.	14–23	337 f. esp. } 360 f.	} 173–88
79–80	67–74	187–90	506–13	47 f.	24–30		
80–82	75–83	191–203	514–22	55–62	31–36	381 f.	189–96
83–84	84–92	204–8	523–36	75 f.	37–47	387–405	197–203
85	93–104	209–13	537–53	99–104	48–62	406 f.	204–16
86	105–11	214–19	554–76	105–11	63–75	451–76	217–29
87–97	112–224	220–2	577–89	114 f. esp. } 125–8	} 76–84	477–85	230–5
97–100	225–33	222–32	590–9			486–505	236–52
101–2	236–57	233–43	600–29	148–58	85–92	523 f. esp. } 533–4	} 253–6
103–13	258–70	244–50	630–44	163 f.	93–103		
114–19	271–321	251–6	645–72	191	104–13	537–53	257–65
119–21	322–9	257–71	673–97	210 f. esp. } 211–14	} 114–19	554–76	266–77
125–36	330–50	272–4	698–726			600 f. esp. } 606 f.	} 278–92
137–9	351–7	275–81	727–38	234 f. esp. } 244 f.	} 120–9		
140–3	358–81	282–4	739–53			630 f.	293–310
144	382–5	295–7	754–63	260 f.	130–46	646–97	311–29
145–7	386–405	298–306	764–70	282 f. esp. } 290 f. & } 309	} 147–59	698–738	330–53
148–59	406–20	309–11	771–88			739–53	354–6
160–4	421–31	335–41	789–808			754–63	357–63
165–7	432–50	354–65	809–37	282 f.	160–5	771–88	364–74
168–72	451–61	390–400	838–92	322–9	166–9	808 f. esp. } 823 f.	} 375–9
172–6	462–76	401–7	893–922	330–6	170–2		
177–9	477–85	408–11	923–32			838–71	380–93

BIBLIOGRAPHY

This is a selective list. Other items are cited in full (in footnotes or commentary) in the places where they are referred to.

PRIMARY SOURCES

(1) *Manuscript*

British Museum, Harley 6641. *Jack Upland.*

Cambridge, University Library, Ff. vi. 2, ff. 71ʳ–80ʳ. *Jack Upland.*

Oxford, Bodleian Library, Digby 41, ff. 2ʳ–16ᵛ. *Friar Daw's Reply* and *Upland's Rejoinder.*

(2) *Printed*

Iack vp Lande Compyled by the famous Geoffrey Chaucer. . . . Prynted for Ihon Gough.

SECONDARY SOURCES

(1) *Manuscript*

British Museum, Additional 38178–38181 and Harley 6895. *The MS. collections for J. Urry's edition of Chaucer, Oxford, 1721.*

Oxford, Bodleian Library, Auct. F. inf. 1. 1.

—— Oriel College 80.

(2) *Printed*

M. Aston, 'John Wycliffe's Reformation Reputation', *Past and Present,* xxx (1965), 23–51.

R. B. Brooke, *Early Franciscan Government,* Cambridge Studies in Medieval Life and Thought, N.S. vii (Cambridge, 1959).

The Philobiblon of Richard de Bury, ed. and tr. E. C. Thomas (London, 1888).

G. Chaucer, *The Complete Works,* ed. W. W. Skeat, 6 vols. (Oxford, 1894).

E. Colledge, '*The Recluse.* A Lollard Interpolated Version of the *Ancren Riwle*', *Review of English Studies,* xv (1939), 1–15, 129–45.

Concilia Magnae Britanniae et Hiberniae, ed. D. Wilkins, 4 vols. (London, 1737).

Corpus Iuris Canonici, ed. A. Friedberg, 2 vols. (Leipzig, 1879–81).

M. Day and R. Steele, edd., *Mum and the Sothsegger*, EETS, os 199 (1936).

M. Deanesly, *The Lollard Bible*, Cambridge Studies in Medieval Life and Thought (Cambridge, 1920).

—— *The Significance of the Lollard Bible* (London, 1951).

D. L. Douie, *The Nature and the Effect of the Heresy of the Fraticelli*, Publications of the University of Manchester, ccxx, Hist. Ser. lxi (Manchester, 1932).

R. Fitzralph, *Defensio Curatorum*, tr. John Trevisa, ed. A. J. Perry, EETS, os 167 (1925).

J. Forshall and F. Madden, edd., *The Holy Bible . . . in the Earliest English Versions . . . by John Wycliffe and His Followers*, 4 vols. (Oxford, 1850).

·P L. Heyworth, 'Christ Church and Chaucer', *Oxford Magazine*, 21 June 1962, pp. 386–7.

—— 'ME *alumere* and *snowcrie*: two ghosts', *English Philological Studies*, x (1967), 57–61.

—— '*Jack Upland's Rejoinder*, a Lollard Interpolator and *Piers Plowman* B. x. 249 f', *Medium Ævum*, xxxvi (1967), 242–8.

—— 'The Earliest Black-letter Editions of *Jack Upland*', *Huntington Library Quarterly*, xxx (1967), 307–14.

E. D. Jones, 'The Authenticity of Some English Works Ascribed to Wycliffe', *Anglia*, xxx (1907), 261–8.

D. Knowles and R. N. Hadcock, *Medieval Religious Houses: England and Wales* (London, 1953).

W. Langland, *Piers the Plowman*, ed. W. W. Skeat, 2 vols. (Oxford, 1886).

—— *Piers Plowman: The A Version*, ed. G. Kane (London, 1960).

G. Lechler, *John Wycliffe and His English Precursors*, ed. and tr. P. Lorimer, revd. edn. (London, [1884]).

Nicholas of Lyra, *Postilla ad Biblia*, 6 vols. (Lyons, 1590).

K. B. McFarlane, *John Wycliffe and the Beginnings of English Nonconformity* (London, 1952).

J.-P. Migne, ed., *Patrologiae Cursus Completus. Series Latina* (Paris, 1844–55).

T. F. Mustanoja, *A Middle English Syntax*, Part i, Mémoires de la Société Néophilologique de Helsinki, xxiii (Helsinki, 1960).

G. R. Owst, *Preaching in Medieval England*, Cambridge Studies in Medieval Life and Thought (Cambridge, 1926).

—— '*Sortilegium* in English Homiletic Literature of the Fourteenth

Century', *Studies Presented to Sir Hilary Jenkinson*, ed. J. Conway Davies (London, 1957), pp. 272–303.

W. A. Pantin, *The English Church in the Fourteenth Century* (Cambridge, 1955).

M. W. Ransom, 'The Chronology of Wyclif's English Sermons', *Research Studies of the State College of Washington*, xvi (1948), 67–114.

J. A. Robson, *Wyclif and the Oxford Schools*, Cambridge Studies in Medieval Life and Thought, N.S. viii (Cambridge, 1961).

F. Roth, *The English Austin Friars, 1249–1538*, ii (New York, 1961).

W. W. Shirley, *Catalogue of the Extant Latin Works of John Wyclif*, revd. J. Loserth (Wyclif Society, n.d.).

W. W. Skeat, ed., *Pierce the Ploughmans Crede*, EETS, os 30 (1867).

—— ed., *Chaucerian and Other Pieces* (Oxford, 1897).

—— *The Chaucer Canon* (Oxford, 1900).

W. G. Smith, *The Oxford Dictionary of English Proverbs*, 2nd edn., revd. P. Harvey (Oxford, 1948).

E. W. Talbert, 'The Date of the Composition of the English Wyclifite Collection of Sermons', *Speculum*, xii (1937), 464–74.

—— 'A Fifteenth-Century Lollard Sermon Cycle', *Texas Studies in English* (1939), pp. 5–30.

—— 'A Lollard Chronicle of the Papacy', *Journal of English and Germanic Philology*, xli (1942), 163–93.

J. A. F. Thomson, *The Later Lollards, 1414–1520* (Oxford, 1965).

J. Wordsworth and H. J. White, *Nouum Testamentum Latine*, edit. min. (Oxford, repr. 1957).

T. Wright, ed., *Political Poems and Songs Relating to English History, Edward III to Richard III*, 2 vols. (Rolls Series, 1859–61).

J. Wyclif, *Select English Works*, ed. T. Arnold, 3 vols. (Oxford, 1869–71).

—— *The English Works Hitherto Unprinted*, ed. F. D. Matthew, EETS, os 74 (revd. edn. 1902).